Hamlet and the Word

Hamlet and the Word

The Covenant Pattern
in Shakespeare

HAROLD FISCH

Now to my Word;
It is "Adieu, adieu! remember me."
(I. v.)

FREDERICK UNGAR PUBLISHING CO.
New York

Acknowledgments

Chapter IV of this book ("From Monologue to Dialogue") incorporates material first published as a contribution to *The Shakespearean World* [Hebrew], edited by Murray Roston and published by Am HaSefer, Tel-Aviv, 1965. Other portions of the same chapter are taken from a paper on "Hamlet and Montaigne" presented to the Tenth Congress of the *Fédération Internationale des Langues et Littératures Modernes,* held at Strasbourg, September 1966. Chapter IX ("All the World's a Stage") incorporates material from an essay contributed to *The Morality of Art: Essays Presented to G. Wilson Knight by His Colleagues and Friends,* edited by D. W. Jefferson and published by Routledge and Kegan Paul Ltd., London, 1969. The Appendix on "*Julius Caesar* and the Bleeding Statue" first appeared in *Bar-Ilan Volume in Humanities and Social Sciences,* Decennial Volume II (1955–1965), edited by M. Z. Kaddari, and published for Bar-Ilan University, Ramat-Gan, by Kiryath Sefer Ltd., Jerusalem, 1969. Acknowledgment is hereby made to the publishers or proprietors of the above-listed items.

In addition, acknowledgment is made to the following publishers for kind permission to quote extracts: to Phaidon Press Ltd., for permission to quote from S. G. C. Middlemore's translation of J. Burckhardt's *The Civilization of the Renaissance in Italy*; to Editions Gallimard, Paris, and to Methuen and Co., London, for permission to quote from Bernard Frechtman's translation of Jean-Paul Sartre's *What Is Literature?*; to Faber and Faber Ltd., and to Alfred A. Knopf Inc., for permission to quote from George Steiner's *The Death of Tragedy*; to the University of Chicago Press for permission to quote from Henri Frankfort's *The Intellectual Adventure of Ancient Man*; to the SCM Press Ltd. of London for permission to quote from G. E. Wright's *The Old Testament against Its Environment,* and to Random House Inc., for permission to quote from F. J. Miller's translation of Seneca's *Agamemnon.*

Bar-Ilan University   H. F.
Ramat Gan
1970

Contents

Introduction

Some years ago I argued for the relevance of Hebraic concepts, in particular the doctrine of covenant, to an understanding of Milton and other seventeenth-century authors.[1] Such spirituality, given new impetus by the Reformation discovery of Scripture, was part of the moral climate of the age. It could operate either as an intellectual challenge or as a dangerous temptation, according to the point of view. Thus Milton in his demand for freedom to divorce, and Jeremy Taylor in his Pelagian stress on a religion of works lean on Old Testament sources and on the practical code of the rabbis, while Bunyan's first warning to Christian in *Pilgrim's Progress* is against seeking salvation by the road of Mount Sinai. When we consider the growth of unitarianism, of religious socialism, and the mid-century vogue of mortalism (in Thomas Browne, Overton, and others), Bunyan's warning is easily understood. In Bacon and Hobbes it was possible to discern the lineaments of a perverted Hebraism in their notion of a this-worldly salvation to be attained by human agency.

While the sources for such an understanding of the literature and thought of the period are clearly available in the seventeenth century itself, where the debate between the covenant of grace and the covenant of works is a persistent theme (to be echoed later on by the novelists Fielding and Smollett), one can also work backward. In fact I was led to this particular inquiry by noting an odd similarity in the pattern of response to certain seventeenth-century authors by critics of the early nineteenth century and onward. Blake, nourishing his own imagination by the Biblical

1

inspiration of Milton, nevertheless recoils from the black rock of Sinai which seems to him to cast its shadow over Milton's poetry and over much of the writing of the age. For Matthew Arnold the poetry of Isaiah with its great theme of "righteousness which tendeth to life" is the source of all enlightenment, and yet seventeenth-century Puritanism, which he identifies as the religion of "the hebraizing Middle Class," is the prime enemy of literary culture! Ezra Pound complains of Milton's "beastly Hebraism," and in T. S. Eliot's warning against the dangers of the Miltonic style there surely lurks a similar motive: he is offended by a type of religious poetry patently less abstract and otherworldly than his own. More recent academic critics have sought to separate Milton's rather eccentric theological notions from his poetry, claiming that the former are somehow unrelated to the latter; or else they have sought to neutralize the unwelcome spirituality of *Samson Agonistes* by the device of typology, seeing the strong-armed Samson as, paradoxically, a figure of Christian virtue and meekness. In all this there is an acknowledgment, explicit or implicit, of a kind of Biblical realism to which the sensibilities of critics are not always attuned.

Something very similar is now sometimes to be found in modern Shakespeare criticism. John Vyvyan, seeking to rationalize his distaste for Hamlet's deeds of violence, remarks that he "disavows the law of Christ to follow the law of Moses; and this in a Christian is sin."[2] Bernard Shaw sees similar Hebraic tendencies in Hamlet: "Born into the vindictive morality of Moses, he has evolved," says Shaw, "into the Christian perception of the futility and wickedness of revenge."[3] Roy Walker considers the Ghost to be an "Old Testament avenger."[4] How are we to account for this kind of critical reasoning, and does it at all correspond to typical audience reaction in our own time or in Shakespeare's time? That Shakespeare and the men of his generation were sensitive to "the morality of Moses" I think there can be no doubt. It was part of the Judeo-Christian tradition inherited from the Middle Ages, and it had emerged as something *sui generis* in the period of the Reformation. We sense it in the chroniclers, in Shakespeare's own *Richard III,* in *Macbeth,* and in the *Henry IV* trilogy with its emphasis on a divine economy working by reward and punishment through the lives of men and nations. Such a consciousness is to be found also in Sir Walter Raleigh's great *The History of the World,* its engraved frontispiece portraying the eye of God surveying human history. He points out grimly and aptly, for instance, that King Henry VIII did "cut off and cast off" so many innocent men and women including a number of his own wives, as a consequence of which "it pleased God to take away all his own without increase."[5] And he concludes by quoting the words of Samuel to Agag:

As thy Sword hath made other Women childless: so shall thy mother be childless among Women.

(I SAMUEL 15:33)

But we err if we suppose that the men of Shakespeare's time did not react positively and sympathetically to such ethical equations. As far as *Hamlet* is concerned, they would feel that the prince of Denmark was a little like King Solomon (by no means the bloodiest of Hebrew monarchs) compassing at his father's command the deaths of Joab and Shimei. And in fact in Belleforest's *Histoires Tragiques,* one of the recognized sources of the play, the analogy between Solomon's deeds and those of Hamlet is explicitly drawn.[6]

Modern critics may have achieved a degree of spiritual refinement that causes them to recoil from the notion of retributive justice (though there is little evidence that the world we live in has advanced so far as to enable us to dispense with it), but we should beware of attributing such fastidiousness to Shakespeare or to his audiences. In a reasonably straightforward performance of *Hamlet* I think it may be assumed that the spectators will still rejoice at the deserved deaths of Claudius, of Rosencrantz and Guildenstern, and even of Gertrude, lamenting only that Hamlet should be destroyed (like Samson) in the overthrow of his enemies. If he also sins through folly or weakness of spirit (like King David) does that make him any less the agent of Providence? Is there not in this whole spectacle something insistently religious, and is that religious note not clearly picked out by Horatio's remarks at the end of the play?

> Good night, sweet prince
> And flights of angels sing thee to thy rest![7]
>
> (V. ii. 373–374)

Do we not ignore such an element in the play at the peril of our critical souls?

Like so many other authors of the Renaissance, Shakespeare has the problem of dealing with violence and aggression. This is the material of nonsacred art at all periods, and never more so than in the age of Shakespeare. At the same time, account has to be taken of that divinity that shapes our ends. How was one to combine the two? In the Hebrew Scriptures human aggressions had been audaciously rooted in the sphere of divinity itself:

> He put on righteousness as a breastplate, and an helmet of salvation upon his head; and he put on the garment of vengeance for clothing, and was clad with zeal as a cloke.[8]
>
> (ISAIAH 59:17)

Such a text and the ethical attitude that it implies may help us to understand the last act of *Hamlet* and the "good end" that Hamlet makes. This does not mean that the last act of *Hamlet* is without its problems. After all, private vengeance is not the same as divine justice, and the Senecan revenge pattern which Shakespeare had inherited with its vicious circle of retaliation is by no means automatically adaptable to the kind of religious awe that we feel at the end of a Biblical drama such as *Athalie* or *Samson Agonistes*. But there is enough of a parallel to justify us in exploring seriously the possibility that *Hamlet* too belongs to that area of Western art in the period of the Reformation which comes near to its Hebraic origins.

This is just one example out of many of the working out of a moral theme in Shakespeare not exactly compatible with the Sermon on the Mount (for Hamlet does not love his enemies) and yet felt by the audiences to be both aesthetically and religiously satisfying. Criticism must respect such intentions and such achievements. In brief, to do justice to the ethical and spiritual norms adumbrated in Shakespeare's major drama, it is well not to bind ourselves beforehand by a prejudice in favor of either traditional

Christian piety or Renaissance secularism. The religious emphasis in these plays is strong, but the need is evidently for a religion by which men can live in the world without hypocrisy or inner contradictions. For Shakespeare this is an aesthetic as well as a moral necessity. His characters must achieve integrity, an integrity which takes in the requirements of their human nature and their sense of a divine destiny and a spiritual purpose beyond. Salvation is a this-worldly business. King Lear is often thought of as a Christ-figure in the last act of the tragedy that bears his name, and indeed there are submerged Christian intimations in the words of Kent at Lear's death:

> he hates him
> That would upon the rack of this tough world
> Stretch him out longer

(V. iii. 315–317)

But we should remind ourselves that Lear had just a moment before told us with becoming pride that he had killed the slave whom he had caught in the act of hanging Cordelia. If Lear is a Christ-figure on the Cross, he also performs an act of violent justice not exactly in keeping with the Christ of the gospels. And yet the audience feels no incongruity here: it is content that its heroes should so act when the need arises. It does not feel disturbed if King Lear in his regenerate phase still behaves like King David or like the prophet Samuel. The elements do not jar. On the contrary there is at the end a sense of balance and wholeness, for Shakespeare has somehow provided a moral syntax which joins together tenderness and vindication, love and terror. The lion lies down with the lamb. If at the end of the play King Lear is a saint, he is also a killer *at one and the same time.* He is a robed man of justice, and wields the sword of justice. At the beginning of the play he was a pagan and a savage, but at the end he has undergone a total moral change, one which governs his actions as a whole and provides a basis on which power and goodness may be combined. We do not feel any longer the old medieval disjunction between Christian pietism and Christian activism. There is instead a synthesis.

Then there is Edgar. At the end of *King Lear* Edgar links his father's past sins of adultery with his later misfortune at the hands of his bastard son Edmund:

> The gods are just, and of our pleasant vices
> Make instruments to plague us;
> The dark and vicious place where thee he got
> Cost him his eyes.

(V. iii. 172–175)

Can we avoid hearing the echo here of Nathan the prophet's warning to David? (Or what is more to the point, could Shakespeare's contemporaries avoid this echo?) There is even the same imagery of dark and light:

> Wherefore hast thou despised the commandment of the Lord, to do evil in his sight? thou hast killed Uriah the Hittite with the sword, and hast taken his wife. . . . Thus saith the Lord, Behold I will raise up evil against thee out of thine house, and I will take thy wives before thine eyes, and give them to thy neighbour. For thou didst it secretly: but I will do this thing before all Israel, and before the sun.
> (II SAMUEL 12:9f)

It has been suggested that Edgar's invocation here of the principle of retributive justice is of pagan origin, that what he has in mind is a kind of nemesis.[9] But this is surely to ignore the whole Biblical dimension of theodicy still so much alive for Shakespeare, for Raleigh, and the chroniclers of the Tudor period. What Edgar is pointing to is not the primitive Greek Ananke, goddess of Fortune or Destiny, nor yet Dike, goddess of Vengeance, who works by the force of an amoral natural law to visit punishment on those who have offended the gods. What we have instead is a Biblical sense of a law justifiable to man, accessible to his reason and his sense of right and wrong. And to balance it we have also in the play a Biblical sense of dialogue, of mutual obligation between man and God, equally foreign to the Greeks. We think of the final scene between Lear and Cordelia and of the still small voice of blessing sounded in it:

> When thou dost ask me blessing, I'll kneel down,
> And ask of thee forgiveness.

(V. iii. 10–11)

The same gentle note of reconciliation is struck in the scenes during which Edgar accompanies his father, Gloucester, on his last trials and wanderings. And yet such Biblical pathos, reminiscent of the final scenes between Joseph and his father, Jacob, is not to be separated from Edgar's stern moral judgments or from the sight of Lear's swift avenging sword.

Such a conjunction is not quite new to the Christian tradition of the West. The medieval knightly code provided for a combination of tenderness and strength employed on behalf of high principles. The armed Christian warrior is a well-established figure. In Shakespeare's time he survives in the noble and virtuous discipline, the strong-armed morality of Spenser's heroes and heroines in *The Faerie Queene*. Redcrosse Knight too employs violence on behalf of the faith. Nevertheless we must be careful to keep in mind the novelty of the Shakespearean model. The Knight Templars of the time of the Crusades were, after all, barbarians dressed up as Christian warriors. Few would quarrel with Scott's summing-up of the knight Bois-Guilbert as a representative of his order, with a faith "which is ever in thy mouth but never in thy heart and practice."[10] And we recall Gibbon's ironical account of the savagery of the heroes of the Cross who captured Jerusalem in the eleventh century, and who, after three days of unbridled rapine and slaughter, "ascended the hill of Calvary . . . and bedewed with tears of joy and penitence the monument of their redemption." There is little sign here of that inner moral change, that genuine "atonement" which we sense in Lear and Hamlet. As for Spenser, at the risk of stating the obvious we may note that Spenser's is an achievement of allegory. We shall not meet Redcrosse Knight or his like in London, Venice, or Denmark. His is a symbolic purity and strength. Shakespeare's characters, by contrast, crave to be located in the world we know, and to be judged by its standards. Lear, Malcolm, Edgar, and supremely Hamlet occupy natural space: their actions express their personalities. These personalities may have an allegorical shading, but this is an extra dimension that in no way prejudices their claim to naturalness. For the dramatic substance in which their actions are embedded is concrete and palpable. If with these characters justice and peace have met and kissed one another, such a meeting is enacted in the here-and-now, in the area of the human and the contingent.

In tracing this kind of religious attitude in the tradition of the West, are we not inevitably drawn to that "old shameless literature of the Old Testament" as J. C. Powys termed it, with "its human anger, its human justice and its human magnanimity?"[11] Shakespeare's generation did not produce a passion play, but George Peele, three years before *Hamlet,* produced a play entitled, *The Loves of King David and Fair Bethsabe,* and in it he celebrated the romantic tale of the house of David, its loves and passions. With the decline of the miracle play or sacred play proper in the Tudor period, a new kind of scriptural drama had arisen based sometimes on the New Testament parables (such as that of the Prodigal Son) but more often on Old Testament narratives, on the lives of Absalom, Queen Esther, and Jonah, or on figures from the Apocrypha and Josephus.[12] The advantage of this material as a counterweight to the new secular drama of the age was obvious: it was divinely vouched for and religiously oriented, and yet its characters were fallible like ourselves, in this unlike the haloed saints of the earlier ecclesiastical drama.[13] Being flesh and blood they could also serve as moral examples and warnings for the audience. There was an "overarching sequence of temptation, sin, and retribution,"[14] the emphasis being on ethics rather than theology and dogma. Above all we have here that unyielding concern with theodicy which stems from the Hebrew Scriptures, for Peele's play illustrates how divine justice works, David reaping through his children the fruit of his sin with Bathsheba. Here was a spectacle calculated to send a thrill of fear (and also pity) through the audience. Shakespeare, as we have said, employs the same principle in *Macbeth,* in *Richard III* and, of course, in *Hamlet* and *King Lear.* In all these examples the Hebrew paradigms are not far absent.

Unlike Peele, Shakespeare never wrote a straight Biblical play but present-day criticism sees a great deal more Biblical substance in Shakespeare than was customary hitherto. There is evident Christian symbolism in *The Winter's Tale* and *Measure for Measure* as G. Wilson Knight has demonstrated.[15] Frank Kermode speaks of fall and redemption in *The Tempest.*[16] Jan Kott sees

King Lear as a pantomime version of the Book of Job.[17] Roy
Battenhouse proposes a host of such "echoes of Biblical realism"
in the imagery and structure of the plays.[18] In the following pages
we shall be pointing to several examples of this kind, some of
them new, some of them already hinted at by earlier critics. But
the main purpose of this book is not to propose Biblical analogues
for specific passages and episodes. I am here proposing to explore
something at once more basic and more intangible, *viz.,* the moral
substance of the Shakespearean drama: how is human destiny
viewed? to what sort of task is man summoned? and in what form
is that summons issued? In the experience of Biblical man the
key to these matters lies in the covenant, a transforming encounter
between man and God, from which many mutual obligations flow,
but also trials, disaster, and salvation as well. It is a dramatic
structure giving meaning and pattern to history.

Is there room for introducing into the canons of Shakespearean
criticism the notion of covenant? The question is not quite fanciful,
for the men of Shakespeare's age were Biblically conscious to a
degree that we do not always appreciate, and the covenant type of
experience was one to which they could easily respond. Moreover,
the covenant presupposed challenges issued to man in his human
condition, possessed of appetites and instincts such as we recognize
in ourselves. It is, we are told (Deuteronomy: 30), neither hidden
from us, nor is it far off. The covenant involves a choice of paths.
To choose aright is a matter of immense responsibility, the sort of
responsibility from which a hero such as Orestes or Oedipus is
exempt, since in their case the path is, in a manner, determined
before they are born. In the covenant type of choice there is, as
we have said, human freedom, but there is also a sense of a commanding voice. Once that voice is heard, its commandments live
all alone within the book and volume of our brain.

At the end of *Henry IV, Part II* we see Prince Hal, for instance, entering into a solemn compact with his dying father,
accepting voluntary curbs upon his freedom in a lodging house
which bears the symbolic name of Jerusalem. Such a dramatic
scene is weighted with religious meaning. It is also a kind of paradigm. Like the meeting between Hamlet and his father's Ghost, it
is accompanied by an exchange of vows and oaths, by the injection

into the life pattern of the hero of a purpose which seems to reverberate beyond the play.

There is no intention here of limiting our understanding of Shakespeare to this one aspect. Shakespeare is not going to be circumcised. But it will be suggested that the Hebraic component of his work—hitherto insufficiently appreciated—may be as important as the Senecan-Stoic or medieval-Christian components, and that the full exhibition of this factor by means of interpretative criticism can enrich and deepen our understanding of the plays. It can be seen emerging through the fable, through the positioning of the characters, through the pattern of the images—especially images of books and writing—and through the structure of the soliloquies. Hamlet's soliloquies are expressions of an intolerable loneliness, but they also imply a search for an answering presence. His inner debate (like that of Angelo in *Measure for Measure*) leads us toward the categories of dialogue.

Francis Bacon warned those who seek to advance learning not to be seduced by the Idols of the Cave, which arise, he says, "from the peculiar nature of every particular person, both with regard to soul and body, as also from education, custom, and accidents." This is surely the fallacy of Christian critics who find crucifixion symbols throughout Shakespeare, and likewise of Marxist critics who find everywhere an endorsement of their dialectical philosophy. In seeking to isolate certain Hebraic patterns and motifs in Shakespeare are we not likely to commit the same offense? And especially so in reference to a play such as *Hamlet* in which every sect and generation have notoriously found a confirmation of their world view. The Romantics found Hamlet to be a Romantic, while the existentialists find him to be an existentialist. Will criticism conducted on the lines proposed here prove to be anything more than a deceptive play of mirrors? Indeed there can be no absolute immunity against this risk. Adapting a phrase of Milton, we could say that assuredly we bring not innocency to the work of criticism: we bring rather our personal freight of opinions and beliefs; and in taking up an author to whom we feel drawn there is the risk of distorting him in the interests of such opinions and beliefs. There is in fact only one method of safeguarding ourselves against this danger, and that is faithfulness to the text. It is the play which must ultimately determine the validity of the interpretation. The interpretation will be proved false if, in order to support it, we are drawn to suppress "some necessary question of the play." Conversely, the value of a reading will be judged by the degree of completeness with which it answers the questions raised by the play itself in its totality. The present study lays claim to such completeness.

The subject of this book is Shakespeare, but it seemed best in every way to concentrate on one work and analyze it in depth. The work selected was *Hamlet.* So that though the other major plays of Shakespeare will not be ignored, the attention in the substantive chapters will be focused on *Hamlet,* its hero and his environment of action. In the concluding chapter some of the insights gained will be applied in detail to three other plays: *King Lear, As You Like It,* and *The Tempest.* An Appendix explores the implications of Shakespeare's images in *Julius Caesar.*

CHAPTER I

A Cry
of Critics

Two vulgar errors are prevalent in Shakespeare criticism: one confines Shakespeare to his own time, and the other confines him to ours. We are all familiar with the first: it is the error of pedants who believe that Shakespeare's meaning is discoverable primarily not from the plays themselves, their universal moral tendency, their imagery and structure, but from long-forgotten Elizabethan treatises on psychological theory, demonology, travel, and the rest. Shakespearean criticism becomes a coral island created by the deposited remains of long-dead literary insects. Thus Reginald Scot's *Discoverie of Witchcraft,* Pierre Le Loyer's *IIII Livres des spectres,* Noël Taillepied's *Psichologie ou traité des esprits,* and Lewes Lavater's *Of Ghostes and Spirites* will tell us infallibly whether the Ghost of Hamlet's father was a good ghost or a bad ghost and whether Hamlet was right or wrong to listen to him.[1] This is the way to the heart of the mystery. One wonders why Shakespeare is still alive for so many nonscholars and nonspecialists.

But the second vulgar error is just as likely to lead us astray as the first. As an example one might consider Jan Kott's much discussed book, *Shakespeare Our Contemporary.* In it he has chosen to ignore Shakespeare's "intention," the Shakespearean "world," the Shakespearean "moment," and all the other concerns of historical criticism. The problems of our own time in the last third of the twentieth century are a good deal more pressing than the needs of academic source-hunting. If Shakespeare has something to say which sounds like the protest of our troubled

13

generation, let us extract that and toss the rest of the business away. All that matters is that our author should be real, meaningful, and alive for us in the year 1961 or 1971.

Thus Hamlet becomes our contemporary, a young existentialist "tormented by thoughts of the fundamental absurdity of existence,"[2] a reader of Camus and Sartre. Hamlet is a symbol of modern alienated humanity, not because Shakespeare so drew him, but because thus we need to portray him for our own purposes. Shakespeare's plays, so Kott assures us, are no more than a scenario, a loose frame into which the critic and producer can fit a play suitable to present-day spiritual and political realities. Kott professes little interest in the play as Shakespeare designed it: it is its re-creation in the theater for each generation that matters. Those parts of the "scenario" that do not fit in with the latest interpretation may be freely dropped or twisted around. In a recent production of *Hamlet* by a Polish disciple of Kott,[3] Horatio could be seen at the end of the play cynically prodding the dead body of Hamlet with his foot, and with obvious satisfaction handing over the kingdom to a brash young Fortinbras. In order to support this, the lines which Shakespeare gave Horatio:

> Good night, sweet prince,
> And flights of angels sing thee to thy rest!

> (V. ii. 373–374)

were conveniently dropped.

Of course Kott does not claim to be writing interpretative literary criticism: he has no responsibility for the whole work in its integrity. He is a little like the Bishop of Woolwich, rewriting the Bible so that we can have what is good for us without a personal God. But the question is whether something of significance for ourselves in the latter half of the twentieth century is not going to be lost if we leave out lines such as those of Horatio. After all, interpretative historical critics could argue that they too (no less than Kott) are in the business because of the enduring significance for the present-day reader and theatergoer of the works they are expounding. If we continue to explore Shakespeare, Milton, and Blake, we do so not for their archaeological interest but because they still have something meaningful to say to us. But who will decide what this meaning is—we or the author? And if the author, how will his meaning reach us if we do not let him have his full say and if we do not allow the work to address us in its own fashion? Let us agree with Kott and against the pedants that Shakespeare's work is for our time, but let us add that it only attains this contemporaneity by virtue of the depth and earnestness with which it explores the problems of his own time; and this is where serious criticism must begin. If history is important—and surely Marxists will be the first to agree that it is—then historical criticism is also important.

To understand the plays of Shakespeare we have to make ourselves members of the Elizabethan audience: we have to learn their language and think their thoughts, for, as Hamlet tells the actors, "the purpose of playing . . . is to show virtue her own feature, scorn her own image, and the very age and body of the time his form and pressure." But the very age and body of the time does not mean Le Loyer and Lavater; it does not mean learned theory or psychological dogma, but something more basic and pervasive. It means something like the spirit of the age, its gestalt, its spiritual ambience. That is of the essence. Let us take a modern example: to appreciate a play such as Archibald MacLeish's *J.B.,* or Beckett's *Waiting for Godot,* one has to share something of the *quality* of life in the mid-twentieth century, in particular the sense of menace peculiar to an age which lives in the shadow of Auschwitz and under the threat of the hydrogen bomb. Now we all devoutly hope that in two hundred years' time these factors will no longer operate on people's minds as part of the actual "form and pressure" of their time. And yet we are entitled to hope that these plays will endure. And if they do, it will be because there will be something of permanent value to men, of permanent admonitory value, in sharing this experience of a bygone age with us. It may be that such works would even at that distance radiate a kind of hope and resilience. But how will this "spirit of the age" be made available to an audience of the future except by means of the techniques and insights of historical criticism? It is such criticism alone that can create a meaningful context of experience within which earlier works of art can retain their power so as to be fully appreciated.

But to return to Shakespeare: how shall we establish a genuine historical context for his work? For the very transitional quality of the Elizabethan age presents a problem. There is no strict medieval system of hierarchies binding all things together in harmony and order, nor is there on the other hand that radical sweeping aside of inherited values that we find in later times. The "form and pressure" revealed by the plays is dialectical, ambiguous. We sense both order and revolt, both security and insecurity, both faith and skepticism. Macbeth has the modern man's ambition, the thirst for power. Rebelling against the divine order of the Middle Ages, he will, if he can, jump the life to come. But his imagination is nevertheless haunted by images of that very divine order against which he has rebelled; the cherubim horsed upon the sightless couriers of the air, the spirit of man which is the candle of the Lord. Hamlet, for his part, has gone further than Macbeth: he is lost, alienated, cut off from the solace and intimacy of man, God, and nature. He is, if you like, a beatnik, but a beatnik of the year 1603. He has attained a more radical emancipation than Macbeth from medieval categories of thought, but even he is still conscious of the breath of angels' wings. He speaks in monologue, but he yearns for the life of dialogue, for grace and mercy at his most need. Hence the torment, the heartache, and the thousand natural shocks. He does not share the absolute skepticism of Horatio, and indeed warns him that there are more things in heaven and earth than are dreamt of in his stoical and secular philosophy. He speaks of the dead Polonius as a modern existentialist would when, on discovering his error, he remarks:

> I'll lug the guts into the neighbour room.
>   . . . This counsellor
> Is now most still, most secret, and most grave
> Who was in life a foolish prating knave.

(III. iv. 212–215)

Here is Hamlet using the accent of the grotesque: he seems to be almost like a clown in the modern theater of the absurd. But he does not speak like a character from Beckett or Ionesco or Pinter when he says in that same scene:

> For this same lord,
> I do repent; but heaven hath pleased it so,
> To punish me with this, and this with me,
> That I must be their scourge and minister.
>
> (172–175)

One who speaks thus does not act in a theater of the absurd but in a dramatic plot overseen and guided by Providence. For the understanding of such a Hamlet we need to bring all our modern sense of alienation, but together with that we need to perform a reconstructive act of the imagination, so as to recover for ourselves the sense of solemnity which invests the circumstances of life overseen by God. Hamlet is not seeking God: on the contrary he is running away from him, but he is still near enough to hear the heavy footstep at his back.

II

The paradoxical, inharmonious character of Shakespeare's age has often led the academic critics astray. Instead of seeing him as striving to accommodate the conflicting tendencies of his age and somehow resolve a meaning out of them, they picture him as having one face of Janus only. D. G. James speaks of his imaginative secularity. Among his contemporaries, Shakespeare most resembles Bacon, the doubter, the apostle of the modern world.[4] This is also the character of Hamlet, Shakespeare's most quintessentially post-medieval figure. L. C. Knights speaks in a similar vein, seeing Hamlet as an image of modernity.[5] Both these critics are genuine students of Shakespeare's time—they are not merely reading back our modern anxieties into Shakespeare's plays—but they are concerned with one dominant aspect of Shakespeare's time, the aspect which has been aptly termed the "Counter-Renaissance," its divisive revolutionary phase.[6] Hamlet is thus not our contemporary, but he is the contemporary of Montaigne, of Bacon, and of the "atheistic" Marlowe. He also shares with the men of the Counter-Renaissance the Calvinist vision of original sin, of a world sunk in depravity:

> How weary, stale, flat and unprofitable
> Seem to me all the uses of this world.
> Fie on't! ah, fie! 'Tis an unweeded garden
> That grows to seed; things rank and gross in nature
> Possess it merely.

(I. ii. 133–137)

Here is no longer the sanctified nature of the Middle Ages, but a world of corruption and brutality. Later on, Hobbes, who draws plentifully from the same sources, will declare that in the "meere state of nature" the life of man is "nasty, brutish, and short."

Another group of critics concentrates on the other face of Janus. They see Shakespeare as the supreme exponent of medieval order. His characters bear witness to a still active faith in the pattern of correspondences linking man, God, and nature in an organic pattern. These critics, in picturing Shakespeare as a traditionalist, again are doing so in full awareness of history: they are mindful that Shakespeare was the contemporary of Richard Hooker and Spenser, and that he was born in the century of Erasmus and Sir Thomas More. Of course Hamlet presents a difficulty, because he is so obviously restless, and because he explicitly denies that the orderly sanctified world of the Middle Ages still exists; "this brave o'erhanging firmament," he says, "this majestical roof fretted with golden fire—why it appeareth no other thing to me than a foul and pestilent congregation of vapors." Many of the traditionalist critics, however, get around this by employing what may be termed the "Ancient Mariner motif." Hamlet is lost, but he undergoes redemption; he is saved by the action of grace in a sound and recognizable Christian manner. He does not actually seek out a hermit to whom he will confess his sins, but it very nearly comes to that. The redeeming moment occurs (again how like the Ancient Mariner) in the course of the sea voyage to England. It was not very Christian of Hamlet to have sent his two friends to their deaths at that precise moment—this is not what the Ancient Mariner would have done in his regenerate phase—but the main lines are there nevertheless, and the recovery of a sanctified order may be discerned with the beginning of the fifth act. C. S. Lewis expressed, in characteristically dogmatic form, what is by now a commonplace of this kind of criticism when he said:

The world of *Hamlet* is a world where one has lost one's way. The Prince also has no doubt lost his, and we can tell the precise moment at which he finds it again. "Not a whit, We defy augury. There's a special providence in the fall of a sparrow."[7]

Irving Ribner,[8] with a fine insight, fixes the moment—the moment that would correspond to the Ancient Mariner's blessing of the water snakes—in the expression of regret that Hamlet utters after his outburst at Laertes:

> But I am very sorry good Horatio
> That to Laertes I forgot myself;
> For by the image of my cause I see
> The portraiture of his.

(V. ii. 75–78)

True it is that these lines give us the measure of the religious depth of this play. The parallels between the fate of Laertes and that of Hamlet—both orphaned, both summoned to revenge the death of a father—serve to reveal to Hamlet the reality of human brotherhood. The parallelism between their fates had done the same for Gloucester and Lear. The exchange of forgiveness between Laertes and Hamlet at the end of that act is therefore no mere stage formality: it marks the affirmation of love—and that, in theological terms, is the manifestation of the category of grace. Hamlet even dresses differently after the sea change of Act IV, when casting his nighted color off he testifies outwardly to the redemptive change which has gone on within.[9] Hamlet is now truly a changed man, and the Christian critics have eagerly identified this change with the Christian notion of salvation. "Hamlet," according to Ribner, "has his Christian religion to guide him," and the end of the play leads the audience toward a "positive affirmation of Christian moral order."[10] Sister Miriam Joseph, with an enviable freedom from any Hamlet-like scruples or from too precisely thinking on the event, declares quite simply that "*Hamlet* is a play with a Christian atmosphere," and that "Hamlet is a Christian prince whose basic moral sensitivity and rectitude fit him to be the hero of a Christian tragedy."[11]

Obviously, if you take the view of Lewis, Ribner, and Sister Miriam, you must reject that of James and Knights, and vice versa.

But these two sets of views do not exhaust the possibilities yielded by historical interpretations. Salvador de Madariaga, drawing upon his knowledge of the Spanish and Italian Renaissance, represents Hamlet not as a skeptical philosopher (D. G. James) nor as a Christian penitent (C. S. Lewis) but as a supersubtle and barbarous Renaissance villain.[12] He comes to look like a member of the Borgia family.[13] After all, the last act has, besides its Christian overtones, certain intimations of Machiavellian violence: Hamlet shows a combination of lion and fox in dispatching his enemies Rosencrantz and Guildenstern, and, finally, Laertes and Claudius. Significantly, many of the critics who share Madariaga's view (with varieties of emphasis) also operate with Christian categories. But they see the play as illustrating the dreadful consequences that follow from the violation of Christian principles. In other words, the ambience of the play is Christian, but Hamlet is to the end the violent disturber of Christian order. John Vyvyan looks upon Hamlet as having been seduced to deeds of barbarism by an evil spirit.[14] The Ghost functions like the witches in *Macbeth,* and Hamlet's actions subsequent to his meeting with it are as grace-less—or almost so—as those of Macbeth himself! The play, says Vyvyan with a certainty equal to that of Ribner, is "a study in degeneration from first to last."[15] Shakespeare is affirming Christian categories, but he is seeking our endorsement of them by holding up the image of Renaissance man in diabolical insurrection against order and piety. There is no redeeming moment, for it is the Devil who enters Hamlet in Act V and drives him on to deeds of blood! Hamlet speaks of himself as having too much conscience, but in fact, says Vyvyan, he has too little!

Other critics have also had reservations about Hamlet's piety. Geoffrey Bush expresses himself with the help of those casuistical formulas that the subtler theologians have always employed when grappling with the problems of nature and grace. Where Vyvyan rushes in, Bush fears to tread. But he treads just the same with a certain angelic caution:

> Hamlet and Orestes are not religious redeemers; yet there are con-
> tradictions about them that approach the paradoxes of religion. Their
> revenge is both an act of horror and an apotheosis; it is a descent into
> barbarism and a leap into sanctity; it is an act of extremity that rep-

resents the contradictions inherent in any human action performed in the context of the world and what is beyond the world.[16]

This makes Hamlet appear a little like a character in a novel by Graham Greene. In Hamlet's revenge, says Bush, we have one of "those moments when our secular lives are crossed by grace."[17] It is clear that Bush is trying to have it both ways. He is powerfully impressed by the Christian atmosphere of the play, by the sense of salvation and grace that pervades the last act; at the same time he is impressed by the fact that such salvation is achieved by fulfilling the instincts of "nature" in an act of revenge. If the powers put on their instruments and if Providence guides Hamlet into the hall where the King and Laertes await him with the foils, it is to enable him to perform a very unchristian deed of bloodshed. That is the descent into barbarism combined with the leap into sanctity. Traditional Christianity of course knows of this tension between grace and nature. Augustine recognized that there is the earthly city and the City of God, and though he recognized that one has to live in both, he nevertheless keeps alive the distinction between them. There is what Bush calls "contradiction" or "paradox." The same would apply to Calvin and the line he draws between the sphere of the civil governor and the sphere of the Church in the last section of the *Institutes*. And despite all the political sagacity that Calvin shows in accommodating the two to each other, they remain distinct and opposed orders. He renders to God what is God's and to Caesar what is Caesar's. There is disjunction rather than conjunction.

While we may agree that Hamlet harbors paradoxes and contradictions, we may well wonder whether Bush is at all justified in proposing a disjunction between "nature" and "grace" as the ground of his conduct at the end of the play. In the last words of Laertes, when he is killed by Hamlet, we have a testimony to the rightness of the act of slaughter in a context which strongly suggests at the same time the categories of love and grace. There is no sense here of what Bush calls "contradiction":

> He is justly served,
> It is a poison tempered by himself.
> Exchange forgiveness with me, noble Hamlet,

Mine and my father's death come not upon thee,
Nor thine on me!

(V. ii. 341–345)

The Biblical phraseology here is important and also the subtle use of Biblical parallelism in the last two lines. Quite contrary to what Bush is saying, Hamlet is careful in Act V to relate his actions to a moral system in which they are justified and even sanctified. Far from conceiving the killing of Rosencrantz and Guildenstern or the approaching liquidation of Claudius as a descent into barbarism, Hamlet is careful to refer them to a system of sanctions in which they become "perfect conscience." The term "conscience" is a key word in the play, and in the last act it carries its full religious load. Of the two unfortunate spies he says,

They are not near my conscience, their defeat
Does by their own insinuation grow.

(V. ii. 58–59)

Nothing could be clearer than this; and of Claudius he declares in similar vein:

is't not perfect conscience
To quit him with this arm? and is't not to be damned,
To let this canker of our nature come
In further evil.

(V. ii. 67–70)

Bush is entitled to regard Hamlet's wielding of the sword of justice as "an act of horror," but Hamlet himself is saying the opposite. He is saying that to refrain from so doing is "to be damned." The contradictions here between nature and grace are not apparent. On the contrary, the religious order intimated in these closing scenes and especially in these speeches of Hamlet is one in which action in this world, even action of a violent and bloody kind, and salvation in the world to come, can support and strengthen one another.

One other highly sophisticated Christian interpretation of Shakespearean tragedy needs to be reckoned with at this point. Roy Battenhouse sets up the nature/grace antithesis in a different form. Arguing in a recent book[18] that Shakespeare is a "Christian artist," he means by this something different from what had been proposed either by Sister Miriam Joseph, or Ribner, or Bush. In such heroes as Hamlet and Romeo, Battenhouse finds neither Christian paradigms nor Christian paradoxes: he sees them rather as representatives of the "Old Adam" of St. Paul—man incapable of salvation or wantonly rejecting Christian truth. But Shakespeare spells out the Christian scheme typologically, that is to say through a plot structure and through episodes which seem to point in one direction but actually point in another. There is a "figurative over-plot." Thus Hamlet's appeal in the ghost scene to "angels and ministers of Grace," or the formula which he proposes at the oath-taking: "So grace and mercy at your most need help you"—seem to suggest that he is invoking Christian standards for his revenge task, but the words, says Battenhouse "ironically signalize for us the values that Hamlet is bypassing."[19] Hamlet's sense of divine election in the meeting with his father's Ghost is merely a parody of such experience, just as his apparent submission to the divine will at the end ("the readiness is all") "means being ready for rashness and the opportunity it can bring to play judge." The reference to a providence in the fall of a sparrow (V. ii) has been universally noted as an allusion to a famous passage in the New Testament (Matthew 10:29), but Battenhouse concludes that such reference "when found in this upside-down context, alerts us to the tragic parody in Hamlet's version of readiness."[20] The whole ending of the play, in which Hamlet seems to seek and attain reconcilement with Laertes and ultimately with his God is seen as a "counterfeit version, an unwitting parody of atonement."[21] Like Richard II in his abdication scene, Hamlet is acting Christ, but doing so in an inverted fashion. He is conducting a Black Mass, a fearful travesty of the gospel account of salvation, acting out his destiny by means of "maimed rites." He points to the truth obliquely, by indirections finding directions out. "His defective action shadows Christian paradigm."[22]

One objection to all this is that such a sophisticated Christian reading requires a kind of mental agility not to be found in common audiences of Shakespeare's time or our own. Battenhouse seems to admit this when, arguing that Hamlet's Christian oaths ('Swounds, 'Sblood) highlight his rejection of Christian standards, he remarks:

> Auditors of the play may overlook this fact while the drama is being
> staged; yet it is embedded in the fabric of the action for our poten-
> tial apprehension.[23]

In other words, the audience, in the excitement of the dramatic
spectacle may not actually share with Shakespeare the metaphysical scheme on which the play is based, but it is there just the same,
even if it is caviar to the general. Criticism has here achieved a
degree of abstraction from the overt meaning of the play which
borders on occultism.

The typological reading has the advantage of serving to relate
seemingly intractable material to established Christian doctrine,
but it has the disadvantage of robbing the literary work of much
of its immediacy and concreteness. The sensual, down-to-earth
elements of *Samson Agonistes*,[24] the Elizabethan toughness of
Hamlet, are all but sublimated away. Typology at one time enabled
the devout to Christianize such a figure as Joshua, the Hebrew
conqueror of Canaan, and see him as a type of Christ whose
kingdom is not of this world. He points beyond himself. Battenhouse is attempting something similar with Hamlet, who bears
witness, against himself as it were, to the true metaphysic, the true
supernatural order of values. Such interpretation fails to register
the strength and pertinacity with which the men of the Renaissance
seized upon the natural world and the natural instincts of man.
This for them was reality. Human love, human ambition, human
effort were not to be gainsaid. Such interpretation also fails to
register the fact that the Bible had now been brought home to
men's businesses and bosoms in a way unknown to the Middle
Ages. Translated (to use the words of the committee of 1611)
so as to be understood of the very vulgar, it had a way of rubbing
up against men's daily lives. Shakespeare's contemporaries, Pem-
broke, Raleigh, Essex, were men of action (even, it is to be feared,
men of blood), but the word of God was not far from their lips.
Rightly or wrongly, they felt they could bring their very worldly
ways within the circumference of the religious life. And Essex has
been thought of as a model for Hamlet. Raleigh's speech on the
scaffold, in which he gives an account to God of his worldly doings,
is one of the most religious documents of the age.

Raleigh's conception of history involves the application of

Biblical categories to the lives of men and nations, but he has at the same time a Machiavellian realism which leaves little room for speculation about worlds beyond our own. And Shakespeare views the doings of Henry V in a similar light. Henry's moral environment is that of human history. The immortality he aims at is the immortal fame of conquest, and when he achieves it on the field of Agincourt he "praises God and not his strength for it." We distort the text if we suppose that such a statement does not carry with it the sentiment of the play, of the audience, and in great measure, of the author. The chronicle plays generate no little religious exaltation, but it is a religion the myth of which is human history, and specifically English history. It is thus related to the doings of men on this earth, even if this earth is, in the Augustinian scheme, the scene of depravity. Augustine keeps before us in an ideal balance the earthly city and the heavenly city, maintaining the reality of both. But the Elizabethan poet and chronicler is clearly much more dominated by the earthly city: it is this which he invests with religious glory. The balance has altered, and a new balance has been struck which belongs peculiarly to the Elizabethan age, the age of Shakespeare.[25]

Erich Auerbach would maintain that even in the figurative literature of the Middle Ages, based as it was on a double world-scheme, the material reality is neither abandoned nor subverted. Even Dante is drawn to sympathize with the earthly hopes and fears, the sorrows and ambitions of his characters in the Inferno. In the case of Dante, this direct experience of life finally overwhelms everything else, including the Thomist metaphysical scheme, and we are left, according to Auerbach, with

> an illumination of man's impulses and passions which leads us to share in them without restraint and indeed to admire their variety and greatness.[26]

I would claim no less for Shakespeare. In *Hamlet,* too, Shakespeare becomes positively involved in the impulses and passions of his hero, and leads his audience to share in them and admire them. There is no hidden censor at work. It may be that not all students of Dante would agree with Auerbach that Dante's world of men and women ultimately overrules the metaphysical scheme, but few would contest his view that in Boccaccio, a little later on, we have a spontaneously sensory world, a representation of the here and now uncontrolled by any "figurative overplot."[27] And Shakespeare surely starts from the naturalism of Boccaccio rather than from the supernaturalism of Dante and his like. His world is that of our fallen nature, of human love, human desire, and human ambition.

Of course, there is "typology," in the sense of a larger myth, a larger pattern of meaning of which the doings of the characters on the stage are merely the index and epitome. The plays have, shall we say, an archetypal quality, a richer, deeper reverberation. Were it not so, it is doubtful whether they would have maintained their hold on the mind and imagination of men as they have done. But such archetypes must be related to the concrete materiality of the action. When the larger myth is seen to rob the play of such concrete materiality, or seriously to undermine it, we may begin to suspect the validity of the interpretation.

We may now go one step further: if the material substance of the action is human history—the doings of men and their fortunes in a this-worldly framework of reality—then the larger drama too is historical. Here we behold not particular events and the fortunes of particular individuals, but rather the forces at work in history, its fundamental pattern. In short, what Shakespeare is offering us at this transliteral level is an interpretation of history itself. And it is, we may add, a religious interpretation. There is an overarching Biblical theme. There is a reading of signs, an illumination of past, present, and future seized as an imaginative whole, proceeding from known beginnings to foreseen endings. The Roman plays exhibit the fortunes of Brutus, of Antony, of Coriolanus; but they also contain a judgment of Roman civilization in its entirety, and even more, of those elements of Romanism which survive in Shakespeare's time, and perhaps also in our own. In an important sense, *Othello, Romeo and Juliet,* and *Hamlet* are all history plays, seeking to define through image and symbolic action the processes whereby men begin to govern their own inherited barbarisms, or the ways in which they confront the challenge of the new. If such plays have a meaning beyond themselves and beyond the conditions of their own age, it is because they illuminate the whole adventure of time, its conflicts and resolutions.

CHAPTER II

Hamlet
Agonistes

Shakespeare is much more Hegelian than Hegel himself gave him credit for being. A. C. Bradley was the first to say this, but Bradley did not go far enough.[1] According to Hegel, tragedy in its true, original form is concerned not merely with individuals in conflict but with historical and religious systems "individualized in living personalities and situations pregnant with conflict."[2] For Hegel the great example of this was the *Antigone* of Sophocles where Creon and Antigone represent two ideologies, the former, loyalty to the state, the latter, loyalty to the family.[3] Here, as Bradley finely phrases it, is "the intestinal warfare of the ethical substance itself." Both principles, though mutually excluding, are good, and for that reason the opposition between them is tragic. We are often told that the *Oresteia* dramatizes the conflict between the patriarchal and the matriarchal principles at a certain critical stage in Greek cultural history: these principles are at war within the soul of Orestes, but they are also objectively realized in the opposition between Apollo and the Furies. The tragic dénouement corresponds with the reconciliation of the two principles—their synthesis—and it is not achieved without death or suffering for the principal parties.

According to Hegel, nothing quite like this is to be found in Shakespeare.[4] In *Macbeth* we have merely the moral insurrection of an evil man who represents only his own evil; in *Othello* we have the torment of a noble mind poisoned by jealousy; and in *Hamlet* the internal private conflict of a man unable to make up his mind. In short we have an interior, subjective situation of great psychological interest rather than a drama revealing the dialectical structure of a whole society or civilization. Such is, approximately, the romantic view of Shakespeare's plays to which Hegel gave a certain philosophical warrant. Shakespeare's characters are seen as burdened with their own tragic pathos and as struggling in a world with which they have little organic connection. But this surely cannot be the view of interpretative, historical criticism. Such criticism will inevitably view Shakespeare's plays as approximating more to the mode of action proposed by Hegel in regard to the *Antigone* or the *Oresteia.*

Othello and Desdemona surely represent more than their own individualities—irreducibly unique though these may be—for they also personify the conflicting forces of the time they live in: they are victims of the clash between old and new. Othello trails clouds of glory from the age of chivalry. Nobly heroic, he looks slightly out-of-date in the new bourgeois environment where Brabantio, the merchant of Venice, has no time for romantic strangers. Othello is a little like Don Quixote, and some of the same ironies invest his person. By the same token Desdemona and Iago are realists of the new age. A handkerchief is a handkerchief, not a magic talisman; Desdemona's father sold them in his shop. Iago, in his Hobbesian fashion, has dropped all such words as "love" and "honor." His advice to Roderigo sounds the accent of a new commercial civilization, "Put money in thy purse." But this is no simple conflict of good and evil. Evil as Iago is, Othello would have been better off with a little of his knowledge of the world. He is far too much concerned with his aristocratic lineage, his honor, and his great doings in the past. After all, army commanders cannot always be charging across the battlefield on horseback or making romantic love like Sergius in Shaw's *Arms and the Man.* The best officers are those who have the practical common sense and administrative ability of Bluntschli. Othello is too much like Sergius: he hasn't yet come to terms with the new world. Had he known how to run a peacetime garrison with its married quarters and its petty intrigues, there would have been no tragedy. Here, in short, is a clash within the "ethical substance" itself, between a new, material, and practical order and an older chivalric order now showing signs of decay. The synthesis marked out for us in Othello's farewell to arms, and in Desdemona's adoption of the best in the romantic code of love and honor, involves a glimpse of a new and happier world in which the harsh discords of an age of transition shall have been assuaged.

Macbeth gives us something similar, a new ambitious Renaissance figure seeking to create his own time in a world still subject to the limitations of medieval sacral order. For Lady Macbeth the metaphysical system (still so appallingly real for Macbeth in spite of his vaulting ambition) is practically nonexistent:

> When all's done
> You look but on a stool.

> (III. iv. 67–68)

According to the new humanism, men can create their own time; they are not subject to the eternal sway of a sacred time-structure ruled over by eternity. Similarly men can twist and pervert the laws of God and nature without fear. Lady Macbeth can dare to revoke her feminine nature, and Macbeth can dare to revoke those sacred ties of allegiance, kinship, and hospitality which should have governed his relationship to Duncan. But the medieval taboos cannot be so easily thrust aside. The Devil will come and Macbeth will be damned: hell-gate is still in its place as in some medieval mystery. There is a fixed and regular subordination of good and evil, powers and spirits. Lady Macbeth will finally succumb to an illness which requires the professional services of a divine, and skin diseases will be cured by the sovereign touch of the Lord's anointed. Nevertheless what finally emerges in the wintry dawn of consolation will be no mere rehabilitation of an outworn system. There is an ultimate irony governing the resolution of the play's conflicts. Macbeth turns to the oracle to seek a metaphysical assurance of his success, and it gives him this assurance, basing its words on the stability of that very orderly subordination which Macbeth and Lady Macbeth have denied. No man of woman born, it says, will overcome him, nor shall he be vanquished as long as the inanimate world obeys the rules set for it. Macbeth cleaves to these words, seeking sanctuary at the altar of medieval natural law. But medieval natural law will reveal its newfound elasticity in terminating Macbeth's career. He will not be dragged to hell by an old-fashioned devil, but woods will move and a man will be untimely ripped from his mother's womb in order to bring down punishment on him. Time and the bell will be suspended in the interests of some newer, more dynamic principle. Macduff asks no questions and seeks no oracles, but charges at Macbeth with the confidence of a new humanistic self-assertion: his voice is in his sword. Nevertheless, the cherubim are still there, in the background, discreetly camouflaged by the moving branches.

Shakespeare was evidently more sensitive to the philosophical currents of his time, to its deep underlying trends and attitudes, than the Romantic critics supposed. The dramatic conflicts between and within the characters are environed by forms and pressures of a universal and collective kind, and these can be defined only with the help of the insights of *Geistesgeschichte.* The study of Shakespeare's plays and the study of the spiritual history of Shakespeare's time are thus in the end two allied concerns. Nor does this make Shakespeare less our contemporary, for our dilemmas and difficulties too may be illuminated by those which find their reflection in Shakespeare's plays and in his time. And if there are also significant differences, the consideration of these may be to our profit and instruction.

Turning now to *Hamlet,* it should be clear that the characters shadow forth a similar opposition of old and new. There is the clash between Hamlet and Claudius; the latter expresses the conventional views on the divine right of kings—

> There's such divinity doth hedge a king
> That treason can but peep to what it would,
> Acts little of his will—

(IV. v. 123–125)

while the former, beloved as he is of the distracted multitude, speaks almost in the spirit of a new republicanism. But there is an even more revealing confrontation of traditional values and their Renaissance aftermath in the relationship between Hamlet and Ophelia.

Ophelia is indeed the ideal candidate for the role of the beautiful but rather inactive heroine of the medieval romance whom the handsome prince gallantly leads off to share with him the dignities of his station. Better still, she would have adapted herself well to the role of the leading lady in a Petrarchan sonnet sequence whom the noble courtier-poet addresses in terms of high compliment. (Hamlet as a matter of fact tried his hand at a few such verses.) He will occasionally present himself before her in all his gallant finery of lace and feathers and she will be duly gratified, though coy. What she is not prepared for is a princely suitor of a different kind,

> No hat upon his head, his stockings fouled,
> Ungart'red, and down-gyved to his ankle,
> Pale as his shirt, his knees knocking together.
>
> (II. i. 79–81)

This is no longer the prince of the romantic fairy tale: it is someone who has tasted the anguish of disenchantment. He is no longer in a position to go through the poses of a Petrarchan minuet. The orderly and artificial world that matches it has gone. This Ophelia is not prepared for.

There is something peculiarly *feudal* about Ophelia's personality, which is perhaps why Hamlet suggests she would be better off in a nunnery.[5] That is where, after all, the heroines of medieval tragic romance frequently ended up. She would have made only a rather run-down version of Guinevere or Heloise, it is true, for after all, the whole spiritual economy on which their behavior had been based is wrecked too. She is sorry that the old order has passed: she laments the passing of the pre-seventeenth-century era, the era of High Renaissance aristocratic dignity and of the spiritual ideal that went with it. She belongs with Sir Thomas More, Spenser, and Sidney, but Hamlet, she notes, has graduated out of that world:

> O, what a noble mind is here o'erthrown!
> The courtier's, soldier's, scholar's eye, tongue, sword,
> The expectancy and rose of the fair state,
> The glass of fashion, and the mould of form.
>
> (III. i. 159–162)

The emblematic imagery may be noted—"the rose of the fair state." It is a perfect medieval touch. Stars, plants, and men are still for her held together by the silken thread of correspondences. She is full of emblematic, medieval folklore, with its doctrine of signatures, and the echoes of it come over with touches of traditional balladry:

> There's rosemary, that's for remembrance . . . There's rue for you, and here's some for me, we may call it herb of grace o'Sundays . . . I would give you some violets, but they withered all, when my father died—they say a' made a good end.
>
> (IV. v. 174–185)

In her speeches and snatches of song we sense as nowhere else in the play the flavor of the old religion with its saints' days and domestic sanctities:

> To-morrow is Saint Valentine's day
> All in the morning betime,
> And I a maid at your window,
> To be your Valentine. . . . .
>
> By Gis and by Saint Charity,
> Alack, and fie for shame!
>
> (IV. v. 49–60)

Here are the folkways of an older world, its charm and quiet, the confessional, the church and the churchyard at the end of the village, where in fact we see the last of her. It is a touching vignette and carries no little tragic pathos.

Interestingly, Ophelia's dramatic tone is throughout elegiac. In every appearance she makes, she is saying good-bye to someone. In her first appearance, it is farewell to Laertes: in her second we hear of her silent parting from the stricken Hamlet. In her third major appearance, she pronounces her elegy on the passing of the chivalric ideal:

> O woe is me!
> T'have seen what I have seen, see what I see.
>
> (III. i. 169–170)

And in her mad scene she leaves us with:

> Come, my coach! Good night, ladies. Good night, sweet ladies. Good night, good night.
>
> (IV. v. 72–74)

She still thinks of herself as a young lady of a courtly romance, departing in her coach. Shakespeare's sense of her personality is fundamentally valedictory. In this, she is not unlike Othello, who is also valedictory, who also laments the passing of a more courtly and chivalrous world: a world of grandeur and romance:

> O, now forever
> Farewell the tranquil mind! farewell content!
> Farewell the plumed troop, and the big wars
> That make ambition virtue! O, farewell!
> Farewell the neighing steed and the shrill trump,
> The spirit-stirring drum, the ear-piercing fife,
> The royal banner, and all quality,
> Pride, pomp, and circumstance of glorious war!
>
> (III. iii. 348–355)

Ophelia (like Othello) knows how to ring out the old; she hardly knows how to ring in the new. The consequence is that between her and Hamlet there can be no real dialogue. The two young creatures who ought to have loved one another are tragically divided, more tragically than Othello is from Desdemona or Romeo from Juliet. Hamlet looks to Ophelia for comfort, but he can find nothing to say to her nor she to him. She goes further: in an act of perverse Petrarchan coyness and out of a feudal obedience to her father and brother she reveals that she has repelled his letters and denied his access to her. She is determined to say good-bye.

Hamlet and Ophelia are thus divided not only by his tragic experiences and her moral insensibility, but more particularly by the fact that they represent divided fragments of the ethical substance; they represent different and opposed strands of culture. Ophelia is a Petrarchan: Hamlet an anti-Petrarchan. In his restlessness, his loneliness, and his self-disgust he is not a little akin to John Donne,[6] the outstanding anti-Petrarchan poet of Shakespeare's time. Hamlet's abuse of Ophelia, widening as it does into a comment on the falseness of womankind in general ("You jig you amble and you lisp . . . and make your wantonness your ignorance" [III. i. 152–154]) and of the parallel falseness of his own sex ("we are arrant knaves all, believe none of us" [133–134]'), echoes Donne's sardonic and insolent anti-Petrarchan lyrics:

Will no other vice content you?
Will it not serve your turn to do as did your mothers?
Or have you all old vices spent, and now would find out others?
Or doth a fear that men are true torment you?
O we are not, be not you so;
Let me, and do you, twenty know![7]

The spiritual likeness between Hamlet and Donne is not surprising since they are both influenced by the Counter-Renaissance,
the new, divisive, and disillusioned phase of the Renaissance, with
its altered image of man, God, and the cosmos. In a phrase that
again might have come out of Donne, Hamlet says, "What should
such fellows as I do crawling between earth and heaven." This is
a far cry from the medieval (and Renaissance) image of the Great
Chain of Being with man poised securely and symmetrically somewhere between the angels and the beasts. For Hamlet as for King
Lear, man is revealed as lower than the beasts themselves. His
situation is unbelievably perilous: his depravity, once he gives
himself up to sin, immeasurable.

With Hamlet the sense of order associated with medieval Christian philosophy has been undermined. According to that system,
God, man, and nature had been securely and organically related,
the three realms upheld and united by the beauty, law, and reason
of the *logos*. Macbeth, in spite of damnation, had retained such
a picture of the universe. Even in his career of crime he had
testified to an orderly arrangement of the cosmos. To do evil was
to violate natural law: he knew what it was he defied, namely, the
sanctified bonds of family, and ultimately the law of God, the
intrinsic knot which held all other bonds in their place. But for
Hamlet this safe and static arrangement has broken down. His
sense of alienation is occasioned precisely by the ruin of the logis-
tic system, the unified world of the school philosophy. And he gives
us a clear, philosophically defined account of his new vision of
the threefold reality. Hamlet's revision of the *logos* is set out in
two passages. The first of them is in Act II, in his speech to Rosencrantz and Guildenstern where he sets out a new image of nature
and man:

It goes so heavily with my disposition, that this goodly frame the earth, seems to me a sterile promontory, this most excellent canopy the air, look you, this brave o'erhanging firmament, this majestical roof fretted with golden fire, why it appeareth nothing to me but a foul and pestilent congregation of vapours. What a piece of work is a man! how noble in reason! how infinite in faculties! in form and moving how express and admirable! in action how like an angel! in apprehension how like a god! the beauty of the world, the paragon of animals! and yet to me what is this quintessence of dust?

(II. ii. 316–329)

The traditional order and beauty of the cosmos which we associate with the High Renaissance idealism of Hooker could not have been caught better than in the ironical phrases that Hamlet uses to describe it—"this brave o'erhanging firmament, this majestical roof fretted with golden fire." In Book I of his *Laws of Ecclesiastical Polity* Hooker had spoken of "the frame of that heavenly arch erected over our heads." It is that vision of a regulated and beautiful cosmos that Hamlet rejects with disgust—"why it appeareth nothing to me but a foul and pestilent congregation of vapours." He is vomiting out the *logos*—the inherited traditional system of Christian philosophy enshrined in the *Summa* of Thomas Aquinas which found in the Bible a confirmation of Aristotle's Golden Mean and Plato's Great Chain. Similarly in his vision of man, the second component of the triple system, Hamlet rejects the traditional optimistic view. Man is no longer "the beauty of the world, the paragon of animals"—again these are the clichés of High Renaissance conservatism. He is reduced, as in the system of Calvin and Hobbes, to "this quintessence of dust." Here is a different style of humanism from that of Pico's great oration on the dignity of man; here is the radical disenchantment of a later generation, the generation of Bacon, Donne, and Montaigne.

As for the clichés of traditional divinity, the image that men had of the third reality, *viz.,* God, it is notable that these are expressed in the play by the two hypocrites, Claudius and Gertrude. We think of such phrases as,

all that live must die,
Passing through nature to eternity.

(I. ii. 72–73)

or else,

> whereto serves mercy
> But to confront the visage of offence?

(III. iii. 46–47)

Hamlet's answer to these clichés corresponds to the above-quoted passage on man and nature, and it is given in the scene with his mother in Act III. Speaking of her betrayal of her marriage vows, he says,

> O, such a deed
> As from the body of contraction plucks
> The very soul, and sweet religion makes
> A rhapsody of words!

(III. iv. 45–48)

His reaction to the gestures of traditional piety is to say that the deeds of Claudius and Gertrude make of sweet religion a "rhapsody of words." If the commentators are right in interpreting the phrase "body of contraction" as a reference to the contract of marriage (parallel to the previous line which speaks of marriage vows becoming as false as dicers' oaths), then the religion which Hamlet is here rebelling against is an institutionalized religion embedded in social forms and practices. Behind the apparently stable structure of family and state he senses panic and emptiness. Claudius reads *The Times* at breakfast while Gertrude butters the toast, but underneath it all rank corruption mining all within, infects unseen, turning the orderly traditional Christianity they profess into a "rhapsody of words." The same corruption has already turned the world of nature into a "foul and pestilent congregation of vapours," and man into a "quintessence of dust."

II

The dialectical structure which we have just examined may also be demonstrated obliquely through the typical imagery of the play. Here in *Hamlet,* the images take part in the "argument" almost as though they were characters, their order and syntax revealing clearly the radical conflicts with which the play is concerned, and the manner in which Shakespeare sought to resolve them.[8] As a fairly simple example, let us consider the way in which images of flowers function in *Hamlet*. Hamlet is a flower-strewn play, and most of the flowers, though not all, center on Ophelia. She is the "rose of May," from "her fair and unpolluted flesh" will "violets spring." It is she in Act IV who gives to the flowers, rosemary, rue, pansies, and violets, their emblematic qualities. She dies amid flowers, "fantastic garlands" of crow-flowers, nettles, daisies, and long purples, and on her grave in Act V are cast the "virgin crants" and the "maiden strewments" (V. i. 255–256) to which she has accustomed us, the rather quaint language underlining the traditional flower lore and flower wisdom which environ her personality. But this extends outward into the play. Hamlet viewed as Ophelia's lover becomes in the words of Laertes, "A violet in the youth of primy nature" and Laertes too develops the image in the rather "precious," allegorical fashion of which Ophelia was so fond:

> A violet in the youth of primy nature,
> Forward, not permanent, sweet, not lasting,
> The perfume and suppliance of a minute,
> No more—
>
> (I. iii. 7–10)

while Ophelia retorts by bidding Laertes heed the moral lessons to be drawn from other items of the florilegium, namely the thorn and the primrose. Again there is the same precise, hortatory exposition of the images:

> Do not, as some ungracious pastors do,
> Show me the steep and thorny way to heaven,
> Whilst, like a puffed and reckless libertine
> Himself the primrose path of dalliance treads,
> And recks not his own rede.
>
> (I. iii. 47–51)

But as the flower imagery extends outward into the play it develops a strong dialectical quality. Gertrude, spiritually linked with Ophelia in the dramatic economy, and sharing with her the same limited medieval piety and sententious wisdom, is likewise a rose, but Hamlet in using this emblematic image in Act III savagely strips the rose from his mother's forehead and substitutes for it—a blister:

                                  Such an act
    That blurs the grace and blush of modesty,
    Calls virtue hypocrite, takes off the rose
    From the fair forehead of an innocent love,
    And sets a blister there.

                                            (III. iv. 40–44)

Indeed the imagery of disease—so prevalent in the play as all the
critics have noted—is rightly to be viewed as an accompaniment,
almost as a function, of the flower imagery. As in Shelley's poem,
"The Sensitive Plant," blight, weeds, and infection take their rise
in the garden of beautiful flowers over which a lady—shortly to
die—had gracefully presided. The world had been disclosed to
Hamlet in Act I as an "unweeded garden," and weeds and blight
continue to manifest themselves in it, choking the fair flowers of
the spring. Laertes anticipates this process in his words to Ophelia
in Act I:

        The canker galls the infants of the spring
        Too oft before their buttons be disclosed.

                                            (I. iii. 39–40)

Hamlet is "Th'expectancy and rose of the fair state" (the rose has
almost the status of a character in the play!) but he is "blasted
with ecstasy." Claudius is a "mildewed ear," as Hamlet tells his
mother, while she herself, fallen into trespass, is bidden not to

                        spread the compost on the weeds
        To make them ranker.

                                            (III. iv. 151–152)

The very crime from which the plot takes its rise is similarly defined. Old Hamlet had been

        Cut off even in the *blossoms* of my sin—

                                            (I. v. 76)

he was a blossoming flower in an orchard suddenly blighted with
the wintry blast. As explicated by the dumb-show and the play-
within-the-play, the same episode is even more firmly located
within a context of fair flowers and foul weeds. The King in his

unsuspecting innocence "lies him down upon a bank of flowers" while Lucianus, in ostentatiously brandishing the bottle of poison, speaks of it as,

> Thou mixture rank, of midnight weeds collected,
> With Hecate's ban thrice blasted, thrice infected.
>
> (III. ii. 272–273)

It is clear that the whole system of disease images in the play has its genesis in the same scene in the orchard with its contrasting motifs of weeds and flowers. The poison is a "leprous distilment," it "possets" the blood and causes an "instant tetter" to break out "most lazar-like" upon the body of the poisoned King (I. v. 64–72). From here the cicatrice, the hectic, the blister, and the ulcer naturally follow.[9] When Hamlet bids his mother not to indulge in self-deception for

> It will but skin and film the ulcerous place,
> Whiles rank corruption mining all within
> Infects unseen,
>
> (III. iv. 147–149)

he is placing her in that same orchard, that same garden grown to seed of Act I. The true *agon*, in short, is enacted not between the characters but between images. It is a symbolic drama about flowers blasted, struck down, replaced by weeds, by blisters, by all manner of evil.

The iterative image of flowers in this play, and their anti-type, *viz.,* the abounding references to weeds, poisons, and diseases, operate, as Matthew Arnold would say, as a criticism of life. They interpret for us the history of Shakespeare's time, marked as it was by the struggle of medieval man to meet the challenge of the new age. In Hegelian terms it may be said that the flowers contain within themselves, like the world-order that Hamlet had inherited, the seeds of their own decay. Ophelia is surrounded by the fading flowers of an ordered feudal world: her death is almost too beautiful, too enchanting to be real. The language in which the description of her end is couched is elegiac, slow, syntactically balanced:

There is a willow grows askant the brook,
That shows his hoar leaves in the glassy stream,
Therewith fantastic garlands did she make
Of crow-flowers, nettles, daisies, and long purples . . .

        . . . Her clothes spread wide,
And mermaid-like awhile they bore her up,
Which time she chanted snatches of old lauds,
As one incapable of her own distress. . . .

                                        (IV. vii. 167–179)

But there will be no ritual descent into the underworld. Unlike Juliet (another flower-strewn heroine), she will be denied the ceremonial obsequies. Death will not suck the honey of her breath: instead, Hamlet will throw aside the virgin crants with which Gertrude is strewing her grave and will set a blister there:

And if thou prate of mountains, let them throw
Million of acres on us, till our ground,
Singeing his pate against the burning zone,
Make Ossa like a *wart*! [*my italics*]

                                        (V. i. 302–305)

The harsh anticlimax matches the violence of the scene with its savage disruption of the orderly pieties of a traditional religious occasion—the "bringing home of bell and burial."

Here, therefore, the contrasting yet dialectically infolded image-systems are used to underline the profound inner conflicts of the play, what Bradley called, "the intestinal warfare of the ethical substance." The same phenomenon may be noted in *Julius Caesar* with its dialectical images of blood and statutes, metal and tears.[10] Indeed, this is a more usual Shakespearean procedure than is realized: in *Antony and Cleopatra* the ethical debate about the nature of love and empire is conducted by means of imagery of cosmic grandeur on the one hand and food and drink on the other. These are not merely different strands of images but contradictory modes of apprehension. Antony can speak of the "wide arch of the ranged empire," thinking of the Roman empire as the vaulted universe in all its infinite extent, and in the same speech he can cynically remark that

                    our dungy earth alike
Feeds beast as man.

                                        (I. i. 35–36)

Antony is both god of war and beastly drunkard: Cleopatra "o'er-picturing Venus" is the apotheosis of love; her longings are immortal longings: yet, paradoxically she is a piece of meat, a tasty dish for tired soldiers requiring stimulation—

>   a morsel, cold upon
> Dead Caesar's trencher.

(III. xi. 116–117)

But *Hamlet* goes further than this. What is remarkable about *Hamlet* is the way in which the imagery interprets for us not simply an ethical conflict, an opposition of attitudes, but an unfolding historical situation, a dialectical movement in time. The blasting of the flowers, the blister substituted for the rose, represent the symbolical collision of the spirit of the Middle Ages and of the Renaissance, a turning point in the history of England, indeed of the Western world as a whole. It is no accident that the disaster symbolized by the onset of weeds, blight, and disease has its genesis in the orchard where the old King is murdered, the point, that is to say, where the Senecan blood cycle is re-inaugurated. The serpent in the garden ("the serpent that did sting thy father's life") is undoubtedly the agent of a universal, an archetypal wickedness. His progenitor is Satan himself in the Garden of Eden. But he is also a very particularized evil manifesting itself at a specifically defined moment of time: he is the neo-Senecan paganism, also the new Machiavellian ambition of the sixteenth century with its abandonment of traditional restraints and pieties, the savage naturalism of a world in which power has been separated from morality; truth has departed from judgment, and *homo homini lupus* has taken the place of *homo homini deus*.[11]

It is not difficult to locate this process of subversion in the history of the period. The men of Shakespeare's time were rightly shocked by Machiavelli's *Prince* with its cool approval of the characteristics of lion and fox for him who would be a successful ruler. But in fact the *Discorsi* with their much more discreet reflections on political conduct are more profoundly subversive, for they assume from the outset and without argument that the ethical values of the pagan world of Livy are automatically adaptable to Christian Europe. It is as though Christianity had not intervened;

and that an unbroken line connected Caligula and Julius Caesar with the men of Florence in the sixteenth century. Here is the challenge to the whole moral order expounded by Sir Thomas More, by Erasmus and Hooker, and derived from the pious doctors of the Middle Ages. This is the precise meaning of the "unweeded garden." Claudius will smile and smile and be a villain: neither murder nor incest will deter him, for the power drives and the desires of the flesh find their justification in the consciousness of the sovereign rights of the ego.

Claudius is—as critics have often noted—a Machiavellian villain, but the new ethic of violence and unlimited self-seeking was part of a more general trend of which Machiavelli was merely the most notorious symptom. The threat to inherited Christian values, to the rose garden of orderly beliefs and dealings, is as clearly revealed in the writings of Valla and Guicciardini. If Claudius had read the *Counsels and Reflections* of Guicciardini (as he might well have done) before embarking on his ambitious plan of murder and usurpation, he would have found at least two passages extremely germane to his enterprise. Here they are:

> States cannot be established or maintained by conforming to the moral law. For if you look to their beginnings, all will be seen to have had their origin in violence . . .

> Frank sincerity is a quality much extolled among men and pleasing to every one, whilst simulation on the contrary, is detested and condemned. Yet for a man's self, simulation is of the two by far the more useful; sincerity tending rather to the interest of others. But since it cannot be denied that it is not a fine thing to deceive, I would commend him whose conduct is as a rule open and straightforward, and who uses simulation only in matters of the gravest importance and such as very seldom occur; for in this way he will gain a name for honesty and sincerity, and with it the advantages attaching to these qualities. At the same time, when, in any extreme emergency, he resorts to simulation, he will draw all the greater advantage from it, because from his reputation for plain dealing his artifice will blind men more.[12]

And it is from the contemplation of this sinister trend, momentarily personified in the conduct and bearing of Claudius in Act I, Scene 2, that Hamlet's first soliloquy takes its rise. The world has become a place of baleful and poisonous weeds:

Fie on't, ah fie, 'tis an unweeded garden
That grows to seed, things rank and gross in nature
Possess it merely.

(I. ii. 135–137)

The outward veneer of piety will make the inner evil more flagrant.
It will spread the compost on the weeds. Moreover, the weeds
themselves will owe their strength and luxuriance to the very
richness of the flowers which they have invaded and on which they
feed. If violets will grow out of the dead flesh of Ophelia, the
foulest of impieties will grow out of the rich flowers of Christian
spirituality once their care has been neglected. The same paradox
is expressed in the imagery of *Measure for Measure,* a play of the
same period and of—in many respects—similar inspiration. "It
is I," says Angelo,

That lying by the violet in the sun,
Do as the carrion does, not as the flower,
Corrupt with virtuous season . . .

(II. ii. 165–168)

Angelo is the devil in the garden, but he takes corruption from an
excess of goodness and virtue. He is the fallen angel of a Christian
order, become infinitely depraved by the loss of grace.

CHAPTER III

My Brother
Jonathan

Hamlet's reaction to the disease of Denmark, to the collapse of traditional order which he witnesses around him is to withdraw into himself. It is not by chance that he is the great soliloquist. All of Shakespeare's major figures speak in soliloquy, but Hamlet is the one to whom soliloquy comes most naturally. The drama centers in his lonely inner life. Othello is lonely enough, but even in his tragic derangement he is bound to another by the covenant of marriage: Hamlet is free from such bonds. When the play opens he is an orphan, and we watch him being driven more and more in upon himself. His mother betrays him; his beloved proves to be cold and false; his friends turn spies. Like Job he is reduced to the depths, but unlike Job he cannot declare that his witness is on high, for the heavens too are closed and God is silent. One could say that Hamlet is alone because Ophelia and Gertrude have withdrawn from him; but it would be equally true to say that he has withdrawn from them. If they spurn him, he no less spurns them. His loneliness is not simply a logical outcome of his dramatic situation; it is equally an outcome of a world view, of a path which he has chosen. Hamlet is exploring his inwardness because he has that within which passeth show, because he is trying to find something different from that which surrounds him.

What does Hamlet hope to gain by his isolation from the world? What new thing is he looking for? The first answer, and the one that a number of well-informed, philosophically minded critics have suggested is, in a word, stoicism.[1] This was the religion-surrogate of the early seventeenth century, the new secular system

44

of faith and action which had been thrown up by the late Renaissance, and the sources of which were to be found in the writings of the wise men of antiquity. Hamlet had surely read the words of the Emperor Marcus Aurelius:

> For nowhere either with more quiet or more freedom from trouble does a man retire than into his own soul—[2]

Or else:

> It is sufficient to attend to the daemon within him, and to reverence it sincerely. And reverence of the daemon consists in keeping it pure from passion and thoughtlessness, and dissatisfaction with what comes from gods or men.[3]

And he had been duly impressed by the stress on personal integrity, self-sufficiency, self-command, and the rest. On the other hand we have a sort of vulgarized version of this egocentric pose in the sententious speech of Polonius to Laertes—

> to thine own self be true,
> And it must follow as the night the day,
> Thou canst not then be false to any man.

> (I. iii. 78–80)

Surely this cannot be what Hamlet was looking for! Probably the immediate inspiration for Polonius was not Marcus Aurelius but the Roman orator, Cicero, in whose *De Officiis* we have the moralizing tendency, the rhetorical gestures, the slightly pompous gravity which Shakespeare is caricaturing in Polonius. Cicero had stressed the ideal of the grave counselor devoted to the public service—exactly the role to which Polonius has adapted himself. This is stoicism of a kind, but clearly not the sort that Hamlet was looking for.

As against this, there was another more up-to-date version for the men of Hamlet's generation, one suggested more by Seneca (the Seneca of the *Epistles*), by du Vair, Lipsius, and above all, Montaigne. This newer stoicism was altogether more individualistic, less public-spirited, more a matter of unassertive self-discipline. It was a secular religion for disillusioned young men who felt that the pompous old men of the establishment had little to offer except fine words. They wanted something more genuinely introspective, more serious, a discipline which might provide the same *frisson* of spiritual achievement that the religions of Geneva and Wittenberg offered their devotees, namely the sensation of grace, but without religious strings attached. In one impassioned speech, Hamlet tells us that he has found this ideal in his friend Horatio: he is the man who has learned to keep the inner "daemon" free from thoughtlessness and passion:

> Nay do not think I flatter,
> For what advancement may I hope from thee,
> That no revenue hast but thy good spirits
> To feed and clothe thee . . .
> Since my dear soul was mistress of her choice,
> And could of men distinguish her election,
> Sh'hath sealed thee for herself, for thou hast been
> As one in suff'ring all that suffers nothing,
> A man that Fortune's buffets and rewards
> Hast ta'en with equal thanks; and blest are those
> Whose blood and judgement are so well comingled,
> That they are not a pipe for Fortune's finger
> To sound what stop she please: give me that man
> That is not passion's slave, and I will wear him
> In my heart's core aye in my heart of heart,
> As I do thee.

(III. ii. 61–79)

Hamlet's admiration is here expressed for the man who (unlike Polonius) has cut himself off from the rewards of public service ("That no revenue hast but thy good spirits") in order to devote himself to virtue. This is the ideal of personal inviolability that Hamlet admires, or professes to admire, in the early part of the play. It is the ideal of the man who faces good or bad fortune with equanimity, and if ever things become particularly difficult or embarrassing, he can terminate them with a bare bodkin. It is the style of Stoic *apatheia* which marks Horatio's attitude to life ("I'm more an antique Roman than a Dane./Here's yet some liquor left" [V. ii. 355–356]) and to which Hamlet more than once turns longingly. The patience of the stoic who suffers the slings and arrows of outrageous fortune, who, having riches within, can bear calmly all the whips and scorns of time—if only he could achieve that!

But of course he does not achieve it. What he accepts at the end is not stoicism, not the Stoic *fatum,* the self-surrender to the sway of the universe, nor the indifference to good or evil which the stoic claimed. Some have seen Hamlet as the type of the Stoic censor.[4] But in spite of his tart comments on life and death, his frequent tendency to scurrilous raillery, he does not have the genuine detachment of the Stoic-Cynic censor such as Apemantus or Thersites. He is ultimately too involved not only in his own affairs but also in the doings of others. The doings of Fortinbras bother him, the actors move him; he cares about things too much for the role of cynic. In fact, Hamlet does not subscribe fully to any of the varieties of stoicism we have mentioned. He is unlike Apemantus, Polonius, or Horatio.

It may seem jejune to ask why Hamlet cannot become like Horatio. But for those who would simply say that there would then be no play, let me remind them that Shakespeare managed to write a perfectly good play about a stoic in the role of assassin, namely *Julius Caesar,* and Hamlet has more than a dash of Brutus in his makeup. Chapman succeeded in fashioning a stoic hero and making him the chief instrument of revenge in *The Revenge of Bussy D'Ambois* (complete with Ghost and all). The exploration of the paradoxes of stoic inaction versus the revenge task was in fact a popular dramatic theme. Hamlet would have liked to get into that play of Chapman, or failing that he would have liked to get into *Henry IV* to play the role of Hotspur, the impetuous antitype of the stoic. Horatio and Fortinbras are the two major planets in Hamlet's universe. They provide him with two alternative reactions to the troubles he had encountered. One is the reaction of Stoic *apatheia,* the other is the reaction of devil-may-care impetuosity, the cult of honor at all ventures:

> Exposing what is mortal and unsure
> To all that fortune, death, and danger dare,
> Even for an eggshell.

> (IV. iv. 51–53)

Here are the two basic possibilities open to the angry young men of Hamlet's time, and they are well personified in Horatio and Fortinbras.

An obvious way of putting it would be to say that Hamlet

has too much passion for the character of stoic frigidity and too much thought for the Hotspur-Fortinbras role. But this is only half the explanation, for he can be as impetuous as Fortinbras (mark the sudden violence he shows in stabbing Polonius and in destroying Claudius at the end) when the fit is on him. The real reason is deeper: it is contained in that very speech of admiration for Horatio quoted above. In the dramatic and philosophical context of the play, the speech has a certain irony which I believe has not been appreciated. The point is that it is a lover's speech addressed to one who is being praised for his imperviousness to all passions, love included!

> Give me that man
> That is not passion's slave—
>
> (III. ii. 76–77)

says Hamlet in a speech of passionate affection! The stoic guards his inner fortress, keeping it free from intrusion by God or man, whereas Hamlet lavishes on his chosen friend the wealth of his affectionate nature. It is notable that Horatio makes no equivalent speech in answer, and the actor who plays Horatio would be well advised to illustrate the irony of the situation by exhibiting a certain embarrassment at this outpouring of Hamlet's feelings. Shakespeare had explored this particular kind of ironical relationship also in the scenes between Cassius and Brutus. Cassius reveals a nature hungry for affection—this is his one redeeming quality—while Brutus remains unmoved in his fortress of stoical egocentricity. Brutus's self-satisfied attitude is summed up in the line:

> I do not like your faults.
>
> (IV. iii. 88)

Cassius's nature is summed up in the line:

> I, that denied thee gold, will give my heart.
>
> (IV. iii. 103)

Here by implication is Shakespeare's exploration of the Roman ideal of virtue and of the profound spiritual and emotional deficiencies which it harbored.

It is necessary here to refine somewhat on this point, for the fact is that the Greeks and Romans, as well as their spiritual disciples in the age of Shakespeare, had a great appreciation for friendship. Aristotle devotes two books of his *Ethics* to this theme, and one of the most attractive of Montaigne's *Essays* is that in which he describes his deep attachment for the poet Étienne de la Boëtie. Friendship is in fact a major theme of Hellenic culture. Normally, it had a more or less avowed pederastic basis, but the philosophers raised it to the level of a marriage of souls possible only to those who have freed themselves from the baser passions. Aristotle makes the distinction between friendship and love: the latter is brief and impetuous, a matter of impulse and pleasure, the former is lasting and based on reason. It is in fact based on more than reason; it is a logical extension of self-love. Only the man who truly and rationally loves himself because he has a perfect and well-integrated soul can, according to Aristotle, offer and receive true friendship.[5] Here we have exactly the point of difference between the classical ideal of friendship as transmitted by the Stoics and the men of the Academy and that which Hamlet is offering Horatio: his gesture is that of an impulsive nature seeking and giving affection, not simply shoring up its own ego.

We are reminded of Henry More's religious criticism of stoicism in the latter half of the seventeenth century:

> For this Kingdome of the *Stoicks* is the kingdome of Selfishness, and *Self-love* sways the sceptre there and wears the Diadem: but in the Kingdome of God, God himself, who is that pure, free, and perfectly *unselfed love,* has the full dominion of the soul, and the ordering and rule of all the Passions.[6]

Self-love *versus* unselfed love—that is how the alternatives appeared to Henry More. Milton, in *Paradise Regained,* speaks to a similar effect of the Stoics who

> in themselves seek vertue, to themselves
> All glory arrogate, to God give none.
>
> (Book IV. 314–315)

Again the "Kingdome of Selfishness." The love which Hamlet is offering to Horatio is in fact more Christian than Greek: it passeth understanding. Instead of that superior self-love based on reason of the Stoics, we have something unreasoned and passionate, beyond philosophical limits. Hamlet is involved here in an I/thou relationship quite outside the Hellenic-Stoic frame of experience. The irony of it is that he fails to elicit a spasm of sympathetic awareness from Horatio. Hamlet is making a gesture in the void. Subtly Hamlet's praise of Horatio's stoic self-control and apathy implies a criticism of stoicism. He praises Horatio for being one who

> in suff'ring all that suffers nothing.
>
> (III. ii. 71)

He is the man with the impenetrably thick skin. Yet Hamlet himself is the man born without a skin: he suffers everything: all occasions inform against him. It is important to recognize such implicit criticisms of stoicism both in this play and elsewhere in Shakespeare. *Julius Caesar* has been mentioned. In that play, the criticism is achieved obliquely through the images. At the center of the play is a bleeding statue.[7] The Romans seem to be blocks of wood or stone, yet paradoxically they weep and bleed. Colossi are shown to have feet of clay. Hearts of stone reveal unexpected weaknesses, those of the flesh. There is a frequent use of the pun on metal/mettle, suggesting that human beings may be conceived as pliable and temperamental or else as having the rigidity of metal objects. There is a basic contradiction about them. Brutus speaks of coining his heart and dropping his blood for drachmas: it is a potent and suggestive image which implies a questioning of the values of Romanism as a whole, a civilization summed up in its statuary, its ideal of rigid self-control, and yet unable to maintain such self-control. Brutus speaks of himself as one

> That carries anger as the flint bears fire;
> Who, much enforced, shows a hasty spark,
> And straight is cold again.
>
> (IV. iii. 110–112)

Shakespeare is clearly exhibiting the inner contradictions of the Roman world; its contrasts of violence and frigidity, of superstition and philosophical skepticism, rational and irrational categories ironically opposed to one another. He also achieves this same criticism by less oblique dramatic procedures. Casca, the "Cynic censor," appears to us at first in his satirical role of commentator on the ceremonies of the Lupercalia; he speaks with contempt of

the vulgar emotions of the crowd and in his reaction to the dinner
invitation extended to him by Cassius he exhibits the precise
manner of Apemantus in *Timon of Athens*. But in the very next
scene we have a different Casca; the Stoic-Cynic self-possession
has all gone; in the ghastly storm he is overcome by superstitious
terrors; and from the prose of cynical detachment he changes to
the verse of emotional involvement:

> It is the part of men to fear and tremble
> When the most mighty gods by tokens send
> Such dreadful heralds to astonish us.

(I. iii. 54–56)

The metal has become pliable, and will yield the more easily to
the impression that Cassius wishes to make on it. In fact the image
of pliable metal is basic in the play, closely associated with the
bleeding statue. But the other characters will undergo the same
emotional awakening as Casca, though without perhaps the touch
of childishness which we note in Casca. Brutus is brought face to
face with Caesar's ghost and at that instant his philosophy deserts
him:

> Art thou some god, some angel, or some devil,
> That makest my blood cold and my hair to stare?

(IV. iii. 278–279)

The same dramatic device is used in *Hamlet*. Horatio the stoic is
confronted early on with the Ghost. When he knows of it only from
hearsay he declares that " 'tis but our fantasy" and he "will not
let belief take hold of him" (I. i. 23–24). But when it actually
appears, his self-possession drains away:

> It harrows me with fear and wonder.

(I. i. 44)

Philosophical skepticism is confronted with the undreamt-of reality:
the trumpets sound and the walls of stoical self-sufficiency collapse.
Shakespeare is a dramatist, not a philosophical poet, and so he
chooses to announce his criticism of stoicism right at the beginning
in dramatic, even melodramatic terms both in *Hamlet* and in
Julius Caesar—two plays which are in this respect very much alike.
"It harrows me with fear and wonder," says Horatio. At the end

of the play, he will bear witness in very unstoical fashion to the religious meaning of Hamlet's pilgrimage:

> Good night, sweet prince,
> And flights of angels sing thee to thy rest!

(V. ii. 373–374)

He has not succeeded in keeping the "daemon" within him free from passion: pity has entered, horror has entered, even most miraculously, love. Hamlet had said rightly:

> There are more things in heaven and earth, Horatio,
> Than are dreamt of in your philosophy.

(I. v. 166–167)

We are reminded of what Joseph Hall had to say, in the same decade as *Hamlet,* about the pagan recipe for happiness:

> When I had studiously read over the moral writings of some wise heathen, especially those of the stoical profession, I must confess, I found a little envy and pity striving together within me.

The envy was for their strength of character, their apparent imperviousness to the blows of fortune: the pity was for their loneliness. They had missed the root of meaning in life, for he who wishes to gain his soul must first lose it. And Hall concludes: "Not Athens must teach this lesson but Jerusalem."[8]

The function of love for revealing the absurdities of the stoic attitude to the passions, and the inadequacy of its ethical system, is a commonplace of later literature. It is found in the eighteenth century in Voltaire, in Fielding, and in Dr. Johnson. As far as Shakespeare is concerned, the so-called stoic plays are really plays in which the I/myself of the stoic is confronted with the I/thou of love. *King Lear,* for instance, has been called a stoic play: others have called it a Christian play. It is in fact both, and yet it is neither: it is a play in which the Judeo-Christian categories of love are brought to bear upon the stoical categories of inaction and *apatheia.* Lear believes that what he needs is patience. "Patience I need." And he is right: he has to learn to curb his violent impatience and anger. But this is only part of the purgation which he must undergo. He will not be saved by patience, but by love, by loss of self. We witness a passionate reciprocity of love (not the

empty gesture of Hamlet to Horatio or of Cassius to Brutus)
between Lear (a "child-changed father") and his restored daughter
Cordelia in Act IV. It is a moment of regeneration, the entry into
the kingdom of heaven for them both. Obviously that scene stands
in dramatic contrast to his first encounter with Cordelia in Act I
where he had sternly and selfishly demanded love. Now he has
learned to give instead of to demand. But the scene indicates no less
a change in the stoical immobility of Cordelia's character. In Act I
her reactions had been negative, "Nothing my lord," had been her
answer to Lear's demand, and she had gone on to say

> Unhappy that I am, I cannot heave
> My heart into my mouth. I love your majesty
> According to my bond, no more nor less.
>
> (I. i. 93–95)

No concession here to passion: all outgoing impulses are curbed
by the concern for the "daemon" within which must be kept free
and uncompromised. By contrast we see her in Act IV pouring out
her feelings without inhibition.

> O my dear father, restoration hang
> Thy medicine on my lips, and let this kiss
> Repair those violent harms that my two sisters
> Have in thy reverence made!
>
> (IV. vii. 26–29)

It is sometimes pointed out that there are echoes in this reconciliation scene of the New Testament parable of the prodigal son.
Cordelia pities her father because, she says, he had been fain

> To hovel thee with swine and rogues forlorn,
> In short and musty straw.
>
> (39–40)

This would suggest that Lear has the role of prodigal son. But a
deeper reading of this scene reveals that Cordelia herself here in
an equal degree acts the part of the prodigal son in the parable.
It is she who has been away and has returned to her father, penitent and seeking his blessing. She who was lost is found, and being
found, she reveals a different nature, full of spontaneity and im-

pulsive concern for others. The difference between her behavior in
Act I and in Act IV is the measure of Shakespeare's sense of the
inadequacies of Stoic *apatheia*.

Clearly, the "Counter-Renaissance" cult of stoicism represented by Cordelia, and in a different way, by Horatio, does not
satisfy Shakespeare, nor does the "Counter-Renaissance" cult of
honor personified in Hotspur, or Fortinbras, or Laertes. Something vital is missing in all these categories of life and thought, and
attractive though they were to the young men of his time, Shakespeare felt bound to explore them with a considerable degree of
critical reserve. Nor can it be said that what he misses in them is
simply the content and form of traditional Christian order. Hamlet
is not finally satisfied by the "philosophies" of Horatio and Fortinbras, but he is equally if not more dissatisfied with the vestiges
of traditional order represented by Claudius and Ophelia. He is
clearly seeking some third force, some synthesis.

How may we begin to define this? For it is the misunderstanding of this factor which has caused the critics to react in such
varying and violently contradictory ways to the puzzle of Hamlet's
character. He has been called variously a good Christian, a modern skeptic, and a Renaissance man of egoistic violence. In fact,
he is a little of all these, but they do not exhaust his variety, nor do
they explain the root of his being and the real object of his search.
By way of suggesting an answer, we may say that the alternatives
offered by the other characters, in particular by Horatio and Fortinbras, are modes of monologue, but Hamlet is seeking the mode
of dialogue. The devotee of honor and the stoic alike are consumed with their own intensities. Self-sufficiency and the assertion
of one's own personality are the ideal: also such characters as
Brutus and Hotspur are hardly aware of the real existence of others:
they have to be forcibly reminded that in this world one does not
only turn upon the axis of one's own ego. Now Hamlet, though in
one way he seems to be the perfect candidate for such lonely self-
involvement,[9] is, viewed from another angle, the man of dialogue,
the man to whom vital communications are made:

> This spirit, dumb to us, will speak to him.

> (I. i. 171)

In his relation to the other characters there is a subtle pattern of attempted dialogue. True, it is frustrated, but there is no doubt of the power and urgency of the attempt. We see him reaching out for union with Ophelia:

> He raised a sigh so piteous and profound
> As it did seem to shatter all his bulk,
> And end his being; that done he lets me go,
> And with his head over his shoulder turned
> He seemed to find his way without his eyes,
> For out adoors he went without their help,
> And to the last bended their light on me.

(II. i. 94–100)

What stands out here is not only the passionate reaching out for sympathy on Hamlet's part, but the lack of any appropriate reaction on the part of Ophelia. Hamlet's first motion of friendship toward Rosencrantz and Guildenstern has the same marks of affectionate reaching out: but realizing their false role, he soon recoils. We have already remarked on the passionate avowal of love for Horatio and the lack of any corresponding spasm of sympathy from the direction of Horatio. For Horatio loyalty means friendship of the Aristotelian or Epictetan variety, in other words, love limited by rational self-possession; for Hamlet it means true dialogue, an I/thou confrontation.

The most striking example of this pattern of attempted dialogue is provided by Hamlet's turning toward Laertes in Act V. In the likeness between his own cause and that of the bereaved Laertes he finds—as we have said—a profound intimation of human brotherhood, and he proposes to turn toward him and seeks his fellowship with regret for his past doings:

> But I am very sorry good Horatio,
> That to Laertes I forgot myself;
> For by the image of my cause I see
> The portraiture of his, I'll court his favours.

(V. ii. 75–78)

Hamlet is as good as his word; in the following scene, he makes a courteous speech of apology and begs Laertes to accept him as a brother:

> Free me so far in your most generous thoughts
> That I have shot my arrow o'er the house
> And hurt my brother.
>
> (V. ii. 256–258)

It may be worth noting that in the last meeting between Jonathan and David, described in the Book of Samuel, David hides in the field, and Jonathan shoots an arrow beyond him as a sign that David is to flee from the wrath of Jonathan's father, Saul.

> And when the lad was come to the place of the *arrow* which Jonathan *had shot,* Jonathan cried after the lad, and said, Is not the arrow beyond thee?
>
> (I SAMUEL 20:37)

Jonathan here is seeking to atone for a bitterness which has grown up between his friend and his father, a triangle of relationship similar to that of Polonius, Laertes, and Hamlet. Jonathan like Laertes is shortly to be slain, and in David's famous lament for him later on, we have the expression, "I am distressed for thee, *my brother* Jonathan." The verbal similarities in Hamlet's speech do not amount to a source—they are more a kind of undertone, an echo—but they do suggest that whole Biblical dimension of selfless love, of which the David–Jonathan story is the great prototype. What Hamlet is offering Laertes is that marriage of souls known to the Judeo-Christian tradition but scarcely comprised in the classical ideal of friendship:

> thy love to me was wonderful, passing the love of women.
>
> (II SAMUEL 1:26)

But what stands out is the ironical counterpointing. Laertes is no Jonathan. His answer to Hamlet's offer of love and reconcilement is to say that he must consult with some expert in the honor code in order to find out whether he may accept Hamlet's friendship.

> I am satisfied in nature,
> Whose motive in this case could stir me most
> To my revenge. But in my terms of honour
> I stand aloof, and will no reconcilement,
> Till by some elder masters of known honour
> I have a voice and precedent of peace
> To keep my name ungored.
>
> (V. ii. 258–264)

Again the reaching out for dialogue, and again the frustration and the recoil.

Hamlet is, in fact, the man who is hungry for love, for the sympathy and understanding of others. He makes his gesture of desperate yearning to each character in turn, but he fails to find a helpmeet for him. There is no answering echo of sympathy. Here is, it seems to me, the fundamental starting point for a study of Hamlet's dramatic posture. He is the great soliloquist, but he is seeking in soliloquy that which he has failed to find in his commerce with the other characters in the play. It is through monologue that Hamlet is trying to achieve dialogue! This is a paradox, but it is the paradox on which the great soliloquies hinge. They are different from other Shakespearean monologues, for they have a form and an inner dynamic which can only be understood in the light of paradox stated above. Hamlet is using the mode of monologue in order to enter the world of dialogue denied to him by his social environment. For it is only in the mutuality of dialogue that genuine life-content is achieved, and as Hall had said, "Not Athens must teach this lesson, but Jerusalem."

CHAPTER IV

From
Monologue
to Dialogue

It has often been noted that Hamlet's soliloquies with their narcissistic brooding on the nature of his motives tend to take us away from the outer business of the play viewed as revenge tragedy. Brutus in *Julius Caesar* is an introspective figure, yet his soliloquies are, unlike those of Hamlet, functions of the plot: they lead on from what has gone before and prepare us for what is to come. His speech beginning "It must be by his death" (II. i. 10) is the hinge on which the whole plot of the conspiracy turns. There is no such direct relation between Hamlet's soliloquies and the ostensible outer drama. William Empson speaks of "the collapse of interest in the story," evinced by the third and fourth soliloquies.[1] Hamlet does not use the mode of soliloquy in order to reach conclusions which will guide him in his subsequent behavior. They are much more radically inward-turned, having reference to an inner drama abstracted from the Ghost and the assassination, and centering on Hamlet's search for the meaning of life. They exhaust themselves in the analytic process itself without serving in any obvious way to advance the action. As a sign of this it is notorious that the order of the soliloquies is to some extent interchangeable. In the bad quarto the positions of the second and third soliloquy are reversed, "To be or not to be" being thus detached from the nunnery scene. There is no obvious dramatic loss, and indeed the changed order was preferred by nineteenth-century producers and is even today sometimes adopted. A quality of radical detachment and also of radical egocentrism mark these speeches and render them different in some fundamental way from the monologues of other Shakespearean characters. Even Richard II, brooding egoist though he is, broods in his monologues (or near-monologues) on his fate as King of England. The dynastic theme is always central. He does not exhibit an autonomous inner realm of moral debate removed from the order of events proceeding without.

A valuable hint as to the formal source of Hamlet's narcissistic soliloquies has been given by Harry Levin in his book, *The Question of Hamlet*. He remarks in one place that:

> In introspection, his mentor is Montaigne; the soliloquies are like the *Essays* in balancing arguments with counter-arguments, in pursuing wayward ideas and unmasking stubborn illusions, in scholarly illustrations and homely afterthoughts which range from the soul of Nero to John-a-dreams.[2]

It is not exactly new to relate Hamlet's skeptical, philosophical, inquiring cast of mind to the influence of Montaigne. This is a well-established canon of *Hamlet* criticism: in fact, more echoes from Montaigne have been found in *Hamlet* than in any other play of Shakespeare.[3] But what is somewhat novel is the suggestion that the soliloquies may have a formal relation to the familiar essay as practiced by Montaigne. For Montaigne is the supreme literary egotist. His essays crystallize the introspective mode. They are monologue in its purest form. As he himself tells us in his prefatory remarks:

> It is myself I portray. . . . I am myself the subject of my book.

Never before had a richer landscape been disclosed, furnished exclusively from the inner stores of one who was convinced that his own life, opinions, and feelings were the most interesting matters that the world afforded. The extraordinary achievement of Montaigne is that the reader too comes to share this sentiment: the world disclosed to us is fascinating and endlessly varied. It has many mansions. He evidently felt no compulsion to step outside and contemplate any other reality, to engage in any other exercise except this endless self-portrait. Like the Stoics, especially Seneca, he sought happiness within through an unmitigated reflexive action of the mind.

There is another more strictly formal resemblance between Hamlet's soliloquies and the familiar essay as practiced by Montaigne. It reveals itself in the balance of the personal and the commonplace, the private and the universal, which characterizes Hamlet's soliloquies and Montaigne's essays alike. Montaigne may start with some particular event or situation, something that had happened to him, maybe in his travels, or he may relate some historical episode that he has read about, but he will leave it behind for a general comment on the human condition, a philosophical maxim or reflection sufficiently abstract or general to cover any case you can think of. There is a movement from the concretely visualizable to the general and abstract, from the personal to the grandly impersonal. Particular experiences and reflections (of which there are not a few) serve as the ground for more universal insights, not always in themselves especially original or arresting. Similarly with Hamlet: his first great soliloquy has as its personal basis his disgust with his mother's overhasty marriage, but this widens into a broadly general statement: "Frailty, thy name is woman!" That is the sort of aphoristic phrase which the essayists loved: it is not very original, but it has that sententious quality of inclusiveness which they were after. Hamlet undoubtedly culled it from his commonplace book, those same tables in which he had jotted down the phrase, "That one may smile and smile and be a villain"—another piece of packaged wisdom of the same type. It was Montaigne who had encouraged Hamlet to develop this habit of jotting down wise saws on his "tables." (He had described the practice in Book I, Chapter 19 of his *Essays*.) If this first soliloquy were to be given a title after the fashion of one of Montaigne's essays, it would be Hamlet's essay on "The Vanity of the World"—a commonplace and popular theme.

If the soliloquies are viewed in this way it would seem that in them Hamlet is primarily concerned with the general universal problems which the introspective essayists, Montaigne and Bacon, loved to handle. The chosen subject of his first great soliloquy ("O, that this too too solid flesh would melt") is vanity; the subject of the second ("O, what a rogue and peasant slave am I") is words; that of the third ("To be or not to be, that is the question") is patience; and that of the fourth ("How all occasions do inform against me") is action. He treats these subjects in something like the same winding personal fashion as Montaigne, with occasional verbal echoes from Montaigne to make the position clearer. Far from reacting to the urgencies of his revenge task, he seems to be gathering material for his brooding mind to work on. The soliloquies do not mark the stages in his progress toward the desired aim of revenging his father—they are eccentric to that. They are in fact achievements in self-discovery, in self-illumination, at the same time as they are mental compositions dealing with grand universal commonplaces larger than the action of the play viewed as revenge tragedy would seem to warrant. The stage on which this inner monologue is enacted is in fact both larger and narrower than the stage in which the outer action is enacted. It is larger because its themes are more universal: it is narrower because it is only Hamlet's inner doubts, problems, and feelings that are at stake. The implication of this might be that here we have the decisive romantic turning-away from dramatic action toward romantic subjectivity: the substitution of the inner consciousness for the outer confrontation with moral experience and the substitution of general wisdom for existential responsibility. It might suggest that the dramatic moment is absent.

II

Now we have only to express the conclusion in this way to realize that we must have gone wrong somewhere. Any producer and any actor will tell you that these soliloquies are the heart of the drama. They may indeed represent digressions from the "main action" (whatever that is), from the logical plot-framework, but they nevertheless constitute paradoxically the most dramatic moments in the play. They are not "essays" nor are they the sentimental reflections of some romantic hero, some Hernani, or Werther, or Manfred. There is some dramatic essence in these soliloquies which such sources and analogies do not reveal. What that essence is remains to be defined, but if drama is the intestinal warfare of the ethical substance, then surely that is present in the soliloquies; if drama is man struggling with his environment that is there; if drama is character defining itself in relation to destiny, that is there too. These factors are as surely lacking in Montaigne as they are present in *Hamlet*. In fact, however attractive the analogy with

Montaigne is (and there is no doubt that Hamlet had been reading Montaigne—he was reading him when he met Polonius in Act II), the analogy between Hamlet's soliloquies and Montaigne's essays will ultimately obscure more than it reveals.

In short, there is a world of difference between Hamlet and Montaigne not only in character but also in respect of their dramatic posture and personality. Montaigne is repetitive, urbane, mellow; he is not forever girding his intellectual loins; he relaxes in an arm chair. In this, incidentally, he is somewhat unlike the Stoics; he lacks their strenuous inner discipline. But he is much more unlike Hamlet. Hamlet never relaxes in an arm chair. He lacks that pleasurable inner life of Montaigne. When Hamlet looks within, it is to show us how ill all's here about his heart: when Montaigne looks within, it is to show us how well all's here about his heart. Montaigne enjoys taking us for this conducted tour of his well-stored mind, a mind where pleasure is reconciled if not to virtue then to reason and intellect. Even death is somehow enjoyable. Montaigne above all has no task, no burden.

The briefest and most comprehensive way of summing up Montaigne is to say that he is the man without a task. While of Hamlet it may be said that he is always and above all the man *with* a task. At that fundamental level they are in exactly opposite situations. Hamlet is anguished and disturbed where Montaigne is at ease. He has this penchant for potted wisdom which Montaigne had made so fashionable, so that at the moment of maximum disturbance he is liable to pull out his notebook and jot down a phrase that comes to mind; but in the final analysis it is not his purpose in these essays to display his collection of such phrases. He is grappling with a problem, viewing his task from all possible angles, walking around it, tormenting himself, and above all, seeking a way out. Montaigne is content to remain in the interior of his mind with its delicate artificial lighting, its Bordeaux tapestries, its well-stocked bookshelves, its calm and consolation. Hamlet is banging on the door, or cocking up his ear to catch the sounds and tremors from the street outside.

When we have said that Hamlet is first and foremost a man burdened with a task we have not said what that task is, and certainly we are not referring to his ostensible revenge task. There is a manifest discrepancy between Hamlet's soliloquies and the movement of the revenge tragedy in which A kills B, and the son of B thereupon compasses the death of A; and it would be a misjudgment to confine the notion of "task" or "responsibility" to this situation. Indeed, the intensity of Hamlet's anguished preoccupation with his problem, whatever that problem is, is only matched by the extent of his nonpreoccupation with the evident and ostensible business of the play conceived as a revenge tragedy. This is the paradox of the soliloquies.

Hamlet is above all, like Christian in *Pilgrim's Progress*, the man with a burden on his back. To act the part of Hamlet in these soliloquies is to realize in dramatic form through every word, gesture, and sigh, through every alternating sign of frustration, woe, hope, and despair the existence which the task-burdened man knows. It is this which makes the soliloquies fundamentally dramatic, just as it is the waiting for Godot which makes Beckett's play dramatic. We do not know who or what Godot is, we do not know what the waiting will yield, we do not know if and when it will end, but the actual suspensive burden of waiting is what counts. And it is Beckett's refusal to enter into explanations that would delimit and define the nature of the "waiting" which surely gives to that situation its metaphysical overtone. We are made to feel by this very undefined quality of the suspense how immensely undefinable it is, how universally real and true, how basic to all experience. In the same way, the soliloquies of Hamlet through their obsessive insistence on the burden of responsibility which Hamlet carries, and at the same time through their lack of coordination with the ostensible task in hand, point to tasks and responsibilities which not merely transcend the task of revenge but which are, in an important sense, which I hope presently to illustrate, at variance with it.

In respect then of the burden which he carries on his back Hamlet is unlike Montaigne, just as he is unlike Horatio and the other characters in the play. This is his unique dramatic quality, that which defines his existence. But there is something more which differentiates Hamlet from Montaigne and his mode of existence, and that has to do with the *nature* of his burden. It is not merely that Hamlet has a task where Montaigne has not, but that it is above all a religious task. Some of the critics have been attracted to the Montaigne echoes in Hamlet's speeches because they seem to support the view that Hamlet's imagination and thinking are secular. Montaigne was the first avowed and systematic secularist, the author of the first autobiography which is not a religious confession. He may have learned some of his technique in the confessional, but he has cast out the demons—as well as the angels—of the medieval imagination. In that sense he is a modern man. And there are those, chiefly D. G. James and L. C. Knights, who believe that Hamlet is just as modern a man living in the same closed world of total and unmitigated self-consciousness. But an examination of Hamlet's words, without a prejudice in favor of a modernistic interpretation, surely shows us in this respect a decisively non-Montaignian dimension. He may echo Montaigne, but he does so in order to contradict him.

This can be demonstrated by having a look at the famous Montaigne echo in the third soliloquy, which all the commentators have pointed out but the significance of which they have not really explored. Hamlet is expressing the stoic death-wish. Death, he says, comes to end

> The heartache and the thousand natural shocks
> That flesh is heir to; 'tis a consummation
> Devoutly to be wished, to die, to sleep!
> To sleep perchance to dream. . . .

(III. i. 62–65)

Hamlet here is echoing Montaigne's essay "On Physiognomie," as translated by Florio, which reads:

> If it [death] be a consummation of ones being, it is also an amendement and entrance into a long and quiet night. Wee finde nothing so sweete in life, as a quiet rest and gentle sleepe, and without dreames.[4]

Now what Montaigne is saying is first that death is the end of all, an annihilation—that is the meaning of Montaigne's word *"anéantissement,"* translated by Florio as "consummation"—and secondly, that because of that it is to be desired as a dreamless sleep. Both of these thoughts pass into Hamlet's speech, but in so doing they undergo an important change. First he is not sure if the sleep will be dreamless, for he goes on to say:

For in that sleep of death what dreams may come?

(III. i. 66)

He has, in short, something of the religious sense of "the other side" which Montaigne, the skeptic and the stoic, has abandoned. There is still the dread of something after death, the echo, the reverberation of something beyond the self-contained inner world of the ego, or the impersonality of the stoic *mundus*. Secondly, the word "consummation" which Shakespeare uses here has an ambiguous quality lacking in Florio. One meaning of it is "consuming away," annihilation—that is the primary meaning here no doubt; but the other meaning is, as in modern English, satisfaction, fulfillment, joy, even ecstasy.[5] In the burial service as set out in the Elizabethan Book of Common Prayer, we read of the death of the elect as "our perfect consummation and bliss." The phrase "devoutly to be wished" brings alive this other more religious meaning of the word "consummation" and reveals Hamlet as, once again, unlike Montaigne, seeking out some reality outside the closed world of the ego. It is an example of what Leo Spitzer calls "linguistic perspectivism." Hamlet is brooding stoically on death, which he views, or tries to view, like Montaigne and the secular philosophers of his time, as the end of all, a bourn from which no traveler returns; and yet another more religious dimension of thinking is embedded in the same words and phrases, a dimension which does not belong to Montaigne at all.

It is impossible to think of Hamlet's reflective monologues except in reference to the introspective "Senecan" tradition represented at this period by Montaigne, but at the same time there is the determined counterpointing. Hamlet does not share the self-sufficient, rational spirit of the secular philosophers of his time. He has gone through it and experienced it, but he has gone beyond it too. This is revealed in the very tone of his soliloquies. They are not urbane, mild, and good-tempered, like the essays of Montaigne, or even Bacon, with their self-controlled calm, their scientific and self-possessed spirit. Hamlet has passion and intensity. His introspection has a quality of deadly earnestness which does not suggest the familiar essay genre at all. It points to another genre altogether.

I am going to suggest that a closer examination of the great

soliloquies reveals another pattern, that of the religious meditation as practiced by Ignatius of Loyola and his followers in
the period sometimes known as the Baroque.[6] The devotional
writings of Ignatius as well as of Luis de Granada and others had
been translated into English, and in Shakespeare's time they had
already had an impact on many writers of prose and verse, on the
verse of Alabaster, Southwell, and above all Donne, and on the
prose of Joseph Hall and many others. Recent exegesis of Donne's
religious poetry has pointed emphatically to this kind of inspiration,[7] and we should remind ourselves again that not only is
Hamlet spiritually akin to Donne, but he is his exact contemporary. He is no stranger to this same tradition. L. L. Martz has
remarked that in Luis de Granada's *Of Prayer and Meditation*
we may note "the very poise of Hamlet in the graveyard scene."[8]
The skull which describes its present bare and empty state while
reflecting ironically on past glories is a commonplace of the
devotional tradition. Some of the practitioners actually kept a
skull in their rooms to meditate upon. Christopher Devlin found
a parallel in a popular Catholic devotional work by Robert Persons
published in 1582. There the skull says:

> Where are all my dalliances and tricks of love: all my pleasant musick:
> all my gorgeous buildings; all my costly feasts and banquetings.[9]

This is not far from the tone, rhythm, and content of Hamlet's
speech to Yorick's skull in Act V.

> Where be your gibes now? your gambols, your songs, your flashes of
> merriment, that were wont to set the table on a roar? not one now
> to mock your own grinning? quite chopfallen?
>
> (V. i. 207–211)

Not only does Hamlet touch on the same themes and adopt
the same poses as the meditation writers, but his meditations are
shaped by the same inner rhetorical structure. His meditations give
us first what the devotional writers called the *compositio loci,* the
descriptive thesis or act of memory; then there is the analytical or
dialectical part, the act of the understanding; finally there is the
vow or resolution, the ultimate fruit of the meditation as it issues
in an act of will. This threefold structure is well known to us not
only from the literary example, such as those of Hall, in the same

decade as *Hamlet*,[10] but also from the manuals of meditation in which the method was well explained and demonstrated as a rhetorical procedure integrating the three functions of the mind: memory, reason, and will, or (in more modern terminology) experience, thought, and feeling. As Martz so aptly puts it,

> There is a tendency to work from a particular situation, through analysis of that situation, and finally to some sort of resolution of the problems which the situation has presented.[11]

Above all it should be insisted that the whole movement is purposive; there is no mere idle musing; trivial episodes are brought purposefully into relation with the major responsibilities which govern our lives. Montaigne's essays may have been collaterally influenced by the Counter-Reformation meditation tradition, but the essential difference is that he enjoys to wander, to discourse on this and that; he strolls around his own garden examining and enjoying all the flowers, the oddities, the little bits of antiquity that are on view; the meditation writers are men who are embarked on a journey, a task; they will not rest until they have found illumination and fruit. They may start from anywhere, the sight of a blackamoor, of an importunate beggar, of a spider, but they will eventually arrive at their destination. A passage from one of Hall's meditations illustrates the psychological pattern of such purposive, task-burdened thinking:

> The motion of this thy heaven is perpetual; so let me ever be acting somewhat of thy will: the motion of thy heaven is regular, never swerving from the due points; so let me ever walk steadily in the ways of thy will, without all diversions or variations from the line of thy law.[12]

This "ejaculatory" meditation shows the digested pattern. There is the *compositio loci* consisting here of the observation of the heavenly bodies undoubtedly suggested by the beginning of the nineteenth psalm: then there is the dialectical application of it to his own condition, and there is the element of prayer or vow expressed in the dialogic, "so let me ever walk steadily in the ways of thy will."

Now it should be said at once that Hamlet's four great soliloquies do not have this assured theological basis. Hamlet is not

praying, and he is not making his vows to God, but he is nevertheless in an existential posture not so very different from that of the
meditation writers, whether Anglican or Catholic. He is aware
of certain religious imperatives (as Montaigne is not), and he has
the same brooding intensity of purpose as he seeks some aim, conclusion, or path. His task is a presence not to be put by, and it
burdens him obsessively at every turn:

> heaven and earth,
> Must I remember?
>
> (I. ii. 142–143)

Yes he must: so it is decreed. He is the man elected for responsibility, the man on whom the inexorable task has been laid:

> The time is out of joint, O cursed spite,
> That ever I was born to set it right!
>
> (I. v. 188–189)

Such a realization informs all the soliloquies, giving them an integrated and single-minded quality. All is morally unified, all is
colored by the same feeling of compulsion. And this is what ultimately makes them dramatic compositions rather than essays, for
the meditation has reference to an inner drama. Its desired end
is not soliloquy but colloquy, not monologue but dialogue. This
is what ultimately differentiates that tradition from the familiar
essay genre. There is, in short, an intimation of dramatic relationships quite foreign to the world of Bacon and Montaigne.

III

The first great soliloquy on the theme of "the vanity of the world"
states the religious problem at the outset:

> Or that the Everlasting had not fixed
> His canon 'gainst self-slaughter.
>
> (I. ii. 131–132)

The notion of an imperative divine command is set beside the image
of the unweeded garden which is the fallen world. Supporting it is
the memory of his father and mother and the bliss they had en-

joyed before the "fall." It is this that his memory contemplates
and on which his reason works by means of analogical argument:

> O God a beast that wants discourse of reason
> Would have mourned longer—married with my uncle,
> My father's brother, but no more like my father
> Than I to Hercules.

(I. ii. 153)

Here is passionate ratiocination; the mind moves nimbly along the
syllogistic path but comes back to the first premise, namely his
own infinite depravity, his sullied or solid flesh, symbolized by
the unbridgeable difference between himself and Hercules. He calls
upon the name of God no less than five times, but his final vow
or resolve is addressed to himself. There is no I/thou confrontation,
no colloquy: he remains in the enclosed world of the stoical or
Montaignian ego:

> But break my heart, for I must hold my tongue.

(I. ii. 159)

Memory, reason, and will have been drawn together in a purposive
search for meaning, for illumination, for a means of dealing with
the challenges of life. But he finds no such illumination. The vow
is self-addressed; it merely echoes around the prison cell of the
personal consciousness; and of course since it is no true vow it is
immediately forgotten and ignored after he meets with Horatio—
as though in fact it were nothing more than a Montaignian "essay."

The second soliloquy has as its starting point or *compositio
loci,* the picture of a weeping actor. It is like an emblem poem,
in which the poet moralizes on some morally significant sight drawn
from the outer world. One of Hall's meditations of 1630 starts
with the portrait of "An Importunate Beggar":

> With what zeal doth this man sue! with what feeling expressions! with
> how forcible importunity!

The sight reminds the devout author of his duty to sue to God
with a similar importunity:

> Why do I not thus to my God? I am sure I want no less, than the
> neediest: the danger of my want is greater: the alms I crave is bet-
> ter; the store and mercy of the Giver, infinitely more.[13]

Hamlet is saying exactly the same thing about the weeping actor, *viz.,*

> what would he do,
> Had he the motive and the cue for passion
> That I have?

(II. ii. 594–596)

There is the same movement from the visualized object to the moral self-questioning, the same pressure of duty, of obligation in both cases. In Hamlet's case, the appearance of the weeping actor functions as the starting point for a meditation on the vanity of mere words, and as a stimulus to finding words which will really give significant moral results. The actor has passion and an infinite supply of words, but he has no urgent personal motive:

> What's Hecuba to him, or he to Hecuba
> That he should weep for her?

(II. ii. 593–594)

What will make Hamlet the true actor is his task, his burden of obligation. This will give him his "cue," shedding upon the histrionic world of make-believe an unexpected new significance, just as the thought of Hall's own importunate needs gives to the sight of the beggar a new significance—raising beggary, so to speak, to a new level. Hamlet's meditation, which has started from the image of the actor, never leaves it behind; the theatrical trope is pervasive, a sign of the thoroughly obsessive nature of the search in which Hamlet is engaged,[14] of the inescapable burden which he carries.

Back then to the play, to the theater. There his task will find fulfillment: there he will know his course. The final resolve seems again to bring the meditating subject face to face with some outer reality. He seems to himself to be moving decisively out of the confines of his own enclosed personality, to be engaged in an act of moral acceptance, an adjustment to a reality outside. The resolve is explicitly religious. He wishes to avoid damnation. Perhaps the devil abuses him to damn him, and therefore the revelation in the theater, if it comes, will carry with it the promise of salvation, of moral justification:

> The play's the thing
> Wherein I'll catch the conscience of the king.
>
> (II. ii. 641–642)

This is a conscience-ridden play. At this level it is not the killing of Claudius that counts, but the confrontation, the challenge, the exposing of his evil, the settling of moral accounts. But Hamlet is wrong: no truly redeeming moment will occur as a result of his decision to mount the play; there will be no colloquy. What he will achieve will be a personal catharsis; he will remain as much as ever before alienated from God and man.

He does not in this second soliloquy call on the name of God more than once or twice, but he is haunted by presences, by an apparent invasion of his privacy. Someone is banging on the outer door of his ego:

> Who calls me villain, breaks my pate across,
> Plucks off my beard and blows it in my face,
> Tweaks me by the nose, gives me the lie i 'th 'throat
> As deep as to the lungs? who does me this?
>
> (II. ii. 607–610)

The element of imposed responsibility is there, the sense of being challenged. Here it is expressed in quasi-comic form, as though he was Bottom haunted by Robin Goodfellow; but the burden is just as inexorable in spite of the queer formulation.

In the third soliloquy, on the theme of patience ("To be or not to be"), the sense of an imposed burden is directly conveyed in the phrase:

> Who would fardels bear,
> To grunt and sweat under a weary life,
> But that the dread of something after death,
> The undiscovered country, from whose bourn
> No traveller returns, puzzles the will,
> And makes us rather bear those ills we have
> Than fly to others that we know not of.
>
> (III. i. 76–82)

The entire meditation is really compressed in those lines. In Geoffrey Whitney's *A Choice of Emblems* (1586) there is in fact a device of a "swimmer with a fardle on his back,"[15] and moral conclusions are worked out on the basis of the device. Shakespeare may or may not have seen the book, but in Hamlet's speech too, a man is visualized sweating under a heavy burden (*compositio loci*); the question is asked why does he go on carrying it? and by means of a dialectical movement of question and answer, the answer is given that he carries it because he is concerned with his eternal destiny, with his soul; there is a mystery about life and death which is not susceptible of dogmatic formulation (here the bad quarto inserts some very trite dogmas in place of the agnostic intimations of our text which speaks of an undiscovered country of which we have no certain knowledge). This exercise of ratiocination leads up to a kind of decision implied in the phrase "bear those ills we have" and in similar phrases throughout this soliloquy, culminating in the final clause which speaks of great enterprises which "lose the name of action."

It is a negative stoical conclusion and again indicates that though Hamlet has advanced in religious awareness, as in the phrase

<blockquote>
a consummation
Devoutly to be wished
</blockquote>

(III. i. 63–64)

he is still only on the threshold of the life of dialogue. As a matter of fact, something is lost by detaching this soliloquy from its context, for having gazed upon being and not being and having recognized the divine mystery in which they are enclosed, a mystery implied again in that word "conscience"—

<blockquote>
Thus conscience does make cowards of us all—
</blockquote>

(III. i. 83)

he meets Ophelia. He himself is not in the posture of prayer, but he is near enough to it to suggest to her that she might care to include him in her orisons, thus achieving by proxy the last stage of the meditative exercise. But the gesture is—as far as the spectator is concerned—ironical. If he cannot save himself, she is even less in a position to save him. Her act of devotion is external only ("devotion's visage"): it cannot bring salvation for her or anyone else. There is no emergence into the world of dialogue.

The fourth soliloquy, on the theme of action ("How all occasions do inform against me"), is the antitype of the third. Again there is the oppressive burden of responsibility:

> I do not know
> Why yet I live to say "This thing's to do"
>
> (IV. iv. 43–44)

but it is a burden that he cannot discharge in spite of his having cause, will, and means. Again there is the sense that his task is ultimately explicable in religious terms only, it is part of a burden imposed on man by God:

> Sure he that made us with such large discourse,
> Looking before and after, gave us not
> That capability and god-like reason
> To fust in us unused.
>
> (IV. iv. 36–39)

The meditation pattern of memory, reason, and will is even clearer in this soliloquy than in the others. The opening composition is visually displayed on the stage in the sight of Fortinbras and his army marching off to Poland. Hamlet registers this sight on his mind and proceeds to ratiocinate about it.

> What is a man? etc.

His argument has a somewhat hair-splitting scholastic flavor:

> Now whether it be
> Bestial oblivion, or some craven scruple
> Of thinking too precisely on the event—
> A thought which quartered hath but one part wisdom,
> And ever three parts coward—
>
> (IV. iv. 39–43)

he loses the thread of the argument a little at this point and returns to the obsessive and importunate demand of his conscience—"This thing's to do." The conclusion, the act of will, comes right at the end in exact conformity with the meditation pattern. It is a resolve to emulate the bloody path of Fortinbras:

> O, from this time forth
> My thoughts be bloody, or be nothing worth.
>
> (IV. iv. 65–66)

And as though to make clear how unsatisfactory a resolve this is and how inadequate it is as an expression of the real nature of his moral burden, Hamlet immediately forgets it and goes off to embark on his voyage for England. It is again a self-addressed vow; it merely echoes around the inner chamber of the meditating consciousness. It has been an essay, nothing more.

IV

After Act IV Hamlet utters no further soliloquy. The burden of his task is still upon him; he has the same keenness of outward observation, the same need to ratiocinate, and the same need to reach conclusions, but this no longer expresses itself in monologue form. Why should that be? Critics of course have often pointed out the important change which comes over Hamlet's outlook and behavior following the voyage to England so strangely and marvelously interrupted as it was. Coming back from this voyage, he has a new adjustment to himself and his task:

> There's a divinity that shapes our ends,
> Rough-hew them how we will.
>
> (V. ii. 10–11)

But critics have not noted that his newfound faith in Providence, this awareness of being, so to speak, in the hand of God may have something to do with the cessation of soliloquy. Surely it is that the soliloquies end because Hamlet emerges from the life of monologue into the life of dialogue.

A similar phenomenon occurs in a modern work of fiction which follows the career of a Hamlet-like man burdened likewise with guilt and responsibility and enclosed for the most part in the world of selfhood. I am referring to Saul Bellow's *Herzog*. In that work the interior monologue takes the form of a compulsive letter-writing mania. Herzog writes letters to all his friends and acquaintances living and dead, even to people he does not know, such as General Eisenhower. His letters start from remembered or experienced events, or from thoughts taken out of books; they proceed through argument and self-questioning to some conclusion or resolve which is never carried out. It is not even clear whether these letters are actually written or only worked out mentally; certainly they are not mailed and they do not reach their destination. There is no contact with the outside world, just the unappeased desire for dialogue. Herzog remains outside the world of human discourse and fruitful communication. Then toward the end, a change comes, a redeeming moment, and in his last letter to God and in his final meditations, he reaches certain insights not dissimilar from those which Hamlet reaches during his sea voyage. He comes to think of man as somehow obscurely saved—he is content "to be just as it is willed." There is meaning after all. The final realization of Herzog is that the letters will now cease. He emerges from his neurotic state, and in emerging he establishes a relation between himself and his environment which is actual and immediate and which can be expressed in dialogue form. The inner consciousness and the outer experience begin to beat in time without the disjunction and dislocations which had hitherto separated the interior world of Herzog from the things that were happening to him and his friends. The last time we see him, he is purposefully waiting for what the future holds in store.

The situation of Herzog (whether or not Bellow had the analogy in mind) resembles that of Hamlet for another reason. His letter-writing monologues are a fundamentally pathological symptom: they represent his state of radical alienation. Herzog lives in the world of monologue because he is sick. Nevertheless it is the sustained self-examination, the intellectual inquiry, and the wrestling with imaginary interlocutors which eventually bring him to health and sanity. He emerges from the life of monologue. The letters are the symptoms of sickness, but they are also a path of purgation. He adopts in them the posture of dialogue; and this desire is finally rewarded in the recovery of a faint but perceptible degree of faith in man and his future. Communication is at last possible.[16]

I have spoken at length of this analogous instance because I feel it is worth pointing out that Hamlet's soliloquies have this same dual character. They are a symptom of sickness of alienation and not merely a convention of the theater like the soliloquies of Brutus and Macbeth. He speaks in soliloquy because he is cut off and alienated. But he is trying not to be, and paradoxically it is through the established discipline of meditation which lurks behind those soliloquies that he seeks and finds a meaningful world with which he may have correspondence. The literary form which underlies the soliloquies is the religious meditation, just as the literary form of Herzog's soliloquies is the letter. Both imply a person or otherness addressed, and in both cases the otherness addressed finally defines itself as a God who both hears and answers.

Thus Hamlet ceases to soliloquize, but he does not cease to meditate. After Act V there is one further meditation, this time not couched in the form of a soliloquy but significantly embedded in a series of dialogic exchanges between himself and Horatio. Yet in spite of this dispersed and interrupted quality, the meditation structure shines through in the established form of protasis, apodosis, and resolution. Moreover, it is a traditional meditation on death, the meditating subject standing before us with a skull in his hand. It is Hamlet's final composition in this genre. The first section gives us the *compositio loci,* the actual concrete image of death gazed upon and made to reveal its secret by the exercise of memory, Hamlet's memory of Yorick:

> Let me see. Alas, poor Yorick! I knew him, Horatio—a fellow of infinite jest, of most excellent fancy. He hath borne me on his back a thousand times, and now how abhorred in my imagination it is! my gorge rises at it. Here hung those lips that I have kissed I know not how oft.
>
> (V. i. 202–207)

After the act of memory—the vivid evocation of the physical concrete fact of life and death, comes the exercise of ratiocination. Hamlet's analytical quest takes the form of a kind of acrobatic exercise of fantastic logic almost in the manner of Lewis Carroll. First he states the argument to be proved

> Why may not imagination trace the noble dust of Alexander, till a' find it stopping a bung-hole?
>
> (V. i. 223–225)

Horatio feels that this is taking analysis too far, " 'Twere to consider curiously to consider so." But Hamlet proceeds to prove the argument;

> as thus—Alexander died, Alexander was buried, Alexander returneth to dust, the dust is earth, of earth we make loam, and why of that loam whereto he was converted might they not stop a beer-barrel?
>
> (V. i. 230–234)

The resolution or act of will comes a scene later. Hamlet has faced death and he has also sensed the working of Providence; now he combines the two in a speech of acceptance, which gives to his meditation a genuinely devotional ending,

> There is a special providence in the fall of a sparrow. If it be now, 'tis not to come—if it be not to come, it will be now; if it be not now, yet it will come—the readiness is all. Since no man has aught of what he leaves, what is't to leave betimes?
>
> (V. ii. 232–237)

"The readiness is all"—the phrase conveys the earnest expectation of the creature for his creator which marks the essential character of Biblical man, but it also echoes Montaigne in his essay on "Learning How to Die."[17] Hamlet has not returned to a medieval Christian order: he is still a modern man sharing with the philosopher of Bordeaux something of his naturalism, his worldliness and realism. But he has gone further than Montaigne: he has achieved a moral and religious perspective which makes death not merely a consummation in the sense of a dissolution, but also a "consummation" in the full religious sense. Underneath are the everlasting arms. In reaching this position of equipoise, which is very far from being synonymous with medieval piety, Hamlet has reached the end of his meditative quest. He has brought his inner life into relation with his outward responsibilities and interests.

In this fifth act where monologue gives way to dialogue, we no longer have a discrepancy between the inner world of Hamlet's thoughts and the "consecutive series of events moving logically towards an appointed end."[18] There is now no discontinuity between the inner emotion and its dramatic manifestation. The speech just quoted directly prepares us for the rapier contest and its ending: it points to the final working-out of the plot; the tragic death of Hamlet himself and of his enemies. All works purposefully together toward the appointed conclusion of Hamlet's task. But what was the real nature of that task? What has been its relation to that Senecan revenge pattern? To explore more closely the nature of the burden laid upon Hamlet is the obvious next stage of our inquiry.

CHAPTER V

Spirit
or Goblin?

There are as many different Ghosts as there are Hamlets in the
literature of *Hamlet* criticism. There is the good Ghost of Bradley,
and of a large number of traditionally minded critics who take
Hamlet's words at their face value—

> Touching this vision here
> It is an honest ghost, that let me tell you.
>
> (I. v. 137–138)

For Sister Miriam Joseph and for Father Christopher Devlin he
is a saved Christian soul temporarily suffering the fires of Purgatory.[1] Then there is the bad Ghost, the evil incubus of J. Vyvyan,
not much better than the witches in *Macbeth,* for he too drives his
victim to deeds of bloodshed in a most unchristian fashion.[2] L. C.
Knights' interestingly associates the specter of Hamlet's father with
the "specter" in Blake's mythology, narrow, self-centered, and
brooding on evil, instead of living, like the "emanation," in the
light of love and imagination.[3] Again there is some support in the
text. It "started like a guilty thing" on the crowing of the cock.
Obviously an ambiguous ghost. I suspect that the first really bad
ghost to walk the pages of *Hamlet* criticism was that of G. Wilson
Knight in his remarkable essay of 1930 entitled "The Embassy
of Death." His summing-up of the character of the Ghost has
become a *locus classicus*:

> Not till it has slain all, is the demon that grips Hamlet satisfied. And
> last it slays Hamlet himself:

78

> "The spirit that I have seen
> May be the Devil . . . "

It was.[4]

Thus far G. Wilson Knight. And since then critics have never been able to see the Ghost in quite the same innocently Christian fashion. Of course, Wilson Knight here, as he openly avows, is applying to Shakespeare the Nietzschean transvaluation of values. Hamlet is the outsider, the superman, corroding with his acid, amoral intellect the fabric of healthy robust Christianity around him, and it is the surly and destructive spirit which drives him to this. Hamlet is the demonic artist, and therefore he is aligned with a demonic Ghost against the normalities of "good" Christian folk like Gertrude and Claudius.[5] Of course this is a paradoxical and deliberately inversive view of Shakespeare's intention, but it lights up the possibility already hinted at, that if the play is the story of Hamlet's salvation it is not quite the conventional Christian salvation that is aimed at; the values symbolized by the Ghost are not exactly traditional Christian values. If not "beyond good and evil" as Knight might say, they are at least beyond the conventional ethics and sanctities of Christian society as inherited from the Middle Ages.

Other critics have felt uneasy about the Ghost but, wanting to retain him in the Christian scheme, they have resolved their uneasiness by distinguishing between his appearance in Act I and that in Act III. Of his later appearance Devlin says,

> The Ghost is "gracious" this time, not hideous; its supernatural power is gentler and more sublime.[6]

Roy Walker speaks to the same effect, and with admirable clarity:

> The Old Testament Avenger of Act One is a New Testament God of Love at the end of Act III.[7]

Walker comes near the root of the matter in giving the Ghost and his commands a kind of divine status. This shows true insight into the special religious solemnity of the occasions, but he has gone astray—along with Devlin—in supposing that there is any real inconsistency between the two appearances of the Ghost. Whatever inner contradictions the Ghost harbors, they surely are present in both scenes, the scene on the battlements in Act I, and the closet scene in Act III.

The command the Ghost issues in Act I and reiterates in Act III is quite clear and categorical, and it consists of two parts. The first part is, briefly, "Kill your uncle!" The second part may be stated equally briefly: it is, "Do not kill your mother!" The command to kill Claudius is comprised in the words:

> If thou hast nature in thee bear it not.

The not-killing of Gertrude is as clearly conveyed in the reservation that immediately follows:

> But howsoever thou pursuest this act,
> Taint not thy mind, nor let thy soul contrive
> Against thy mother aught—leave her to heaven . . .
>
> (I. v. 84–86)

The key word in the first part of the command is "nature": the key word in the second part is "heaven." It may seem rather strange to us that the possibility of Hamlet wishing to kill his mother should be raised at all, and not only raised, but given such emphasis. That this is a major element of the Ghost's command, however, the text makes clear beyond the least doubt. It is the emphatic note on which the speech ends. And it is that part of the command even more than the first to which the last line of the Ghost's command has reference:

> Adieu, adieu, adieu, remember me.
>
> (I. v. 91)

The terms of the Ghost's second appearance in Act III correspond precisely to this twofold instruction. The first part of the command is reiterated in the words—

> this visitation
> Is but to whet thy almost blunted purpose—
>
> (III. iv. 109–110)

a statement that can only refer to the killing of Claudius. The concern for Gertrude and the concern that Hamlet should show her a proper filial regard are conveyed in the lines that follow:

But look, amazement on thy mother sits,
O step between her and her fighting soul.
Conceit in weakest bodies strongest works,
Speak to her Hamlet.

(III. iv. 111–114)

Hamlet's reaction to this shows a remarkable degree of introspective insight: it is to say that the observance of the second part of
the Ghost's instructions, *viz.,* solicitude and pity for Gertrude,
might well prejudice the execution of the first part by undermining
those springs of wrath and ferocity needed to nourish it:

Do not look upon me,
Lest with piteous action you convert
My stern effects, then what I have to do
Will want true colour, tears perchance for blood.

(III. iv. 126–129)

The "piteous action" relates evidently to the gesture that accompanies the Ghost's references to Gertrude; the "what I have to
do" as clearly refers to the revenge task which the Ghost has im-
peratively laid upon him. The Ghost has not developed; there is
no change of plan, no conversion from a pre-Christian avenger to
a post-Christian God of love. When the Ghost develops he does so
by disappearing from sight altogether. The new and more integrated
understanding of his task which Hamlet achieves in Act V is
marked by the disappearance of the Ghost from the play. By then
he is neither seen nor mentioned. But in Act I and Act III he remains the same figure with the same ethical (or unethical) mission.
Ambiguous he may be, but his ambiguity is constant. If he is a
Christian ghost in Act III, then he was this already in Act I, and
if he was a Hebrew avenging ghost in Act I, he is still a Hebrew
ghost in Act III.

But before we take up the question of the Hebrew avenger—
a ghost indeed, and one we shall have to lay before long—let us
take up this second and to my mind more significant and more
truly religious part of the Ghost's instructions, which may be
paraphrased in the words, "Thou shalt not kill Gertrude!"[8] Was
Hamlet in any danger of performing so "unnatural" a deed? The
answer of course is that he most certainly was in such danger.

Orestes, the Greek prototype of Hamlet, kills both his mother Clytemnestra and her husband Aegisthus (likewise a close kinsman) in revenge for his father's death. In fact, the killing of Clytemnestra is the culmination of the whole revenge cycle, the final working out and exorcism of the curse which had infected the house of Atreus for three generations. It is to this consummation that the oracle of Apollo savagely and relentlessly drives Orestes on, until he is left wracked with horror, bereft of reason, and drenched in kindred blood. It is not necessary to prove that Shakespeare had any direct knowledge of the *Oresteia* of Aeschylus or the parallel treatment in Sophocles: all the ancient revenge tragedies, both in the Greek original and in the sensationalized form in which Shakespeare would have found them in Seneca, turned on "unnatural" crime, parricide, fratricide, child-murder, and incest. Nor is this simply a gruesome incidental feature of the old revenge tragedy. Kindred blood is of its essence. The killing of Gertrude by Hamlet would have been the logical and inevitable sequel to fratricide and incest. In telling Hamlet that this is just what he must not do, the Ghost is telling him as clearly as he can that he must break out of the vicious circle of pagan revenge tragedy with its unnatural crime and its unbridled savagery. But it is not easy to break out. Hamlet feels the terrible pull of the old archetypal instinct, and the killing of his mother toward which this would inevitably point is an actively present horror in his imagination. Before his meeting with her in Act III, he has to steel himself against this temptation:

> O heart lose not thy nature, let not ever
> The soul of Nero enter this firm bosom,
> Let me be cruel not unnatural.
> I will speak daggers to her, but use none.

> (III. ii. 418–421)

Nero had killed his mother who had been married to his stepfather Claudius. The coincidence of names and functions is too close to be fortuitous. Hamlet is in real danger of becoming another Nero, not only by taking away the throne from Claudius—as Nero had done—but by dispatching Agrippina-Gertrude-Clytemnestra in the same fashion. This is to transgress the religious part of the Ghost's command, and so he must renounce the path of Nero:

The soul o   let not ever

And yet the i   *32 - Last P Quote*   natural
a sequel to th   e first
part of the s]   it can
only with difl   r but
use none.   *33 -*
  It is not   es to
killing his m(eizes
her by the ar

  What wil

This is no rh   and
in front of hi   nes-
tra: there ca]   had
Polonius at   onius
behind the a   s the
blood lust which had been mounting up _____ ching
the eavesdropper. It is a mistake to think of Hamlet at this point as primarily intending to kill his uncle and killing Polonius in error. The hope that he has killed the king is an afterthought. His savage anger throughout this scene has reference to his mother not his uncle: she is the target, and Polonius becomes a substitute not for the King but for the Queen. Hamlet draws the moral equation himself a moment later, making his deed correspond with that of hers for which it very nearly became the retribution:

QUEEN: O what a rash and bloody deed is this!

HAMLET: A bloody deed—almost as bad, good mother,
    As kill a king, and marry with his brother.

(III. iv. 27–29)

At this moment his matricidal instinct finds its justification in the supposition of his mother's direct complicity in his father's murder.
  The danger of killing his mother has now been averted for

the moment through the opportune appearance of a "ram in the
thicket" whose death, though opprobrious, will not come upon
Hamlet as the death of Gertrude might have done, but Hamlet's
anger still has in it something dangerous. She herself echoes his
own phrase in the Nero soliloquy when she says,

> O speak to me no more,
> These words like daggers enter in mine ears.
>
> (III. iv. 94–95)

And it is at the point where Hamlet's fury rises once again to the
point of uncontrol that the Ghost appears for the second and last
time to enforce his double command on Hamlet. The word is once
again, "Kill the King," but also, "Nor let thy soul contrive against
thy mother aught."

We should not underestimate the supreme difficulty of the command thus placed on Hamlet, the daunting contrariety of the two
aims when their full implications are understood. He must strip
the revenge task of its most customary feature; he must limit his
operations to one person, the actual murderer himself. Here is the
moral and psychological novelty of the Ghost's command. "The
soul which sinneth, it shall die" (Ezekiel 18:4)—that is what the
Ghost is saying. "Kill the murderer, but leave his wife and children untouched." This is exactly what is meant by "taint not thy
mind." Beware of being carried away by the whirlpool of indiscriminate savagery like Orestes, like Medea, like Nero, like Atreus
himself, like all the revengers of antiquity. Here is the departure
from the law of the jungle to the law announced at Sinai. It is a
momentous turning point.

I am always struck with amazement—perhaps because I was
not fortunate or unfortunate enough to have received a classical
education during my tender years—at the moral horrors with which
the imaginations of young children in Western society are fed at
school. Could darker violence be imagined than that contained
in the Senecan tragedies of *Thyestes, Medea,* and *Agamemnon*?
And yet this is "Christian Seneca." It is a central part of that
Renaissance culture which in the sixteenth century of Roger
Ascham, Sir Thomas More, and Sir Philip Sidney was absorbed
into the warp and woof of Christian education. I quote from the

words of the Ghost of Thyestes at the beginning of Seneca's tragedy
of *Agamemnon* in the translation of F. J. Miller,

> By my dread crimes will I outdo them all—
> But not my brother's crimes. Three sons of mine
> Lie buried in me, yea, mine own dear flesh
> Have I consumed. Nor this the only blot
> With which dire fortune's hands hath stained my soul;
> But daring greater sin, she bade me seek
> (O foul impiety!) my daughter's arms.
> Bold for revenge, I dared and did the deed,
> And so the fearful cycle was complete:
> As sons the sire, so sire the daugher filled.
> Then were the laws of nature backward turned:
> I mingled sire with grandsire, sons with grandsons;
> Yea, monstrous! Husband and father did I join,
> And drove the day back to the shades of night.
> But fate at last, though doubtful, long deferred
> Hath had regard unto my evil plight,
> And brought the day of vengeance near; for lo,
> This king of kings, this leader of the Greeks,
> This Agamemnon comes, whose royal flag
> A thousand Grecian vessels following
> Once filled the Trojan waters with their sails.
> Now ten bright suns have run their course, and Troy
> Has been o'erthrown, and he is close at hand—
> To place his neck in Clytemnestra's power.
> Now, now, this house shall flow again with blood. . . .[9]

Surely no morally sensitive person can forbear a shudder of horror
at this recital. And even the seemingly limitless vision of blood and
unnatural crime which this speech contains does not reach to the
final horror, the ultimate climax to the whole blood-soaked history,
namely the killing of Clytemnestra by her own son Orestes at the
end of the cycle.

Hippolyte Taine had a feeling for racial and cultural characteristics, but led astray by his own spiritual dependence on the
classics, he saw things in a remarkably idealized fashion:

> On reading a Greek tragedy, our first care is to figure to ourselves
> the Greeks, that is to say, men who lived half-naked in the gym-
> nasium or on a public square under a brilliant sky in full view of
> the noblest and most delicate landscape, busy in rendering their
> bodies strong and agile, in conversing together, in arguing, in vot-
> ing . . .[10]

When I read Greek tragedy, I regret that my care is to figure to myself a man who, pursued by an evil demon, slays his father and cohabits with his mother, or a woman who, in order to help her lover, slays her own brother and leaves his mangled limbs on the wayside, and who afterward consumed by jealousy on account of that same lover's infidelity kills their two children before his eyes. Perhaps before the twentieth century it was possible to treat these stories as fantasies or as profound images to be taken in a quite transferred nonliteral way: it seems to me that faithfulness to the truths of contemporary history no longer permits such idealization. The deeds of violence which occur from time to time in the Hebrew Bible pale by comparison with such catalogues of crime and horror as we find in the Greek and Roman classics. And yet this was the normal diet of schoolboys in Shakespeare's time, and still is the staple of upper-class education in many Western countries. One can only speculate on the psychological distortions to which such images must inevitably give rise, and at the same time feel thankful that a majority of pupils are too much occupied with problems of grammar and syntax to pay much attention to the Thyestean banquet of atrocities which is set before them. Classical scholars write and discuss these matters with enviable sang-froid. The impression they give, as far as Seneca is concerned, is that the whole thing was little more than a rhetorical exercise, a form of closet drama not to be taken up in terms of moral approval and disapproval. I find such an attitude rather strange. Is literature to be thus separated from the main concerns of our lives? Can it be thus separated? It is hardly conceivable that the men of the Renaissance made such academic distinctions, and we must reckon with the fact that the revenge tragedy, which was a central part of the cultural experience of the sixteenth century in England and elsewhere, became part and parcel of that upsurge of paganism to which the elegant term "Renaissance culture" is customarily given.

The Renaissance was an ugly time to live in. It looks pleasanter to us in historical retrospect. But let us remind ourselves that *Romeo and Juliet* is a Renaissance tragedy: the vendetta between the two houses takes its toll of one young life after another until the two old bloodthirsty fathers of the feud face one another over the tombs of their fairest offspring. It is not far from the life of the times. Jacob Burckhardt relates of an actual vendetta in Italy:

> In the district of Acquapendente three boys were watching cattle, and one of them said: "Let us find out the way how people are hanged." While one was sitting on the shoulders of the other, and the third, after fastening the rope round the neck of the first, was tying it to an oak, a wolf came, and the two who were free ran away and left the other hanging. Afterwards they found him dead, and buried him. On the Sunday his father came to bring him bread, and one of the two confessed what had happened, and showed him the grave. The old man then killed him with a knife, cut him up, brought away the liver, and entertained the boy's father with it at home. After dinner, he told him whose liver it was. Hereupon began a series of reciprocal murders between the two families, and within a month thirty-six persons were killed, women as well as men.[11]

The only difference between this and the story of Thyestes and the house of Atreus is apparently in the larger number of victims and the more concentrated quality of savagery in the later vendetta which instead of being spread over several generations occurred within a month. Pagan inspiration had broken away from the traditional restraints of Christian civilization.

The Montagues and Capulets or the people of whom Burckhardt is writing in the above passage were presumably not readers of books, but the cultured class was morally no better. Savagery ran free in the pages of Seneca and in the strange and unbelievable deeds of violence and brutality recorded by Plutarch, by Livy, Herodotus, and the rest. It is from the ancient historians that the new political science of Machiavelli took its rise with its moral realism, its objectivity, its cool analogy between man and beast. The ethical sanctities of the Judeo-Christian tradition are forgotten, and political philosophy is based squarely on what men do, not what they ought to do. There was much true poetry and art in the Renaissance, and the glories of man's soul were newly discovered and revealed. But on the other hand there was much fear of violent death. A Christian gentleman carried one or more sharpened knives in his belt; when insulted he would jump at his fellow Christian's throat. This is not just literature: not just an exercise in rhetoric. Marlowe was slain in a drunken brawl. Ben Jonson, a very moral Christian poet, killed his man in a duel.

In case the drift of the foregoing remarks is not clear enough, let me simply state that the Renaissance cult of honor, which found its expression in literature in the revenge genre, and in life in the duel, was produced—insofar as literary sources are in question—through the influence of Greek and Roman classicism, and not in the least through overconcentration on the Old Testament Scripture. The interesting question is why so many critics have jumped to a demonstrably wrong conclusion about this: they include G. B. Shaw, Roy Walker, and Geoffrey Bush, all of whom see in the Ghost's urging of Hamlet to revenge and in Hamlet's acceptance of this bloodthirsty mission an example of a Mosaic attitude and ethic. It is no part of this study to attempt an investigation of the aberrations of criticism: Hamlet's aberrations are our business. But it may be noted that the confusion of the critics is part of a more widespread confusion—one of those idols of the tribe which may be traced in the history of the West. Marlowe's reaction to Machiavellianism in *The Jew of Malta* takes the form of a Jew play; Shakespeare, in reacting against the new Calvinist economics of usury, again focuses on the Jew; Blake, in his violent rejection of the moral code of Puritanism, confounds it with the "rock Sinai," and in the nineteenth century, Matthew Arnold and Samuel Butler both throw the blame for the dark Victorian Sunday and the harsh family life of the nonconformist middle class upon "Hebraism." They do not stop to ask whether all these various and often conflicting standards really have their roots in Old Testament Scripture or in the social pattern of Jewry: the identification is made at a subrational level.

The same applies to the linking of the Jewish god with the Senecan revenger and his ghostly prompter. It is a case of "psychological substitution." The Jewish god is made guilty of those sins against the spirit which he explicitly came to root out. It is Hebraism that had commanded "Thou shalt not murder." This was a disturbing commandment when so much murdering was being done, and some of the disturbance gets directed against the author of the command. The fact is that the Jewish god in the West has fought hard to control the still active remnants of paganism, but he has not always succeeded. The most common text quoted in the sixteenth and seventeenth century by the moralists in condemning private vengeance was from Deuteronomy: "Vengeance is mine, saith the Lord, and I will repay." There were texts from the New Testament as well, such as "Resist not evil," but these were not always so effective in argument because they tended to go too far. It was reasonable to demand of an insulted man that he should submit his grievance to some higher authority, divine or human, and seek restitution in that way. It was not quite so reasonable to ask him to turn the other cheek or condemn him for seeking legal redress at all as Paul does in his letter to the Corinthians. The Jewish god addressed himself to man in his natural condition: St. Paul demands of him that he root out the "Old Adam" and be reborn in grace. The first approach could become the basis of effective social legislation; the second could not: it did not confront nature on its own ground and consequently very often left man just as unregenerate as it found him. Tawney has described how the combination of an evangelical ethic and the new advances in science and economics produced the characteristic evils of unbridled capitalism in the West during the period immediately following the time of Shakespeare.

But to return to the Jewish god and to Hamlet, for whose evil impulses as a revenge hero the Jewish god has been held responsible, it may help us with our understanding of this play if we put a somewhat finer edge on the Old Testament attitude toward private vengeance. Along with the great command "Thou shalt not murder," the Mosaic legislator did take account of the psychological fact of the revenge instinct and did provide for it. He set aside for the accidental slayer six cities of refuge to which he could flee in order to escape the hands of the incensed relatives of the slain man. There he could remain unharmed until such time as he might "stand before the congregation in judgment" (Numbers 35:12). The revenger of blood was only at liberty to slay the man who had omitted to place himself in the protection of one of the cities of refuge. The object of this structure of legislation is "that innocent blood be not shed in thy land" (Deuteronomy 19:10). There is no question here of the Mosaic legislator urging the avenger of blood to kill: here is rather a structure of law which accepts human nature for what it is, but is determined to impose upon that nature the principle of respect for human life, the horror of indiscriminate slaughter of man, woman, and child through which the land becomes tainted and infected. The object of such law, in fact, is to rid the ancient Hebrew polity of that taint of bloodshed and unnatural crime which reeks from the ancient tragedy of the Greeks and Romans.

How did sixteenth-century Christianity, that is, the ethical civilization to which Shakespeare's plays have reference, react to the threat to the moral stability of society and its inherited Judeo-Christian tradition which the Renaissance cult of honor and un-restricted personal vengeance undoubtedly posed? There were, I suppose, two broad solutions: one was that of what is generally termed "Christian humanism," which meant soaking up as much of the pagan culture as could be made compatible with Christianity and allegorizing or somehow humanizing the rest through inter-pretation. This was the medieval method which had worked well when classical culture was rather more restricted in scope and had less power over men's minds, and it continued to work for a great many people who had conservative, traditionally ordered minds. Spenser, in Shakespeare's time, is a great harmonizer of Christian and classical themes. But Shakespeare does not resemble Spenser much in this. A second method, ultimately more effective, but at the same time more sinister, was cleanly to divide the inner spiritual life from the outer activities of man as a social, cultural, and political animal. This was in line with—or at least could be easily adapted to—the evangelical principle of rendering to Caesar that which is Caesar's and to God that which is God's. It gives a free and unrestricted scope for all the secular concerns of the new Renaissance man, including any violent homicidal tendencies that he might have. Nature is separated from grace, and becomes a zone no longer sanctified by religion but given up quite delib-erately to the Devil, who is thought to rule our fallen world. This division of the human personality into secular and religious halves is chiefly, I suppose, associated in the Reformation with the doc-trines of Luther (we remember how vividly present the Devil was to him), and from it, by a discernible historical thread, German totalitarianism with all the inhumanity it implies may be seen to take its rise.[12]

Now there is a great deal of both these attitudes in Shakespeare's plays, but they are not attitudes that could completely satisfy a poet of real moral power and insight. Neither of these solutions creates order out of the chaos resulting from the new Renaissance drives as they clashed with the new Reformation biblicism. I am not trying to argue that a poet—even if he is Shakespeare—must necessarily be a moral genius. But I am trying to suggest that when a poet is as sensitive as Shakespeare was to the form and pressure of the times—its conflicts and contradictions—his very artistic integrity will drive him to seek something better than either the Calvinistic and Lutheran division of spheres or the timeworn compromises of Christian humanism. That something better is what Shakespeare is feeling toward in all his great tragedies, and nowhere does it reveal itself more sharply than in *Hamlet*.

II

The Ghost has been there all the time. Even when we have been talking about other things he has been down there in the "cellarage." And now we must bring him up and take a closer look at him. He is, of course, a Senecan ghost, first of all. That is the tradition Shakespeare inherited. He transforms him—indeed sanctifies him—as he had transformed and humanized the anti-Semitic image of the old bloodthirsty Jew in *The Merchant of Venice*. But just as Shylock remains attached to his hoary origins in the Jew-Judas-Devil complex of medieval tradition, so Hamlet's father remains the bloodthirsty Senecan ghoul whom we glanced at a little earlier in the character of Thyestes announcing the forthcoming crime of Aegisthus. The reference to his own evil past is in the Senecan tradition. Thyestes had said,

Then were the laws of nature backward turned . . .
Yea monstrous! husband and father did I join,
And drove the day back to the shades of night.

Similarly the Ghost of Hamlet's father speaks of the "foul crimes done in my days of nature," and goes on to say that he had been

Cut off even in the blossoms of my sin,
Unhouseled, disappointed, unaneled,
No reck'ning made, but sent to my account
With all my imperfections on my head.
O, horrible! O, horrible! most horrible!

(I. v. 76–80)

The words "O, horrible! etc." refer ambiguously both to the crimes of old Hamlet and to the crime of Claudius in dispatching him, as well they might, the point being that the revenging ghost of the old tragedy was generally as bad as the person whom he was execrating. There is the same ambiguity in the "Yea monstrous" of Thyestes. It is a vicious circle of one criminal calling down vengeance on another criminal; the avenger whom he summons will in his turn invert the laws of nature and become an equally execrable monster. There is, in the strict economy of the Senecan revenge tradition, no way out of this progressive imbrutement of the human species except the ultimate holocaust in which the chief parties on both sides lie dead and a wintry peace ensues. This moral pattern—if it can be so called—lies deeply embedded in the tradition which Shakespeare inherited in *Hamlet*. Shakespeare does not give us any details of the foul crimes done in the days of old Hamlet's nature—but there is no doubt about the emphasis given to this, an emphasis which must occasion surprise to any reader or spectator who is not attuned to the spiritual *ethos* of pre-Christian Senecan revenge drama. It is obvious that these "foul crimes" do not refer to the small peccadilloes of an otherwise good Catholic prince who has been unlucky enough to have died without receiving absolution; the insistence on the horrible nature of the crimes is too great. Moreover the punishment was made to fit the crimes, and the punishment for old Hamlet's crimes was such that the recital of it would cause young Hamlet's

knotted and combined lock to part,
And each particular hair to stand on end.

(I. v. 18–19)

In all this we clearly have an inheritance from such Senecan ghosts as Thyestes, whose monstrous crimes match those of his enemies. There is no doubt too that unless someone can put an end to the grim infection which abolishes all moral distinction between revenger and revenged, young Hamlet too will end by committing equally foul crimes which will in turn cause his descendants' hair to stand on end.

This part of the Ghost's recital, in spite of the superficial references to purgatorial fires, contains in fact no real Hebraic or Christian sentiment. The appeal is, as in the Senecan revenge tradition, to nature and the violation of its laws: old Thyestes had spoken of "the laws of Nature being backward turned": old Hamlet speaks of "the foul crimes done in his days of nature," he speaks of the poverty of Claudius's "natural gifts" and of the poison coursing through "the natural gates and alleys of the blood." And finally, in the name of the same god whom he had followed in his "days of nature," he appeals to young Hamlet with the words "If thou hast nature in thee bear it not" (I. v. 81). This succession of murder, usurpation, and incest, in which each offender becomes in turn a victim, is thus referred to the rhythm of an endless nature-cycle. This impersonal and instinctual rhythm it is which finally sees to it that violations of natural law are visited on their violaters. There is, strictly speaking, no salvation at the end of the journey: there is just the eternal revolving movement of nature, as in the succession of seasons. Indeed, as the anthropologists have taught us, the original myths on which many of these tragedies are based are nature myths intended to express primitive man's sense of this cyclical movement of the seasons.[13] Old Hamlet had been a winter god: he "smote the sledded Polacks on the ice" (I. i. 63). Claudius is a summer god, the usurper who comes along in high summer when old Hamlet is sleeping in his orchard in the afternoon. When the play opens, some months have passed (according to one passage two months, according to another, four) and it is again winter: in the first scene and again in the fourth scene of the first act we are informed of how bitter cold it is. Young Hamlet dressed in black is the winter god all over again, and he will be unseated by another spring god who comes at the turn of the year. At this level there is nothing to suggest any appeal beyond the instinctual life of nature, the rhythm of the seasons: birth, copulation, and death. It is not in the name of any higher justice that Claudius must be slain, but in the name of blood loyalty, family honor, and above all, nature.

But the Ghost is nothing if not ambiguous: the stress on his depraved nature, on the monstrous character of his crimes, and on a purely natural rhythm of usurpation is contradicted by other indications in the same speech. In comparing himself with Claudius, he speaks elsewhere of Gertrude's deplorable lack of judgment in failing to discern the difference between the two brothers:

> But virtue, as it never will be moved,
> Though lewdness court it in a shape of heaven,
> So lust, though to a radiant angel linked,
> Will sate itself in a celestial bed
> And prey on garbage.
>
> (I. v. 53–57)

The key words here are "heaven," "angel" and "celestial," and they are clearly used to define his own absolute moral superiority to Claudius. Old Hamlet claims to be a radiant angel, and his bed was a celestial bed. The grammar and syntax of the sentence are clear. Nothing here of his vile imperfections, of unspeakable crimes done in his days of nature which would level him with Claudius. The Ghost identifies himself here as an angel; elsewhere he presents himself as a devil. It is not surprising that Hamlet wonders from the beginning whether he is a spirit of health or goblin damned, whether he brings with him airs from heaven or blasts from hell. Clearly he brings both.

If the Senecan side of the Ghost's "personality" issues in the cry for blood revenge pure and simple, based on the instinct of nature, then it is his "heavenly" character, his quality of "radiant angel" which issues in the second command:

> Taint not thy mind, nor let thy soul contrive
> Against thy mother aught—leave her to heaven . . .
>
> (I. v. 85–86)

It is the restriction of the vengeance to the one guilty party and the explicit prohibition against involving Gertrude which raises the encounter to the religious level of a high moral duty. The proposed deed will in this way become something other than the savage release of instinct; it will be canalized and directed, hedged around with intimations of divinity. "Leave her to heaven"—in

these words Hamlet's attention is drawn to obligations and sanctions other than simply blood loyalty.

Now this ambiguity in the nature of the command placed on
Hamlet governs the entire movement of the play and the inner
life of its hero. Two contrasting movements are set up: one is the
ostensible plot movement based on the Senecan revenge pattern
with its circle of retaliation, its inevitable rising and falling movement, its sequence of A kills B, a son of B kills A after being
temporarily foiled by A's counterplot. This is the rhythm to which
the first part of the Ghost's command refers. But in contrast with
it, though subtly interwoven with it, is another rhythm set up by
the second, the more religious part of the Ghost's command. Here
is the burden set on Hamlet's back, the burden of moral self-
discovery and self-determination. Here is an invitation to the wayfaring soul to discover some kind of destiny not comprised by the
term "nature." Instead of the circular advance of the Senecan plot,
there will be a hesitant and persistent search for meaning, for foot-
prints of divinity in the outer world and in the inner world of the
soul. There will be no clear progress along a well-defined path of
practical endeavor, but rather an ever-defeated and ever-renewed
quest for illumination, a never-ending attempt to break out of the
confining barriers of egotism and to seek communion with some
otherness. This is the rhythm which we have noted in the four great
soliloquies. And their relative detachment from the ostensible
Senecan revenge plot—a phenomenon which we observed in the
previous chapter—is to be explained by this metaphysical disjunction in the heart of the play.

It is thus to the second half of the Ghost's command that the
four great soliloquies have reference, and this explains their religious *charge,* their link with the tradition of religious meditation,
and their purposive movement from observation, through ratiocination to an act of will, a moment of resolve which will be in no
necessary way coincident with the foreordained purposes of the
revenge hero of Senecan melodrama. But the first part of the
Ghost's command, with its appeal to nature and instinct, also bears
fruit in Hamlet's thoughts and actions—at least until the regenerative change which occurs at the end of the play. If he is the man

who bears a burden of religious responsibility, he is also the man who has been told, "If thou hast nature in thee bear it not." There are contradictions here, and part of the intellectual burden of Hamlet's soliloquies consists of the grappling with these very contradictions. There is one additional soliloquy, indeed, in which it is the first part of the Ghost's command, the nonreligious part, which is uppermost and which controls the movement of thought and feeling. I refer again to the Nero speech (III. iii) in which, after the Mousetrap scene, Hamlet prepares himself for the actual execution of his task:

> 'Tis now the very witching time of night,
> When churchyards yawn, and hell itself breathes out
> Contagion to this world: now could I drink hot blood,
> And do such bitter business as the day
> Would quake to look on.

(III. ii. 413–417)

We remember that in Ben Jonson's tragedy of *Catiline* written a few years after *Hamlet,* Catiline actually calls for one of his slaves to be killed that he might drink his blood. Hamlet feels ready to respond to the call of savagery. But this call, if followed, will lead in a direction appropriate to a Catiline or a Nero. As we noted earlier, his "nature" will drive him toward the deeds of Nero, such as the killing of his mother, but he proclaims that his "soul" will never consent that his words should be sealed by such a deed:

> I will speak daggers to her, but use none:
> My tongue and soul in this be hypocrites.

(III. ii. 421–422)

He recognizes in his recoil from the full exercise of savage instinct an element of hypocrisy. His words (the "daggers" that he will speak) will be true to the original purposes of the revenger; they will suggest the unlimited play of appetite, the vicious circle of retaliation; but his soul, in affirming a different standard, will betray the utterance of his lips.

On the way to his mother's chamber, he comes upon Claudius at prayer. The revenger mentally identified with Nero comes upon his victim, and at this point the full inhibiting and disabling effects of the conjunction of Senecan and Christian standards become evident. At the sight of Claudius at prayer, Hamlet's conscience recoils. Just as in the soliloquy quoted above, the Neronic standard has overflowed its bounds, so that to deviate from it seemed no less than hypocrisy, so here the second part of the Ghost's command comprised in the words "Leave her to heaven" has overflowed its bounds, so that the very validity of the first command—"If thou hast nature in thee bear it not"—is cast in doubt. It is not easy to connect two such mighty motives and hope that the man on whom they are enjoined will know how to harmonize them. They are more likely to get out of line with one another and each will claim sovereign rights. This is the significance of the dramatic sequence of events in this scene. There is the image of Hamlet, Catiline-like, drinking hot blood; and there is the image of Claudius at prayer. The Nero speech shows us Hamlet being swept along by the force of nature to ignore the religious summons of the Ghost with its appeal to heaven. The second event, the sight of Claudius at prayer, causes Hamlet to ignore the revenge task, the appeal to nature, and see himself as subject only to the grace and authority of heaven. After all, a strictly evangelical concept of that grace and authority rests on the command "Resist not evil." Such a passive and pietistic religion is dramatically symbolized by Claudius's posture. He is the quintessential image of medieval Christian piety. He sins and seeks forgiveness. His speech begins and ends with the word heaven:

> O my offence is rank, it smells to *heaven* . . .
>
> (III. iii. 36)

and ends with . . .

> Words without thoughts never to *heaven* go.
>
> (III. iii. 98)

and its fundamental terms are sin, mercy, and atonement. In short, it evokes the full forces of Augustinian Christianity. Its implication is the suppression of nature. Hamlet, for the moment, is taken in: he is near enough to the spiritual world of Claudius to believe that a villain on his knees—possessed of the fruits of all his crimes —can obtain the grace of God, and that if he dies in such a posture, he will be "fit and seasoned for his passage." This kind of religion will be called in question later in the seventeenth century, notably by the Arminians, and by Jeremy Taylor in his *Unum Necessarium*. He will challenge the efficacy of deathbed repentance whereby bad-livers had made good ends both in literature and life down the centuries. Later in the play, Hamlet too will have achieved a different standard of godliness, but that is still to come.

At this stage, then, Hamlet is swayed by two standards, each representing, during the period of its sway, a total and exclusive mode of existence, and both of them referable to the Ghost's communication in Act I. Hamlet's problem is to reconcile them, but he has not yet achieved the sort of inward balance, the quality of vision which will enable him to adjust these mighty forces to one another in one integrated framework. This is the fundamental meaning of the antithetical expression with which he reacts to the sight of Claudius at prayer:

> And now I'll do't, and so a'goes to heaven,
> And so am I revenged. That would be scann'd.

> (III. iii. 74-75)

His problem is to scan the unscannable contradiction between heaven on the one hand and revenge on the other—both of them imperatives.

A great deal of critical subtlety has been expended on the interpretation of this speech, and it has been pointed out that in refraining from killing Claudius, and in postponing the deed until he finds Claudius in a less religious posture, Hamlet is proving himself an unbelievably execrable monster. He desires to kill his victim's soul as well as his body. But it is surely to consider curiously to consider so. The simple dramatic truth of the encounter is that Hamlet, out of religious considerations, recoils from the assassination of Claudius. The sight of Claudius on his knees has evoked the accumulated forces of traditional Christianity: the desire for grace, which is just as strong a motive in Hamlet as the desire for revenge, has for the time led him to the ethics of the Sermon on the Mount, to a denial of instinct more radical than that which the Ghost had demanded. The rationalizations Hamlet uses to explain his recoil are of no greater "objective" significance than the reasons Macbeth thinks up in his soliloquy "If it were

done when 'tis done." Macbeth also comes out in favor of leaving
his victim alive and gives as his reason that

> We still have judgement here, that we but teach
> Bloody instructions, which, being taught, return
> To plague the inventor.

(I. vii. 8–10)

In other words, he supposes that the reason for his hesitation is
fear of the police: we know that his real and deeper reason, unex-
pressed at this point, is his horror at the moral obloquy of the
crime itself. This is precisely the state of Hamlet's mind also. He
speaks of denying his victim a place in heaven; but his real motive
is fear of losing his own place in heaven. At this point, the sanctions of grace, evoked through the words and acts of Claudius,
have called up in him the sense of religious obligation inherent in
his task. He has surrendered to the covenant of grace. His text
is "Resist not evil." He has not yet learned to adapt grace to
nature: the two are at war within him and consequently each
claims sovereign rights. A little earlier nature had temporarily
ousted grace: here grace has temporarily ousted nature.

When Hamlet comes into his mother's closet he is a man in
whom the two principles of action are as yet unreconciled: viewed
in one way it is a Nero who enters with drawn sword into Agrip-
pina's chamber: viewed in another way he is the seeker after
salvation come to bring his mother back to grace ("Mother, for
love of grace" [III. iv. 144]) and confession ("Confess yourself
to heaven" [III. iv. 149]).

We have stressed how very incompatible are these two intentions which guide Hamlet's actions up to this point in the play.
He exhibits to the full the disjunction between nature and grace
which medieval Christianity had known in its combination of the
worldly and the otherworldly, cloister and tourney, murderer and
saint. It is the religion of conquistadores and crusaders: its devotees
could oscillate between the surrender to lust on the one hand,
and spiritual rapture on the other. Calvinism was going to try and
adjust the two realms to one another in a more logical and integrated fashion, but what it finally bequeathed to the Puritan
middle class was a system which notoriously lent itself to hypoc-

risy, a legitimation of burning zeal combined with active rapacity. Here, then, is that Christian oxymoron which we recognize in so much Western literature from Augustine onward. There is the City of God, and there is the earthly city, and though we abide in them both, they remain distinct and divided spheres. This is the problem with which Hamlet is grappling in action and in meditation.

Macbeth too is a play about the conflict between nature and grace; usurpation and blood lust on the one hand, and the fear of the "cherubins" on the other. But *Macbeth* is a play about damnation, while *Hamlet* is a play about salvation. Its hero will not remain in distinct and divided spheres; he will seem to be saved. The path on which the Ghost has launched him in imposing upon him his double task will turn out to be the path of virtue. He will learn to transform himself from revenger to redeemer. He will emerge from monologue to dialogue, and the trumpets will sound for him on the other side. We may well wonder what it is in the life-experience of Hamlet that enables him to come through with some measure of triumph, however small, where so many had failed. He will finally reject the religion of Claudius, the naturalism of Laertes and Fortinbras, the stoicism of Horatio: he will spurn Ophelia and bid her go to a nunnery. For himself he will begin to see something better, more realistic, and more integrated. What is this something better, whence is it derived, and in what dramatic and imaginative form does it gain admittance into the play? The initial answer to this is to be sought once again in Hamlet's encounter with the Ghost, not so much this time in the content of the Ghost's command, the ambiguous communication itself, as in the manner of the communication, the form and structure of the encounter as Hamlet experienced it. Here is to be found a vital key for the understanding of the play, and perhaps of more than the play.

CHAPTER VI

The Covenant Task

As we have seen, the meeting with the Ghost derives originally from the Senecan melodrama in which customarily the ghost of the departed urged on the revenger to deeds of blood and so hastened the final catastrophe, at the same time providing an opportunity for the introduction of the element of the horrific. This is the tradition Shakespeare inherited and he exploits it openly, though perhaps not without a touch of burlesque. The full-blooded rhetoric that the Ghost uses in the description of the prison house, and the hair-raising account of the murder in the orchard are all in the Senecan tradition of blood, spooks, and fustian. But crossing this and emphatically engrafted on it is the tradition of another mode of meeting, that of the covenantal encounter. Let us see how this is intimated. Hamlet meets a visitor from the other world who imposes a solemn task upon him. A "commandment" is given, a promise asked. Above all, the quaking human frame, transfixed as it were with the terror of the occasion, is bidden to *remember*. "Remember me." The covenant event, according to Buber, is characterized by the stress on Event and Memory, *"Ereignis und Erinnerung"*:[1] the memory of the incomparable moment in which the divine and human worlds meet is carried alive into the heart with passion, never to be effaced. The memory of the encounter is that which will accompany the unwilling clay on its pilgrimage of self-discovery and in moments of weakness will enable it to recover the strength needed for the imposed task. The meeting with the Ghost as a dramatic shadowing forth of a meeting between the human and the divine has been noted by critics from Bradley onward. The point is made most clearly by Roy Walker:

> Alone on the spiritual heights, he [Hamlet] will receive a revelation setting him forever against his uncle's world below, putting a distance even between him and the friends from whom he has roughly wrenched himself free.[2]

The emphasis on Hamlet's loneliness at this moment of confrontation with the divine otherness is extremely germane. It is not a collective or institutionalized religious experience which is here being suggested but a call to the soul's depths, in a lonely encounter that will mark Hamlet off even more sharply from his fellows.

I would like to suggest that the Biblical metaphors which accompany and underscore this encounter force upon us the comparison with such Biblical covenant occasions as the revelation at Sinai or the dark covenant with Abraham (Genesis 15:17). The commandment is written down in a book:

> And thy commandment all alone shall live
> Within the book and volume of my brain . . .[3]
>
> (I. v. 102–103)

Furthermore, the memory of the covenantal encounter and the knowledge gained therein are inscribed upon "tables":

> My tables, meet it is I set it down.
>
> (I. v. 107)

The weight of verbal suggestion is impressive, but I would not rest my case on that alone. I am concerned with the momentous quality of the encounter as a dramatic episode, with the sensation, which is entirely in accord with Biblical experience, of entering upon a new path in life whereby all previous bonds and loyalties are wiped away. The covenant creates new responsibilities. In the Biblical form the human partner usually receives a new name to indicate the new path on which he is launched. Abram becomes Abraham, Jacob becomes Israel. A new personality is forged out of the terror and the transforming quality of the occasion. And thus Hamlet:

Remember thee?
Yea from the table of my memory
I'll wipe away all trivial fond records,
All saws of books, all forms, all pressures past
That youth and observation copied there,
And thy commandment all alone shall live
Within the book and volume of my brain,
Unmixed with baser matter.

(I. v. 97–104)

All that has gone before is rendered insignificant, and yet in another sense this command to remember is the ratification of preexisting bonds rooted in the flesh and in the covenant history of the race from its beginnings. It is a covenant between two partners who are already bound by the most intimate ties. The God of Sinai enters into a covenant with a nomadic tribe and thereby transforms them into a new entity, welds them into a nation, "a kingdom of priests," but the partners to the covenant are not strangers: they are already bound by the nearest ties of kinship. "Israel is my son, my first-born son" (Exodus 4:22). It is between father and son that the covenant symbol applies with peculiar force and poignancy. In Wordsworth's poem "Michael," the father makes a solemn covenant with his son Luke over the stones of the sheepfold which they have jointly laid (recalling the covenantal heaps of stones in Genesis, 28:22; 31:44). Again there is the brooding sense of solemnity and sanctity, the exchange of promises, the bid to remember:

When thou art gone away, should evil men
Be thy companions, think of me my Son,
And of this moment; hither turn thy thoughts,
And God will strengthen thee. . . .

The Biblical tone and echoes are in a sense too obvious here. In fact, Michael explicitly terms it "a covenant between us." Wordsworth's mode of experience is essentially covenantal. In Book IV of the *Prelude,* awed by the solemnity of nature in the lakes, and meditating on its meaning, he arrives at a moment of dedication in which he senses an exchange of vows, although he personally remains passive:

                    I made no vows, but vows
Were then made for me; bond unknown to me
Was given, that I should be, else sinning greatly,
A dedicated spirit.

                                                    (334–337)

The Biblical character of the occasion is clear, even though in
Wordsworth's case the *dramatis personae* are no longer Biblical.
The Stoic *mundus* has taken the place of the God of Abraham.

The Shakespearean episode we are examining embodies the
features of the covenantal encounter in a far more oblique and
inexplicit form, and yet the encounter is more actively Biblical than
in Wordsworth. The Biblical imagery is working underground—
even unconsciously it may be—and emerging through a super-
structure of Senecan rhetoric and melodrama. But there it is, nevertheless, the outline of an act of self-dedication, clearly apparent in
the dramatic stance of Hamlet and in the words he uses:

                    Remember thee?
Ay thou poor ghost while memory holds a seat
In this distracted globe.

                                                    (I. v. 95–97)

He will do, he will be obedient. The "word" is spoken ("Now to
my Word,/It is 'Adieu, adieu, remember me.' ") and from that
creative fiat of revelation, the whole history of trial, suffering, sin,
and salvation will follow.

Hamlet's dramatic situation in relation to the other characters
before and after the encounter with the Ghost also brings to mind
vividly such Biblical "covenant" moments as the revelation on
Mount Sinai. He is the prophet who ascends the mountain alone
to receive a revelation amid thunder and lightning. The momentous
word is spoken; it is inscribed on the tablets: then he descends to
meet his followers who have been waiting anxiously below, and
shortly afterward (as in the Biblical paradigm) he brings them
by oath into his fellowship, the unseen spirit prompting them and
urging them to "swear by his sword." And so, overwhelmed by
the wondrous strangeness of the occasion, they are made partners
in the revelational moment and in the promise which it portends:

So grace and mercy at your most need help you.

                                                    (I. v. 179)

Hamlet himself gives the final seal to the occasion as a covenant occasion involving the election of a chosen vessel on whom special unique responsibilities will be placed when he says:

The time is out of joint, O cursed spite,
That ever I was born to set it right.

(I. v. 188–189)

He is bidden to become a savior, a redeemer.

Again, it needs to be emphasized that it is this injection of religious solemnity and purpose into Hamlet's task which gives to his four great soliloquies their special timbre, their meditative and yet dramatic movement, and their relative disconnection from the overt Senecan revenge plot. The Senecan pattern is, at this level, absorbed into another, more morally challenging pattern. There is an entry into a new sphere of reality. Viewed in literary terms, the encounter involves dramatic relationships and symbols not merely different from, but opposed to the self-assertive cry for private vengeance. There are echoes of profounder responsibilities altogether than can be comprehended in the term "revenge tragedy." Hamlet's problem is to discover what those responsibilities are. Certainly he will have to kill Claudius, but he will have to do it not as a revenger but as a reformer of society, a purger of the commonweal. Moreover he must draw a line: there must be no savage release of instinct. He must stop short of indiscriminate slaughter. "Leave her to heaven." In these words Hamlet's attention is drawn to obligations and sanctions other than simple blood loyalty. With the circumscribing (or should we perhaps say, "circumcising"?) of the revenge task in this fashion, it becomes an act of justice, a dread command. In short, it becomes a covenant task.

Of course the Ghost cannot spell out this task for him in an integrated form. He can only insist on the call of nature ("If thou hast nature in thee bear it not"), and on the call of grace ("Leave her to heaven"), but without showing Hamlet the syntax by which the two are to be combined. He cannot define the road of righteousness, for, after all, as he tells Hamlet, he has himself a pretty heavy prison record to live down. It is rather like Magwitch trying to tell Pip how to become a gentleman. He can point the way to salvation by hints and gestures, and Hamlet will have to learn the real integrated meaning for himself. He will have to learn how to translate revenge into justice. Bacon had called revenge "a kind of wild justice": Hamlet will have to tame it. Also he will have to learn how to bring grace down to earth to live with men. It will not do to return to a pietistic religion of faith without works in the manner suggested by Claudius's soliloquy. Prayer alone, confession alone, atonement alone will not do, if society is not at the same time purged of evil. Hamlet is summoned to activity, to responsibilities almost too heavy for his frame to bear. But they must be discharged in deeds: grace will only come to the man who will know how to act righteously. This is the implication of the burden placed on Hamlet's back. Natural instinct will remain, but it will have to be governed by moral law, and thus raised into the sphere of religion. Nature is to be united with grace, and grace with nature.

Hamlet's problem is thus, in large measure, a theological problem. He has to heal a breach not only in his family history but in the history of the reformed church in the West. He must try to define ways of living that shall be true to the kindred points of heaven and home, God and world. The covenant is enacted between God and man upon the stage of the world: it thus brings together in dynamic existential form the three realities that medieval man had sought to combine intellectually and philosophically. They will now unite by means of a dramatic encounter: even the Devil, cast out by Luther, will have to be brought back into the sphere of moral existence. Wilson Knight says that the spirit Hamlet saw was the Devil. How true that is! But we should remember that in the Book of Job Satan is a member of the divine family. It is later, in the gospels, that he is expelled as the black sheep of the family, and only in the Book of Revelation that he is seen as the great red dragon who must at all costs be uprooted and cast down. In the Hebrew Scripture it is almost possible to say that the diabolical is part of the divine: the aggressions within us may, when morally directed, open up for us the path of salvation. There is a mystery here which Hamlet is trying to solve. His meeting with the Ghost beckons toward it; for the form and environment of that meeting is, at one level, Biblical, Hebraic. It suggests a command, a deed to be done, but done for the sake of heaven. To accomplish it in this way, i.e., for the sake of heaven, means bringing together divided and opposed life principles. The world, the flesh, and the devil must be brought back into the sphere of religion, and a new unity devised for them. There is a turning aside here from all Pauline formulations of Christianity whatever.

I am not suggesting that Shakespeare had grasped this theological problem in the way I have just outlined it above. I am not even claiming that Hamlet in his life and death fully achieves the kind of balance implied in the terms "covenant," "election," and "righteousness." The divisions and disjunctions which we noted in the personality of the Ghost run right through the play and right through Hamlet's character as a functioning part of the play. But there is a positive movement, an increasingly emphatic religious pressure, and a kind of catharsis at the end, the nature of which can hardly be conveyed without the use of such theological vocabulary as I have been employing in this chapter. Moreover, Hamlet is not alone in the seventeenth century in making this kind of attempt, in seeking out a more ordered spirituality which should provide for human freedom and effort within a context of divine authority. And here the insights of historical, interpretative criticism come to our aid. Instead of relying simply on literary intuition based on image-reading, we may helpfully look for analogies amid the known facts of intellectual history.

The covenant imagery and language which we have discerned in Hamlet's encounter with the Ghost gain significance against the background of the increasing emphasis upon covenant theology from the mid-sixteenth century onward. The "covenant" had become a central kind of religious experience for Puritans, from the secret "Covenant of Grace" vouchsafed to the elected saints, to the Covenant by which the Scottish covenanters governed their political existence.[4] The seventeenth century later on knows of public covenants entered into solemnly with exchange of vows and oaths; this was customary in New England when new colonies were established, and the covenanting parties had in mind such Biblical prototypes as the public covenant mentioned in Jeremiah 34.[5] By the early seventeenth century the covenant idea had become a central, one might almost say, an all-embracing theological concept for the Puritans. But it is not to be thought that Hamlet is a Puritan! Though the Puritans did more than anyone else to introduce the dynamic categories of covenant into both public and private life, the orthodox Puritans were committed to a decidedly Pauline type of religion which involved a strict exclusion of the world, the flesh, and the devil from the sanctified area of religion. There were confusions and contradictions here which are not our present concern, but briefly it may be remarked that theirs was not a solution that Hamlet could ultimately find helpful. Their life-denying piety could scarcely be more satisfactory from his point of view than the cloistered type of piety suggested by Claudius and Ophelia.

But it was not only the Puritans who made use of this theological mechanism: the opponents of the strict Puritans, *viz.,* the Arminians, and those on the right wing of the Church such as Jeremy Taylor later on, felt no less its quality of urgent purpose and obligation, as the spur to their more practical type of religion. The same note is struck by the Levelers, those early democratic reformers, whose entire program was based on what they called "Agreements of the People," i.e. freely undertaken solemn vows for social betterment. In Milton, the term "covenant" has considerable centrality, both as a means of understanding relations between men, and between man and God, and with him too it is above all a covenant of works, involving practical righteousness and a search for salvation which does not eschew the world, the flesh, and the devil. At the center of *Paradise Lost* is the image of a garden. A command is given to Adam and Eve that they may freely eat of the fruit of the garden except for one tree which is forbidden to them. It is respect for that prohibition which raises the enjoyments of the gifts of nature into the sphere of grace. His is a peculiarly Hebraic formulation of the covenant experience.

Hamlet is far from such an assured position and from so clear an apprehension of the meaning of his task as Milton's Samson or Adam, but the intimations are there nevertheless. He knows he is embarked on a covenant enterprise, and he knows that (unlike the Calvinist covenant of grace which we find adumbrated in *Pilgrim's Progress*) it is an enterprise to be performed in Vanity Fair itself, using the tools, instruments, and instincts that the world provides. He does, in fact, anticipate a central theme of much later seventeenth-century theology, and though he defines the issue with less dogmatic and philosophical clarity than Milton, Jeremy Taylor, and the rest, he experiences it with greater existential acuteness even than they do, for his life and death are nothing if not dramatic.

II

I lay this kind of stress on *Hamlet* in spite of the fact that it is, in many important respects, Shakespeare's most secular drama. D. G. James is right in insisting that its hero is a secular hero, terribly conscious of living in a nonsacred environment. That is the ground of his intense loneliness. And yet it appears that his dramatic situation and the nature of his task are covenantal, Biblical. Again to the student of seventeenth-century intellectual history this need occasion no great surprise. The covenant motif in the period shows up often in a nonsacral, even an antisacral form. Hobbes's philosophy of social contract is essentially covenantal. Primitive man is liberated from the brutal and fearful state of nature, and is privileged to enter into a state of "civil society" founded upon justice and law. This miraculous transformation is the result of a pact, a solemn mutual exchange of promises in which each man agrees to forfeit certain rights and to burden himself with certain duties. The primordial contract, says Hobbes, was the original of all community, the source of unity among men. Yet the oath was not taken between man and God. On the contrary, it is human reason alone which defines the terms of the covenant, and as a result, their promulgation ushers in, not the "Kingdom of Heaven," but a powerful authoritarian state which becomes a "mortal god." Such a conception, while retaining the dynamic quality, the feeling of a stupendous turning point in human affairs which belong to the essence of the Hebraic covenants, points to a secular, even antireligious mode of application.

In the period of the Reformation and Renaissance we often note the release of the peculiar energies of Hebraisim in a context from which the spiritual overtones and imaginative coloring of Hebraism are absent. This is a larger subject which we need pursue no further at this point, except to say that what appealed to the men of the new age about the covenant idea as brought forward by the reformers from its Biblical sources was the sense of purpose that went with it. It provided a means of breaking free from the passive attitudes of medieval society with its static, Aristotelian order. Instead of following immanent laws, man is *summoned, charged, made responsible*. In this atmosphere, the growth of modern free enterprise in industry and commerce, in fact the whole history of the modern middle-class revolution is made easier to understand. The covenant idea appealed to the Renaissance sense of human freedom, to its stress upon the limitless value of the human personality, for after all in the covenant theology man is directly addressed and made a partner in providential purposes. The human partner is free to accept or refuse the divine offer: his power over his own fate is incomparably great. Moreover it is as an individual that he is addressed. In Bunyan, the individual wayfaring Christian, with a book in his hand, enters the wicket gate which leads from the City of Destruction to the Heavenly Jerusalem. Helpless and alone, he is yet supported by a divine promise. Translated into secular terms, as it so often was, such a conception of the dynamics of human life could and did lead to an extraordinary sense of liberation, to a revolutionary ardor, a quality of self-reliance made the greater for the feeling that success is somehow guaranteed to him who will strive in his pilgrimage. This is the psychological background of American capitalist democracy: but it is no less the psychological background of communist totalitarianism, for that too is sustained by the sense of a purpose working through history which will lead us inevitably to salvation, if only we will dedicate ourselves to its fulfillment.

This has taken us some distance from Elizabethan literature but not as far as might appear at first sight. Marlowe's *Dr. Faustus* is no less a covenant-type drama than *Hamlet*. Dr. Faustus enters into a covenant with the Devil. It is solemnly ratified in blood: every now and again Mephistophilis returns to bid Faustus remember, and the unwilling soul is screwed up once again to the sticking point. Moreover, it is from this diabolical covenant with the dark powers that opportunity, success, and power will flow. Marlowe presents the signing of the contract with almost comic meticulousness: it becomes a parody of the Calvinist Covenant of Grace.

FAUSTUS: Then, Mephistophilis, receive this scroll,
A deed of gift of body and of soul;
But yet conditionally that thou perform
All covenant articles between us both.

MEPHISTOPHILIS: Faustus, I swear by hell and Lucifer
To effect all promises between us both.

(II. i. 89–94)

Faustus's turns away from the time-ordained pieties, from the sense of feudal subordination and restraint, to face an epoch of self-aggrandizement marked by voluptuousness, power, and knowledge. This makes of him a paradigm for revolutionary post-Renaissance man and his fate. He is, of course, doomed, and it is the terms of the covenant which doom him. And yet he is not doomed in the same way that Agamemnon or Oedipus is doomed. They are under the curse from the beginning. Fate is supreme and fate does not invite their participation or consent to its decrees. We can behold, suffer, and acknowledge the rightness of the laws of nature, but they are utterly beyond our control. To suppose otherwise would be, on our part, the most incredible *hubris*. The covenant mode of interpreting human life, whether it is conceived as a diabolical or divine covenant, is the opposite of this. Instead of blind fate or the cyclical laws of nature, we have a moral history flowing from our freely undertaken acts. There is a balance, a reciprocity between our decisions on the one hand and the providential order which guides us on the other. Our problem is to adapt ourselves to this situation.

All this surely marks a dividing line between Shakespearean and Elizabethan tragedy generally and that of the Greeks. With the Greeks, it is either Medea or Oedipus, either the completely self-motivated, self-directed human act unallied to any divine order, or the totally ordained, totally determined plan over which human beings have no influence. There is no means of integrating the two, i.e., the kingdom of self-will and that of iron necessity. Similarly, in the tragedies of Seneca, such as *Hercules on Oeta,* the human subject may turn with horrible eagerness toward Nemesis, toward

Juno and the powers of evil, but Deianira never really makes her exit from the world of monologue. The gods do not yield her their secret; they do not make her a partner in their enterprises, good or bad. It is only in death that Hercules or Deianira may achieve communion with the powers beyond: only the dissolution of the human frame makes possible the meeting between man and what is beyond man. That is why death is the true cathartic moment, the untying of the knot. It is a covenant with death, but in death there is no dialogue. As the Psalmist says (6:5):

> For in death there is no remembrance of thee: in the grave who shall give thee thanks?

There is, in fact, no moment in classical drama comparable to the above-quoted piece of dialogue between Faustus and Mephistophilis. Such a moment would be inconceivable in terms of pagan naturalism. *Dr. Faustus,* it may be claimed, is not a Christian drama; it symbolizes rather the rebellion against Christian beliefs and attitudes: in its thirst for this-worldly satisfactions, for glory and power it reflects rather the sensuousness of the Renaissance, the abandonment of the sacral universe, and yet its fundamental conception of man in relation to his fate is explicable only in the terms of the doctrine of covenant, its forms and structures.

III

Shakespearean drama is fundamentally covenantal. This does not only apply to *Hamlet.* It applies to many other plays. Macbeth's moral history, for instance, and that of Lady Macbeth take their origin in a freely undertaken pact with the powers of darkness. The witches are, in this respect, unlike the oracle of Apollo: they do not merely announce; they invite, they seduce, they summon: without the free will of Macbeth they are nothing. The first event that occurs as Macbeth enters the new realm of existence signalized by the meeting with the witches is the change of his name and title. This is precisely in accord with the Biblical pattern. No sooner are the witches off the stage than Ross enters and brings Macbeth news of his new title:

He bade me, from him, call thee, Thane of Cawdor:
In which addition, hail, most worthy Thane!
For it is thine.

(I. iii. 105–107)

Macbeth's reply is again in accord with the psychology of covenant meetings. He feels that he has undertaken something that is too much for him. It is a moment full of destiny, and he quails before it:

The Thane of Cawdor lives. Why do you dress me
In borrowed robes?

(I. iii. 108–109)

There is a similar adoption of a new personality as Lady Macbeth makes her pact with the powers of darkness and pronounces her dreadful oath:

Come you spirits
That tend on mortal thoughts, unsex me here,
And fill me, from the crown to the toe, top-full
Of direst cruelty!

(I. v. 41–44)

And having entered upon this new path, she senses the momentousness of the occasion, its transforming quality:

Thy letters have transported me beyond
This ignorant present, and I feel now
The future in the instant.

(I. v. 57–59)

Macbeth, prompted by the new sense of power and opportunity which the covenant encounter has afforded him, proceeds to create his own time, his own order. He is no longer subject to the orderly sanctified world of the Middle Ages. He is free in a new and terrifying sense. The existential perils associated with the change from the medieval sacral universe to the post-medieval universe are at the very heart of the play's meaning. It is no wonder that Macbeth boggles at them. For the covenant mode and the freedom that goes with it have, as we know, proved to be of immeasurable consequence for good and ill to us all. The equivocal character of the witches is in this respect highly prophetic. They hold the key to the future ("What will the line stretch out to the crack of doom?"), but Macbeth can never know whether they bode ill or good for the race. "Fair is foul and foul is fair." The ambiguous nature of the new post-medieval mode of existence has never been more powerfully expressed. Man is invited to participate with the "metaphysical powers" to embark on a joint enterprise, but he cannot tell for what it is they invite him. It may be infinite blessing, or it may be an infinite curse.

We need not wonder why so often in the post-Reformation world the covenant or contract is represented in the diabolical form as a pact with the powers of darkness. The men of the new age sensed the threat to the traditional orderly inherited world of medieval Christendom which the covenant theology posed, with its more dynamic, challenging, and earthbound ethical character, and consequently the imagination prompted them to visualize it in the form of a pact with the Devil. Only thus could they express the combination of fear and fascination which it inspired. Something similar happens in *The Merchant of Venice* where a contract is signed at the beginning of the play between Antonio, a member of the new merchant class, and the Jew, conceived as "the devil incarnal." This contract, which will disrupt the ivied peace of Belmont and its aristocratic inhabitants, will finally force us to acknowledge a new cash-nexus, a different concept of civil society, less feudal, less static than that of the Middle Ages, more dependent on individual private enterprise, energy, and zeal. For this disturbing change in men's lives (actually the result of the rise of the new Puritan middle class) the Jew is held responsible. This is historically somewhat out of line, but there is no doubt of Shakespeare's historical intuition in representing this revolutionary change in the form of a contract or pact freely undertaken. That is of the essence of the change.

Measure for Measure begins with a moment of election. The Duke, whose divine or semi-divine status is well indicated in the play, delegates overwhelming authority to Angelo, the chosen vessel. The solemn moment is emphasized by the handing over of a written commission or scroll:

There is our commission,
From which we would not have you warp . . .
For you must know, we have with special soul
Elected him our absence to supply,
Lent him our terror, drest him with our love,
And given his deputation all the organs
Of our own power.

(I. i. 13–21)

Ironically, the Duke, in referring to the responsibilities he is imposing upon Angelo, the Puritan, uses the covenant terminology
of the Puritans. It is an election by special calling. But there is a
difference; in the end Angelo will be judged by his deeds. "Grace
is grace," but men are tested by their actions:

hence shall we see,
If power change purpose, what our seemers be.

(I. iii. 53–54)

In covenant drama a man is tested and tried: the dramatic tension
is provided by the quality of unpredictability, by the paradoxical
conjunction of infinite human possibilities on the one hand and
wretched inadequacy on the other. Angelo's name carries this
paradox within it. We shall see whether he is angel or devil. He is
free to be either one or the other. The play provides a cutting
critique of Puritanism, but it does so by using those dramatic structures and mechanisms on which the Puritan world-view is based,
down to the election moment and the stress on calling and justification. All in accordance with the Biblical paradigms, Angelo
seeks to ward off the trial to which he feels himself unfitted:

Let there be some more test made of my metal,
Before so noble and so great a figure
Be stamp'd upon it.

(I. i. 48–50)

Moses had said the same at the burning bush. Angelo is free to
choose whether he will be angel or devil, but choose he must; he
is not allowed to withdraw from the trial: that is of the essence.
A man is invaded, confronted, challenged. It is this which makes
the covenant drama so intensely dramatic. There is genuine dialogue, genuine meeting, and the momentousness of the meeting

seems to reverberate beyond the confines of the play itself on each
occasion. It seems to touch the core of a universal human experience.

I believe that the covenantal or contractual pattern can be
discerned at the heart of Shakespeare's major drama even when
no supernatural visitors or watchers are introduced. The moral
chaos of the vendetta in *Romeo and Juliet* is met and brought to
an end through the solemn contract of marriage between the two
lovers. Indeed marriage and the vows that accompany it are for
those who have absorbed the scriptural sense of existence (see,
for instance, the prophecy of Hosea) an almost indispensable
analogy for the covenant dialogue. This is the case in Milton, whose
ode to "wedded love" in *Paradise Lost,* Book IV, represents the
institution of marriage as the fundamental climactic turning point
in the history of civilization. By it moral chaos and lust are "driven
from men." This is what happens also in *Romeo and Juliet.* The
high solemnity of the occasion on which the two lovers address one
another in the loneliness of their encounter surrounded by enemies
and darkness takes on in Shakespeare a religious, prophetic quality.
It is a contract—Juliet says, "I have no joy in this contract to-
night"—and it is a contract from which the most momentous consequences will flow for good or ill. In one sense it is freely
undertaken by the covenanting partners. In another sense it is
somehow imposed upon them by their moral destiny. The contractual moment marks a turning point in their lives. (Notice also
the discussion of names: Juliet even suggests that Romeo might
renounce his name and adopt a new one.) For them both there
begins a life of active responsibility. Juliet seems suddenly to grow
much older: Romeo ceases his moping contemplation and becomes
a man of purpose. Meaning has suddenly been injected into an
erstwhile passive mode of existence. At the beginning of *Othello*
there is likewise a marriage, and from it all the sad and terrible
history proceeds, and it is toward marriage as the means of bringing peace and order into society that Shakespeare's major comedy
invariably points.[6] The inauguration of the "brave new world," i.e.,
the new post-medieval world with all its problems, is, in *The
Tempest,* symbolized by the marriage of Ferdinand and Miranda,
a marriage very deliberately hedged around with sanctity and moral

restraint, suggestive of a wider, religious transformation in the affairs of men.[7] The difficulty here is not in finding sufficient evidence for the centrality of the covenant structure in Shakespeare's plays: on the contrary the danger is that one might find too much. In the history plays, the kings, bearing their high and lonely responsibilities, regularly turn toward heaven (as does Henry V before the battle of Agincourt) in an act of dedication which involves the mutual exchange of vows. Then again there is the solitary solemn communion between Henry IV and his son Hal when the father is lying on his deathbed in "Jerusalem": there too we note the handing down of a task from father to son amid vows and promises. That moment of dedication will govern the future and prepare us for what Hal calls, "The noble change that I have purposed" (II *Henry IV*, IV. v. 153). These are the moments which feed such drama and give it its forward momentum. But here in the chronicle plays, Shakespeare is operating, it seems, not with the covenant in its newer dynamic form, but with the medieval man's ideal of a hierarchical community bound by a permanent sense of mutual dependence. The king's "partnership" with the king of kings is the extension of the social bonds which bind him with his subjects according to their various ranks and stations. The arrangement is static, and no doubt the inspiration of the chroniclers here is at work, keeping Shakespearean drama to the traditional paths of order.

This brings us back to the special novelty of *Hamlet*: there the feeling of a sanctified hierarchical order has vanished. The lonely encounter between Hamlet and his father's ghost will not lead us back to a secure feudal commonwealth, a happy peaceful coexistence of church and state, with every man keeping degree, priority, and place, presided over by the planet Sol. It is rather the evil Claudius who utters the timeworn commonplaces of degree and order, and pronounces his speech on the divine right of kings like Richard II himself:

> There's such divinity doth hedge a king,
> That treason can but peep to what it would,
> Acts little of his will.

(IV. v. 123–125)

Such guarantees securing the rights of kings no longer have the same meaning in the new revolutionary world of *Hamlet*. Hamlet is more like the puritan political theorists and leaders, for whom the new experience had swept away all the traditional loyalties in a violent new upsurge of republican idealism. It is significant that Hamlet "is loved of the distracted multitude." Claudius senses a threat here not simply to his own tenure of the throne but to the whole feudal order that his sovereignty implies. This too is part of the meaning of the revelational experience that has been vouchsafed to Hamlet, and the exchange of promises which followed it. It has swept from his mind

All saws of books, all forms, all pressures past

(I. v. 100)

—among them all the inherited monarchical ideals, the sacral kingship which underlies Shakespeare's chronicle plays. We are in the presence of a disturbing and essentially post-medieval notion of man. Not only will his own life be ordered differently from now on, but this new sense of existence will finally transform society at large. If we read *Hamlet* aright we find ourselves on the threshold of the changes for good and ill which, from the seventeenth century on, have transformed the relations of men and nations.

CHAPTER VII

The Book
of the
Covenant

We spoke earlier of the *agon* enacted between the flower images on the one hand, and disease and mildew on the other. Through this and related image-patterns, the play's thesis and antithesis are defined. We witness the medieval rose-garden blighted with weeds. A blister is set on the forehead of an innocent love, as a savage anti-Petrarchianism sweeps away what is left of the courtly graces of an earlier day. Political self-seeking personified in Claudius infects society, and the fair blossoms of a sacral universe seemingly governed by moral law are withered at the root. Such is the conflict intimated in the play's dialectical image-system.

We may now note that the *agon* is enlarged. Shakespeare is not content to set up his vision of inherited charm and order subverted by decay. There is a synthesis. A third image, or rather a third complex of images and symbols, makes its appearance with the encounter between Hamlet and his father's ghost. The answer to the blight in the orchard, to the "mildewed ear blasting his wholesome brother" (III. iv. 64–65) (the Biblical source of this in Genesis 41:23–27 has evidently not been noted) is the word, the book, the commandment, the manifold and unmistakable covenant imagery which accompanies the revelation to Hamlet in Act I, scene v.

> Yea, from the table of my memory
> I'll wipe away all trivial fond records,
> All saws of books, all forms, all pressures past
> That youth and observation copied there,

119

And thy commandment all alone shall live
Within the book and volume of my brain,
Unmixed with baser matter—

. . . Now, to my Word,
It is "Adieu, adieu, remember me."

(I. v. 98–111)

Never was there a play in which the written word was so mani-
festly central a concern. And if the flower imagery has its focus in
Ophelia, and the weed imagery in Claudius, then the book and
writing imagery is certainly centered in Hamlet himself. He writes
down on his tables the phrase which comes into his mind after
the meeting with the Ghost. Hamlet is a scholar; so is Horatio
("Thou art a scholar, speak to it, Horatio" [I. i. 42]). This is the
chief impression which their personalities would convey to the
Elizabethan audience. And the scholar is the man who reads and
writes. His epistles to Ophelia in both verse and prose are the
theme of Polonius's conversation with the King and Queen in
Act II. When a little later in the same scene Hamlet himself appears, he is reading a book and he even discusses its satirical con-
tents with Polonius. Hamlet's interest in the written word is crucial
to the meeting with the Players, at the end of which he arranges to
write "a speech of some dozen or sixteen lines" to be inserted in
The Murder of Gonzago.

A basic question which arises out of the frequent references
to writing and books is the degree of truth in the written word.
The book of satires that Hamlet is reading in Act II is true but
Hamlet wonders whether it was honesty to have it thus set down.
On the other hand the speech he writes for the Player is clearly
fiction and yet it will have the power of revealing the truth of
Claudius's life. The written word has in fact an extraordinary
potency, for good and evil. Ophelia is bidden to "read on this book"
in Act III. It is a book of devotions, but the false purpose to which
it is put turns the act of reading into evil:

'Tis too much proved, that with devotion's visage
And pious action we do sugar o'er
The devil himself,

(III. i. 47–49)

—says Polonius. Sacred writ may be emptied of its holiness and perverted to profane use. But on the other hand the ordinary word used in a secular context may become the word of revelation, for guilty creatures sitting at a play may be struck to the very soul.

Sartre has a passage on the revelational power of words which could without any alteration whatever be applied to the Mousetrap scene and to Hamlet's stated intention therein of revealing the truth to his uncle and the truth of his uncle to himself:

> If you name the behaviour of an individual, you reveal it to him; he sees himself. And since you are at the same time naming it to all others, he knows that he is *seen* at the moment he *sees* himself. The furtive gesture, which he forgot while making it, begins to exist beyond all measure, to exist for everybody; it is integrated into the objective mind; it takes on new dimensions; it is retrieved. After that, how can you expect him to act in the same way? Either he will persist in his behaviour out of obstinacy and with full knowledge of what he is doing, or he will give it up. Thus by speaking, I reveal the situation by my very intention of changing it; I reveal it to myself and to others *in order* to change it. I strike at its very heart, I transfix it, and I display it in full view; at present I dispose of it; with every word I utter, I involve myself a little more in the world, and by the same token I emerge from it a little more, since I go beyond it towards the future.[1]

There is no reason to think that Sartre is here thinking of Hamlet's situation, yet the relevance to the play of what Sartre is saying is quite remarkable. Hamlet too, by speaking, by uttering the word, causes the "furtive gestures" of Claudius to "exist beyond all measure." He strikes at the very heart of the situation, he radically changes it through formulating it in words. The triumph of Hamlet is the triumph of language, language not as a means of communication simply, but as a revelational medium, a moral force.

Hamlet does not cease writing after the play scene. At every turn in the play, words are written, letters are sent and received. But the final and crucial use of the written word was in the ship where Hamlet broke open the letter sent by Claudius to England by the hand of the two spies, Rosencrantz and Guildenstern, importing his own immediate death, and substituted for it a letter in his own hand commanding the deaths of the spies themselves.

Hamlet had once thought it a baseness to write fair, but in the ship it did him yeoman's service. On this point, he too had evidently like Claudius been reading Guicciardini, the political realist, who had said:

> In my youth I made light of such superficial accomplishments as dancing, singing, and playing, nay, even of writing a fair hand, knowing how to ride, how to dress becomingly, and all other like arts, which savour more of show than substance. Since then, however, I have seen reason to change my mind.[2]

Hamlet, it appears, has adapted something of this same Machiavellian wisdom to his own needs. In this, Hamlet much resembles Sir Walter Raleigh who at this same time was also accommodating the new political realism of Machiavelli and others into his fundamentally religious view of history as governed by the providence of God.[3] This is part of the spiritual synthesis offered by Hamlet in Act V. He will combine the new political sagacity of his time with the pieties of an earlier age. It is this synthesis which underlies the writing symbolism of Act V. Here is political trickery on the part of Hamlet, but also an awareness of the grace of heaven. The newly fashioned ethic of Hamlet is still a Biblical ethic, although it is notably far removed from the Sermon on the Mount. In resealing the commission given to Rosencrantz and Guildenstern with his father's signet, as Hamlet tells us, "heaven was ordinant," and though the words he inscribed in that document were a command to kill, they were clearly words of moral power, revelational words charged with the justice of heaven. Hamlet had written them, but he had done so by the prompting of that divinity which in the marvelous provision of a heaven-sent opportunity was clearly shaping his ends. His part was to inscribe the prompting in language, the sort of language which controlled the destinies of men.

Though clearly the persistent imagery of reading and writing has its focus in Hamlet, scholar, playwright, and statist, it nevertheless extends outward, as the flower imagery does, into the world of the play. Polonius is a kind of burlesque version of Hamlet in this respect. He too is a literary man with an absurdly pedantic taste for phrases and foolish figures. "Beautified" he thinks is a vile phrase. He gives his daughter "prescripts" which he hopes will lead to the truth, will unkennel all occulted matters (like Hamlet's speech for the players).

> If circumstances lead me, I will find
> Where truth is hid, though it were hid indeed
> Within the centre.
>
> (II. ii. 157–159)

He too bids the Queen not suppose that

> I had played the desk or table-book—
>
> (II. ii. 136)

for like Hamlet he had his tables in which he was wont to write down all the foolish figures and sentences that occurred to him, hoping to make use of them in the great affairs of state. The same imagery of words of command written on the tablets of the brain which Hamlet was to employ in his reaction to the communication of the Ghost is already given currency earlier on in Polonius's pompous commands to Laertes—another father laying a charge on another son:

> And these few precepts in thy memory
> Look thou character.
>
> (I. iii. 58–59)

The word "character" still bears in Shakespeare's time its authentic meaning of forming letters by inscription on a tablet, as in Sonnet 108

> What's in the brain, that Inck may character?
> Which hath not figur'd to thee my true spirit?

The religious, indeed covenantal nature of this image is made clear in the continuation:

> but yet like prayer divine,
> I must each day say o'er the very same;
> Counting no old thing old, thou mine, I thine,
> Even as when first I hallow'd thy fair name.

The same word used in *Measure for Measure*—

> There is a kind of character in thy life
> That to th'observer doth thy history
> Fully unfold
>
> (I. i. 27–29)

—underlines likewise the covenantal nature of Angelo's situation. He is (like Hamlet, and like Laertes) charged with responsibility laid down in written prescripts (he is actually given a scroll of rules and regulations), and in the very next scene the notion of how that written covenant is going to be transgressed is comically intimated in the badinage of Lucio, who speaks of

> the sanctimonious pirate, that went to sea with the Ten Commandments, but scraped one out of the table.
>
> (I. ii. 7–8)

Angelo is clearly the sanctimonious pirate, just as the Duke is the author of the commands he transgresses. It is noteworthy that the Duke too writes many letters, and that he too has a signet ring bearing his seal with which, like Hamlet, he controls the fate of the characters in the play. In *The Tempest,* likewise, the book and the staff of Prospero are clearly the signs of his divine authority, the power he has of imposing his will on the world and its people, of raising up and bringing low, of making marriages and renewing the bonds of brotherhood.

Shakespeare is sensitive in a special degree to the religious symbolism of the act of writing itself, its revelational implication, and in *Hamlet* this kind of reference occurs with almost obsessive frequency. We are constantly made aware of commands being written, of mysterious or nonmysterious instructions being conveyed, charactered on books, on scrolls, on the brain itself. Claudius himself, in a travesty of the divine privileges of his kingly office, puts his communications in writing, bidding Cornelius and Voltimand carry them to old Norway. But the misuse of the written character by Claudius and the burlesque use of it in the speeches of Polonius merely light up the more clearly the true saving quality of the written word in its authentic use, that use which links all written words to the divine *logos,* the Word itself by which the world had come into being. The word does not merely report; as Sartre points out in a passage quoted earlier, it directs, it changes, it even creates things new that never were in nature: it is the intimation of that which can save us.

This is the basic implication of the image, but it must be insisted that the book-writing-reading image cluster has within it certain inner contradictions with which the play is much concerned. We may arrive at this by glancing at the words of Claudius to Cornelius and Voltimand to which we have just adverted. Claudius says, in handing to them the message of warning to old Norway, that in doing so he is

> Giving to you no further personal power
> To business with the king, more than the scope
> Of these delated articles allow.
>
> (I. ii. 36–38)

There is a sense of constraint. The words written rob the human subject of his freedom: they are a dictate. There is likewise a sense of constraint, though of a more solemn religious kind in the words of acceptance that Hamlet uses after the task is laid upon him:

> And thy commandment all alone shall live
> Within the book and volume of my brain,
> Unmixed with baser matter.
>
> (I. v. 102–104)

From this point of view the revelational word stands at the opposite extreme from the notion of human freedom: the constant suggestion of words being written is that of a dread and ineluctable force controlling both thought and action, though paradoxically freedom of action is given at the precise moment that the task is laid upon the subject. Polonius likewise seeks to lay a controlling hand upon Laertes at the very moment that he lets him leave the parental roof, and in the effort to enforce the "precepts" which he has bid him "character" in his *memory* (the same appeal to the memory which Hamlet's father makes in his words to Hamlet) he sends after him a servant to spy on his actions and behavior while abroad. This is one implication of the writing image, *viz.,* that of powerful, paternal constraint—but on the other hand, the lines which Hamlet inserts into *The Murder of Gonzago* represent the absolute exercise of human freedom, a total license. Hamlet is exercising to the full the right of free speech in the very presence of the King. He does so entirely on his own initiative. The word is free, the artist shaping it entirely in response to his own private vision and interests, unbound even by the limits set by preexisting words. Hamlet does not bother to ask himself whether the play will allow of free alteration or rearrangement of the kind he proposes. He treats the text as being entirely at his disposal. In this sense he is the new poet of the new secular world unbound by church and state, testing out his own inspiration in words of defiance to God and the Devil. He responds only to the urgent summons of his own peremptory nature. This assertion of personal will, which is the sign of the unconstrained freedom of the literary artist, is well conveyed by the sequence of "I'll have," "I'll observe," "I'll tent," again "I'll have," and "I'll catch" in the following speech in which he states his determination to test his uncle—and by implication also the ghostly author of the commands he had received in Act I—by means of the play within the play:

> *I'll have* these players
> Play something like the murder of my father
> Before mine uncle, *I'll observe* his looks,
> *I'll tent* him to the quick, if a' do blench
> *I know* my course. The spirit that I have seen
> May be a devil, and the devil hath power
> T'assume a pleasing shape, yea, and perhaps
> Out of my weakness and my melancholy,
> As he is very potent with such spirits,
> Abuses me to damn me; *I'll have* grounds
> More relative than this—the play's the thing
> Wherein *I'll catch* the conscience of the king.   [*my italics*]
>
> (II. ii. 631–642)

Here then is the dialectic of the book image itself. It may represent the divine *logos* which orders human life after the manner of the pagan oracle, or it may point toward a free creative act carrying within itself a similarly free creative act on the part of man, even an act of defiance. This ambivalence can be illustrated in a more unmistakable fashion from other uses of the same image elsewhere in the Shakespeare canon. In *Romeo and Juliet* it is clear that the repeated use of the book image is hellenic: it suggests a fatal decree. Romeo's life is not a book which Romeo writes but one which is written for him: of Paris, he says, that he was

> One writ with me in sour misfortune's book.
>
> (V. iii. 82)

Both are controlled by fate. In *Macbeth,* on the other hand, the image has the effect of enforcing the impression of Macbeth's totally self-willed, self-determined evil. Says Lady Macbeth:

> Your face, my Thane, is as a book, where men
> May read strange matters.
>
> (I. vi. 63–64)

She suggests that he conceal the signs of his authorship, the evil text which they two are writing.

> To beguile the time,
> Look like the time . . .
>
> (I. vi. 64–65)

But the words of Lady Macbeth are highly ambiguous. Macbeth, after his meeting with the witches, is launched on an adventure in which only his ambition will guide him, and yet there are other forces at work in the play controlling him, and these too are intimated in the lines quoted above, for the strange matters referred to by Lady Macbeth may be understood as signs of remorse and fear and not only as signs of homicidal intent. In fact, in the development of the play Macbeth's face is going to betray more of the former than of the latter. The love of God, albeit denied and spurned, will constrain him. She is already in Act I, scene v, in effect warning him by the image of the book of the danger of succumbing to such constraint.

The book image in *Hamlet* likewise comes to support either the notion of total constraint, of a prescript, as in Act I, or the notion of a total self-determination, as in the written word of the artist which Hamlet will use in Act III. Both are relevant to the discharge of his moral task. But in this respect also the fifth act provides a synthesis. The final exercise of the written word in Hamlet's writing of the new commission on the ship represents the integration of the two. He will write what he will write as an expression of his freedom of will, but it is a God-given freedom, just as his will is ultimately referable to the will of heaven. Not only in the idea of writing the substitute letter but even in the happy circumstance of the signet ring he had in his purse . . . "even in that was heaven ordinant." Hamlet is not simply following his own prompting: he is in a genuine dialogue situation, en-

gaging in a covenant drama, making choices which are nevertheless the result of divine assistance. There is a shaping hand,
a ratifying and consenting will at work in his environment. He is
no longer alone. The words he writes are words which are simultaneously written above. There is now no longer any need of a
Ghost to voice commands and press his task hard upon him. This
is a humbling as well as an exalting experience, for "there's a special providence in the fall of a sparrow." The experience of God's
special dealing with him might cut him off from the world, giving
him an inflated sense of his own importance, of the majesty of
his own will, but it does not. On the contrary, he is made aware
of how similar are the situations of all other creatures in the world,
though they may not know it. As he says of Laertes,

> For by the image of my cause I see
> The portraiture of his . . .

(V. ii. 77–78)

The wheel is come full circle. Laertes also is subject to the same
Providence, the same divinity. Indeed, the emergence of Laertes
into the world of active responsibility in Act I had been accompanied, as we have seen, by the same imagery of book and written
prescript. We are all, in short, in the hands of God, our deeds
written down in a book. But that book we write ourselves. Such
is the meaning which Hamlet apprehends in the course of the play.

CHAPTER VIII

A Time
of Forgetting

The most celebrated modern example of the covenant type of drama is undoubtedly Goethe's *Faust*. It represents once more the diabolical form of the covenant with the newfound opportunities offered by it being traced to the Devil. As in *Macbeth* and *The Merchant of Venice*, so in *Faust*, the change from the static to the dynamic form of existence—the latter bringing with it new sources of power both in man and in the world he inhabits—is conducted in terms of a written pact between the hero and the powers of darkness. It is as though men were seeking to shift the blame for their misuse of the newfound freedom into the metaphysical realm. Of course, the covenant with Mephisto in Goethe's play is only half-serious—an inheritance from the old Faust story—but the psychology of the new man begotten by it is unmistakable. The entry into the covenant is the signal for a new intensity of feeling and experience in an atmosphere of boundless freedom:

*Dem Taumel weih' ich mich, dem schmerzlichsten Genuss
Verliebtem Hass, erquickendem Verdruss.*[1]

The hero explicitly "dedicates" himself, as it were, to some task; but along with this dedication he can assert his freedom of will and welcome the new opportunities for its exercise. *"Allein ich will,"* he declares. It is almost unnecessary to point out that Faust too, like Hamlet, becomes a symbol for the new individualism— especially that of the artist and writer. He too is, for the most part, alone, cut off from traditional ties and institutional loyalties. Like Hamlet or Lady Macbeth, he wipes away all saws of books, all

129

forms, all pressures past, and gives himself up recklessly to the pursuit of what is untried in feeling, in knowledge, in experience.

There is one particular aspect of this new sense of reality on which we may pause. Faust expresses it well:

> *Stürzen wir uns in das Rauschen der Zeit,*
> *Ins Rollen der Begebenheit!*
> *Da mag denn Schmerz und Genuss,*
> *Gelingen und Verdruss*
> *Miteinander wechseln, wie es kann;*
> *Nur rastlos bethätigt sich der Mann.*[2]

Here the emphasis is on activity in the realm of time, on the fluidity and unpredictability of historical existence—*"das Rauschen der Zeit."* The realm is the here and now with its mobility and its sense of a pulsating movement forward. Events are not neatly arranged: they occur in a violent, disorderly fashion. It is not merely that the things the hero does and the things that happen to him are different from what went before: the time dimension itself in which they occur is experienced differently in the covenant drama: it is no longer the time of myth and ritual with its rounded regular expectancy, but the time of history. In this, Goethe belongs not with Aristotle but with Hegel.

The Greeks had little understanding of history, of *"das Rauschen der Zeit."* As Tom F. Driver in his book, *The Sense of History in Greek and Shakespearean Drama,* has aptly made this point, we can do no better than quote some of his more compact conclusions:

> The dimension of the historical was not a constituent part of the Greek situation. Its place was taken by nature, which led to the time-less.[3]

It is the Hebrews who "invented" history:

> The Greek genius was a particular outgrowth of a nature orienta-tion . . . The Hebrew genius, if one may call it that, was directed toward history. It emphasized the significance of action taken in the historical present.[4]

And what gives pattern and meaning to history is the "covenant." "It is in the relation of the covenant God with a covenant history that the Old Testament is to be understood."⁵ Students of the Old Testament are generally agreed that the covenant is the specific Israelite mode of expounding history. It is what gives meaning to the experience of men and nations as they emerge from the obscurity of their past and move forward to the challenges of the future. The covenant takes creation as its starting point and salvation as its terminus. Along the road between these two there is revelation, the all-important annunciation of the meaning and purpose of the whole process. The covenant provides the syntax whereby the three "moments," which, so to speak, straddle the whole history of mankind, are coordinated. Creation itself is a covenant act. (In Isaiah 42:5–6 the Hebrew word *bara*, meaning "create," is linked with the word *berit*, meaning "covenant."⁶) Creation is the beginning of a program of which the chief features will be revelation and redemption. Ancestral memories are linked with messianic promises and the whole is given tension by the moral burden placed on us in the historical present. The relevance for *Hamlet* of this Biblical time-scheme is evident. The grave-diggers "hold up Adam's profession," and they make houses that will "last till doomsday."⁷ Such remarks bite as deeply into the central meaning of the play as the remarks of the Porter in *Macbeth*. Every moment is loaded with meaning and peril. Yet it is not with the grand eschatological plan of human history that Shakespeare is primarily concerned: he is writing drama not epic. He focuses on the lives of individuals, but these too are conceived as a covenant history. In the Biblical view of man, what determines the rhythm of human life is not the cyclical return of the seasons but the individual's interior moral growth. A man will be walking along the road and he will meet someone (cf. Genesis 32:1; Exodus 4:24): that meeting will change his life for good or ill. Similarly, lives are shaped by the moral choices we make: these have their inexorable consequences. Time is held in place by the memories of our youth and the grave promises of old age. Thus Gloucester cries out:

He that will think to live till he be old,
Give me some help.

(*King Lear*, III. vi. 69–70)

The history of man from his youth up is a moral history. As Silas Marner says, "There's dealings." Life may follow a seemingly wayward plan, but there is a plan nevertheless, and to arrive at old age and do one's duty on the way to it requires an awareness of the reality of time and its onward progress as somehow directed meaningfully toward ourselves. It requires that a man should meet the challenges that come to him, should be conscious of being tested, and of being subjected to a final judgment at the end. It is rather like living under examination conditions. Instead of a three-hour paper, however, it is a period of threescore years and ten. One's decisions are significant: they will affect the path one is treading from youth to age. Similarly, the history of nations, though full of seemingly meaningless by-paths and vagaries, ulti-mately testifies to a plan. Nations can also choose: they can go wrong; they can repent. Their going wrong or their repentance have consequences. A thousand years in the life of nations are but as yesterday, so that nothing is in the end forgotten. The blood of Richard shed on Pomfret stones is finally atoned for on Bos-worth field. Men are called upon to have long memories, to make connection between the present and the past. But such connection only has meaning if time really advances, if we visibly sense its progress, if we feel that not merely is King Lear a wiser man in Act IV than he was in Act I, but that he is an older man; he has had time to learn, he has endured, he has undergone the stress of events. The scene in Act IV where he kneels before Cordelia and asks her forgiveness gains its full meaning only when we (and the parties involved also) make a comparison with the scene in Act I where he sits high on his throne and demands that she declare her love for him: and this comparison owes its force precisely to the sense of the intervening journey through madness and exile, the grim passage through the Slough of Despond and the Valley of the Shadow of Death. There is, in other words, the possibility of *real* change, and for real change there must be *real* time.

Such a sense of time and the reality of its passage is as ger-mane to Shakespearean drama as it is foreign to Aeschylus, Seneca, and Sophocles. What concerns us in *Oedipus Rex* is not the his-tory of Oedipus but his *situation*. The past is needed in order to make ever clearer the outline of his situation, which has remained unchanged throughout, its grim dénouement already determined before his birth. The history of Orestes again is no true history, but a cycle: A kills B, the revenger of B kills A, the revenger of A kills the revenger of B, etc. There is no salvation, no promise at the end of the journey except in the deaths of the entire dynasty, and the beginning of a new dynasty which shall be marked by a similar history of murder and usurpation. The origin of such cultic dramas has been illuminated in a series of remarkable scholarly works beginning with Sir James Frazer's *Golden Bough*. The Kings of the Wood in their sacred grove at Nemi regularly perished by the swords of their successors. This is a fertility ritual: it guarantees the succession of the seasons, the fertility of the land. In Mesopotamia, similarly, the death and rebirth of Tammuz in the summer is meant to assure the coming of the seasonal rains. In Phoenicia there was the myth and ritual of Adonis. In ancient Greece there was the cult of Dionysus, and the connection between that and the beginnings of the drama is too well known to require recapitulation. The Hebraic noncyclical concept of the time cuts right across this and in the period of the Renaissance radically undermines the pattern of the drama which the Elizabethans had inherited from antiquity.

All this has a manifest applicability to *Hamlet*. If he is caught in a pagan time-cycle by virtue of the revenge plot and its inevitable movement, he is also, especially in his great soliloquies and in his chance encounters and meditations, reliving the life experience of Biblical man. He is precisely at the junction of the two roads. It would be worth quoting here a passage from Henri Frankfort which describes the loneliness of Biblical man, cut off from the supporting rhythms of nature. His account will surely have special interest for students of Shakespeare, and in particular of *Hamlet*:

> It is a poignant myth, this Hebrew myth of a chosen people, of a divine promise made, of a terrifying moral burden imposed—a prelude to the later myth of the Kingdom of God, that more remote and more spiritual "promised land." For in the myth of the chosen people the ineffable majesty of God and the worthlessness of man are correlated in *a dramatic situation that is to unfold in time* and is moving toward a future where the distant yet related parallels of human and divine existence are to meet in infinity.

Not cosmic phenomena, but history itself, had here become pregnant with meaning; *history had become a revelation of the dynamic will of God.* The human being was not merely the servant of the god as he was in Mesopotamia; nor was he placed, as in Egypt, at a pre-ordained station in a static universe which did not need to be—and, in fact, could not be—questioned. Man, according to Hebrew thought, was the interpreter and the servant of God; he was even honoured with the task of bringing about the realization of God's will. *Thus man was condemned to unending efforts which were doomed to fail because of his inadequacy.* In the Old Testament we find man possessed of a new freedom and of a new burden of responsibility. We also find there *a new and utter lack of eudaimonia, of harmony— whether with the world of reason or with the world of perception.*

All this may help to explain the strange poignancy of single individuals in the Old Testament. Nowhere in the literature of Egypt or Babylonia do we meet the loneliness of the Biblical figures, *astonishingly real in their mixture of ugliness and beauty, pride and contrition, achievement and failure.* There is the tragic figure of Saul, the problematical David; there are countless others. *We find single men in terrible isolation facing a transcendent God*: Abraham trudging to the place of sacrifice with his son, Jacob in his struggle, and Moses and the prophets. In Egypt and Mesopotamia man was dominated, but also supported, by the great rhythm of nature. If in his dark moments he felt himself caught and held in the net of unfathomable decisions, his involvement in nature had, on the whole, a soothing character. He was gently carried along on the perennial cosmic tides of the seasons. The depth and intimacy of man's relationship with nature found expression in the ancient symbol of the mother-goddess. *But Hebrew thought ignored this image entirely. It only recognized the stern Father*, of whom it was said: "he led him [Jacob, the people] about, he instructed him, he kept him as the apple of his eye." (DEUT. xxxii, 10)   [*my italics*][8]

The relevance of this (especially of the italicized portions) to Hamlet's situation is obvious. He too is condemned to unending efforts which are doomed to fail because of his inadequacy, and yet the burden of responsibility is laid upon him. Unlike the pagan who is "caught and held in the net" (Agamemnon!), Hamlet is charged with a task, a burden. Time will pass and he will not succeed in discharging it. On the contrary, he will find himself pushed to and fro by events of a seemingly arbitrary kind, and by the weaknesses of his own nature, for real historical existence lacks the "eudaimonia"—the harmony—of an orderly and cyclical cosmos. He will stumble through many pitfalls: he will (like Jonah) go off on a sea journey, but he will be brought back to his task by a profounder will which, barely perceptible in the seemingly unpatterned flux of events, is nevertheless at work beneath, inscrutably shaping our ends. Such a sense of time has, on the one hand, a quality of purpose and direction, and on the other a quality of indirection, of concreteness, and untidiness as of real human existence in the world we know. After all, we do not experience time as a circle, we experience it as vocation, meeting, marriage, journey, failure, success. We feel it as a creeping on of old age still burdened with memories of youth growing ever fainter, but nevertheless often staying startlingly with us in odd troubling details which have gathered some special meaning into themselves.

Where in all this is the principle of unity? For we could not endure the passage of time if we did not, in spite of the kaleidoscopic variety of events, sense some relation between the past and the present, between the present and the future. It is here that the notion of election and covenant comes in. Unity of life experience is by the Hebrew derived from the will of God and the freedom of man: for the Greek it had been derived from the cosmos, its circular movement. It had been based on "the eternal recurrence of the same." For the Greek, no one can say

> The time is out of joint, O cursed spite,
> That ever I was born to set it right!
>
> (I. v. 188–189)

No one is ever born to change the world: no one is elected, picked out from the herd like Moses or Jonah, and issued with a unique summons. Nor does the world really need to be changed. The cosmos will proceed on its circular course, and no matter how hard we strive we will find ourselves in the end at the place where three roads meet. We have been there before, and our successors will be there again.

Such a notion of existence has great advantages: it has order, harmony, and above all, beauty. Frankfort in this connection does well to remark on the absence of harmony which marks the life of Biblical man. He does well also to point out the mixture of ugliness and beauty which reveals itself when we observe their careers. We note the fearful ups and downs of Jacob, the mixture of the utterly noble and the utterly shameful in David. This is the way real life is lived by real people in the dimension of history. It is not beautiful in the Greek sense: it is not aesthetic. The Hebrew idea of what is "beautiful" it seems to me is best conveyed by the verse in Isaiah 52:

> How beautiful on the mountains are the feet of him that bringeth good tidings, that publisheth peace, that bringeth tidings of good, that publisheth salvation; that saith unto Zion, Thy God reigneth.

Such beauty could not be caught in some Greek frieze illustrating the herald Mercury alighting on a heaven-kissing hill. That is a beauty of situation; but the beauty of the herald's feet in the passage from Isaiah is not inherent in his situation: it is inherent rather in his mission. He is moving from one place to another, and the message he brings is one of salvation; that is what sheds beauty on him. This is not the beauty of form, of *stasis,* but of a fulfilled historic promise. The pattern that is being discerned is a historical pattern, an ordering of the events of time whereby the past and the present fall into a significant and purposeful shape. It is the beauty not of being, but of becoming, not of rest but of motion. It is a dynamic beauty where the beauty of the classical *logos* had been static.

II

Three aspects of *Hamlet* would seem to be especially amenable to new interpretation in the light of the distinctions just made. First, we may take another look at the notorious untidiness of the plot; then we might consider the double time-scheme; and finally, we might see whether the Biblical pattern in any way helps us with that famous crux—Hamlet's delay.

Some wise remarks of Erich Auerbach will here be relevant. Comparing the Biblical pericope of the binding of Isaac with the Homeric description of the scar of Odysseus, Auerbach in his now-famous first chapter of *Mimesis* suggested that the thoughts and feelings of the Biblical characters "have more layers, are more entangled.""⁹ There is not that straightforward, clearly defined quality of Homer. There is more conflict, more complexity. There is also a greater degree of inwardness. Such narratives open up the possibility of a kind of literary work for which the criterion will be, not beauty, but reality. They are, in fact, a major source of realism in modern literature, especially, one would think, in the novel. And for this reason, Auerbach, with a masterly insight, places his analysis of the Hebrew mode of storytelling at the beginning of his study of realism in the West. Hebrew story points forward to a mode of existence fraught with tension, with conflict, with change. There is a quality of unexpectedness because there is no knowing how the man on whom responsibility is placed—the chosen vessel, so to speak, who is elected to put things right—will finally discharge his task:

> God bends them and kneads them, and without destroying them in essence, produces from them *forms which their youth gave no grounds for anticipating.* [*my italics*]¹⁰

The real life of man which is the subject of Biblical storytelling has room for the unexpected, the arbitrary, even the irrelevant. Such arbitrariness, such irrelevance is noticeable also in the medieval miracle plays, in their mixture of the comic and tragic, of different tones, different times, prefiguring and typology. In *Hamlet* it is so noticeable as to make this play unique in the Shakespearean canon. There are other untidy plays, but none as untidy as this one. *King Lear* has two well-defined plots which unfold in relation to one another with a certain parallelism and a certain dialectical force, but *Hamlet* has at least three loosely related and simultaneous plots. There is the Hamlet, Gertrude, Claudius triangle which is the theme of the Ghost's commands: then there is the Laertes, Ophelia, Polonius triangle which likewise has a tragic ending: then there is the whole story of Fortinbras, his father and uncle which, as critics have noted, parallels the relationship of Hamlet with his father and his uncle. But such an account by no means exhausts the play's digressive tendency. Instead of keeping to the three plots in which he is already well engaged, Hamlet from time to time seems to lose interest in them all and takes the stage with Rosencrantz and Guildenstern, or with the players, or with

Osric, or with the grave-diggers, or with Horatio. Whenever he does so, the ostensible plot or plots recede into the background. Such a meandering story has worried critics who come to *Hamlet* with expectations derived from more unified, classical drama. Goethe's Wilhelm Meister complained of hanging ends in *Hamlet*:

> Among these external relations I include the disturbances in Norway, the war with young Fortinbras, the embassy to his uncle, the settling of that feud, the march of young Fortinbras to Poland; and his coming back at the end . . . *All these circumstances and events would be very fit for expanding and lengthening a novel*; but here they injure exceedingly the unity of the piece, *particularly as the hero has no plan,* and are in consequence entirely out of place. [*my italics*]11

Goethe with a sure instinct pointed to the novel as the proper vehicle for such a digressive and loosely constructed plot. For the novel imitates our own mode of experiencing time with all the fortuitous and circumstantial and incongruous details that life offers—a tendency carried to extremes in modern novels from *Ulysses* on. In *Hamlet* this is already anticipated. In this respect it exactly contradicts the principle of artistic unity laid down by the ancients: here Aristotle, speaking of the nontransferability of the parts of the tragedy (or the epic), remarks:

> [It] must represent one action, a complete whole, with its several incidents so closely connected *that the transposal or withdrawal of any one of them will disjoin and dislocate the whole.* For that which makes no perceptible difference by its presence or absence is no real part of the whole.   [*my italics*]12

Here is a crucial passage in the *Poetics,* perhaps the most crucial, for it contains the essence of the Aristotelian aesthetic. In a truly unified work nothing can be taken out and nothing can be removed from its place. A poem, according to this conception of Aristotle, is like a perfect circle, in that every part supports the whole and is essential to its unity. Now here *Hamlet* marks the decisive rejection of all Hellenistic categories whatever. It is remarkable how many parts of *Hamlet* are regularly omitted in productions. And can we honestly say that their omission destroys the dramatic unity of the piece? Hardly, for the unity of *Hamlet* is immanent, organic, capable of maintaining itself in despite of amputations or the transposal of its parts. We remarked earlier that the two great soliloquies in Acts II and III and the accompanying stage business were transposed in the first quarto, and as is well known, many nineteenth-century productions reverted to the altered order. Only the pedants would maintain that the unity of the play is thus basically injured. Nor is this lack of formal coherence due to the fact that Shakespeare did not sufficiently understand or appreciate what Aristotle had so perfectly stated. Just a year or two before *Hamlet* he had composed a play, *Julius Caesar,* which had beautifully exhibited the classical principle, the principle of economy, unity, relevance, and the necessary interdependence of parts. In fact, it is the unity of its design which constitutes the chief virtue of that play. It will stand up to Aristotle's acid test; for let any manager try to transpose any of the episodes in *Julius Caesar* or cut any passage of more than a few lines and the fault will immediately become apparent. Such an experiment would serve very well to illustrate what Aristotle meant by the unity of action. But *Hamlet* is obviously a different matter. If it has unity it is of a different kind.

The point is that the digressive movement forward, the wayward structure of *Hamlet,* is bound up with the sense of the time being free; we have an "open" time as against the "closed" time of the Greek and Roman drama. The pattern is not imposed externally by God, and since that is so it cannot be imposed externally by the playwright. It has to be, in a way, discovered by the hero himself: he has to be left to pick up the trail of his destiny out of the random circumstances of real life. In real life we might indeed hear the call of destiny, but thereafter there would come all sorts of odd and seemingly irrelevant distractions. Waking up in the morning after the fateful encounter in which his life's purpose is seemingly marked out for him, the hero will read in the newspaper of a Norwegian army moving to the main of Poland; he will go out into the street and come upon a cry of players; he will return home to find a letter from Ophelia who is about to jilt him; he will meet two old friends from the university; he will have a bitter and upsetting quarrel with one of his parents. All of these things require attention. Throughout it all, the great question of the meaning of life, the task, is lurking in the background: it is not being abandoned; indeed, he can no more abandon it than he can abandon the sound of his own voice. He is discovering reality in the varied forms of the real. The seemingly trivial is the straightest path to the overwhelming. That is exactly what is meant by saying that "there's a special providence in the fall of a sparrow."

If critics have sometimes complained of the incoherence and irrelevance of *Hamlet,* actors and theatergoers have, I think, found this its chief attraction. It has the tang of reality, not because it does not hang together, but because it challenges us to find meaning in the seemingly meaningless, unity in the seemingly unorganized. This is the chief difference between *Hamlet* and the modern theater of the absurd; the data may be the same, but the attitude to the data is different. In *Hamlet,* as in Beckett's play, all sorts of odd, disturbing, and irrelevant things will happen while we are waiting for Godot, but in *Hamlet* unlike the version of Beckett, Godot will finally come forward and explain things. The readiness is all.

This is briefly, I think, why things happen thus in *Hamlet.* Goethe is wrong about the hanging ends. *In the end* everything fits purposefully into place. But this is not a *foreseen* design; it is an *afterseen* design. The design is itself the fruit of time. It evolves with the characters, the things that happen to them, the choices that they make. The chance meeting with the players becomes a thread leading eventually to Hamlet's sharp encounter with his mother in Act III; the accidental killing of Polonius in that interview—a seemingly fortuitous event—precipitates both Ophelia's death and Laertes' return from France; and the latter will provide the ground and occasions for the rapier contest in which Hamlet finally will destroy his enemy and save his own soul. Rosencrantz and Guildenstern, the friends who are really traitors in disguise, provide a timely escort for Hamlet going to England, and the "providential" discovery of their infamy makes him finally realize that there's a divinity that shapes our ends: it shows him the directing hand behind the accidental flux of events. Here is no epicurean concourse of atoms, but a plot so ordained that the numerous and seemingly unconnected parts will finally cohere. Even the affair of Fortinbras, the most obstinately unrelated part of the jigsaw, will finally fit into its place. There is incoherence, but there is also a determined interweaving of the seemingly incoherent in a fashion not a little reminiscent of some episodic nineteenth-century novel. But this is the fundamental nature of moral history. The design is itself a product of history; it is not fixed in advance but rather revealed in the stress of circumstance. When we have achieved the proper understanding of such history, every event, every meeting becomes unique. We never cross the same river twice.

III

The splaying out of the story in *Hamlet,* its seemingly digressive, episodic movement, is bound up with that well-known phenomenon in all Shakespeare's major drama—the double time-scheme. Oddly enough this phenomenon has not received as much attention in relation to *Hamlet* as it has for instance in regard to *Othello.* There a novel, by Cinthio, had been compressed into a compactly dramatic thirty-three hours while the outline of the longer time-scheme, according to which the alleged infidelity of Desdemona could have proceeded for many weeks, is left in numerous indications of greater or lesser emphasis. At the risk of noting the obvious let me say that the longer time-scheme is needed in *Othello* for the accomplishment of a pattern of moral history and change, the shorter for the creation of the tragic intensity that the sense of an inevitable doom requires.

In *Hamlet* it is the other way around. The inherited design of the revenge play clearly provides for a short time-scheme with no long-drawn-out and subtle character development, but rather a sustained fury and violence of emotion culminating in the dread and inevitable action of Nemesis. But Shakespeare deliberately expands this. Again and again in the play the characters emphasize the passage of months.[13] When the play opens, Hamlet's father has been dead for two months. In Act I Laertes goes off to France and the ambassadors leave for Norway. By Act II the ambassadors have made the journey both ways, and a new plan of campaign for the army of Fortinbras has been announced. In Act III, Ophelia

asks, "How does your honour for this many a day," and tells
Hamlet that she has "longed long to redeliver" his letters—though
this could only have been since Hamlet's decline and Polonius's
warning in Act I. In the play scene Ophelia says that now "twice
two months" have passed since the death of Hamlet's father. The
disclosure of this interval is not casual or accidental. Hamlet begins
by suggesting that they are acting in a play governed by the short
time-scheme, and Ophelia quickly corrects him. The correction
gains emphasis by contrast:

> HAMLET: What should a man do but be merry, for look you how
> cheerfully my mother looks, and my father died within's two
> hours.
>
> OPHELIA: Nay, 'tis twice two months, my lord.
>
> HAMLET: So long?
>
> (III. ii. 133–138)

The realistic long time-scheme is again emphasized by contrast
with the theatrical and highly unrealistic dumb-show in which the
King is poisoned and the Queen accepts the love of his murderer
all in one or two minutes of acting time. Hamlet hastens the actors
on, emphasizing the speed necessary for the accomplishment of
the traditional revenge:

> Begin murderer. Pox! leave thy damnable faces and begin! Come—
> "the croaking raven doth bellow for revenge."
>
> (III. ii. 267–269)

He is making fun of the conventional revenge plot. In fact the
whole of the Player King's two speeches is intended to underscore
the rapidity of the action. The Player King and Queen have been
married for thirty years ("Full thirty times hath Phoebus' cart
gone round, etc."), but the marriage will be undone in less than
as many minutes, and the rest will follow with comparable rapidity

> Our wills and fates do so contrary run,
> That our devices still are overthrown,
> Our thoughts are ours, their ends none of our own;
> So think thou wilt no second husband wed,
> But die thy thoughts when thy first lord is dead.
>
> (III. ii. 223–227)

The changes that determine our lives are sudden and fateful, our wills being subject to the swift and inexorable reversals of fate. We do the things that the plot requires us to do, and we do them in the heat. This is art. But is it life? Hardly. There is still another journey. Hamlet is shipped off to England; Laertes has a chance to get back from France after hearing of his father's death; Fortinbras crosses the kingdom on his way to Poland. Finally, during the "two months" since the visit of Lamord from Normandy, who had reported on Laertes' skill with the rapier, Hamlet has been "in continual practice" (V. ii. 221). If Shakespeare had desired to emphasize the passage of time and to stretch it out to as many months as possible, he could not have given a stronger series of indications. It is as though he is deliberately slowing down the clock, expanding the time of the action, giving Hamlet time to grow, to search his cause, and the meaning of life, to try all ways of coming to grips with reality. Where *Othello* compresses the time of a novel into that of a quick-acting drama, underlining by repeated careful indications the fact that the whole occurs between one Saturday evening and the following Monday morning, *Hamlet* takes short dramatic time and expands it into the time of the novel, mentioning on three separate occasions an interval of two months as dividing one stage of the plot from the next. Indeed we sometimes feel the intervals to be of years rather than months, such is the illusion of long time which Shakespeare deliberately creates. At the beginning of the play, Hamlet is a student fresh from the university: in the fifth act, he is stated to be thirty, and inclined (according to his mother, who should know) to be out of breath. There is time for growth.

It may be claimed that the long time-scheme is a feature characteristic of the covenant-type drama mentioned earlier. *Dr. Faustus* enjoys his pleasures for twenty-four years and it is a main object of Marlowe to provide a dramatic structure which will support the feeling that a period of such a kind is indeed elapsing. He does it by means of a divaricating episodic technique, frequent journeys, lurches of tone from the humorous to the tragic. He does not entirely succeed—the first and last scenes, in which time is measured out in minutes, come over better—but what Marlowe is trying to do is clear: it is to create the sense of the passage of many years, during which the parties perform or do not perform the terms of their agreement, and to emphasize the periods of threatened breaches of contract. *Macbeth* again is a story of degeneration during which the metaphysical order is gradually put in reverse: the end comes when "Macbeth is ripe for shaking" (IV. iii. 236–237). The long years implied by Goethe's *Faust* and by such history-oriented dramas as Brecht's *Mother Courage* are patent examples of the same thing: Brecht indeed deliberately explodes the economic design of the Ibsen-type play in his attempt to make the stage portray the immanent laws of history. But *Hamlet* at the beginning of the modern era is the most notorious example of this process of deliberate decompression, and the object of it is to show us the aspect which life presents when governed by the categories of covenant as that which molds and kneads the human clay and conditions its growth. The outcome may be salvation or it may be damnation, but it will not be reached by some sudden fall or some sudden peripeteia: it will come as the end product of a long series of accidental judgments, casual slaughters, and purposes mistook, through all of which an ultimate providential purpose gradually makes itself manifest.

IV

We are now in a position to take a look at that most argued-about Shakespearean puzzle—Hamlet's delay. This is not, as is sometimes thought, a discovery of those Romantic critics such as Coleridge and Goethe's Wilhelm Meister who sought in Hamlet a reflection of their own indecisiveness, and their own tendency to morbid introspection. For Dr. Johnson (surely no sensitive flower of the Romantic type) had already drawn attention to it in the mid-eighteenth century:

> After he has, by the stratagem of the play, convicted the King, he makes no attempt to punish him, and his death is at last effected by an incident which Hamlet has no part in producing.

But we can go further back than Dr. Johnson. Hamlet himself had drawn attention sharply to his own procrastination. In the second soliloquy he declares

```
                    it cannot be
But I am pigeon-livered, and lack gall
To make oppression bitter, or ere this
I should ha' fatted all the region kites
With this slave's offal.
```

(II. ii. 612–616)

And again in the great soliloquy in Act IV he declares

```
                I do not know
Why yet I live to say "This thing's to do,"
Sith I have cause, and will, and strength, and means,
To do it.
```

(IV. iv. 43–46)

The Romantic critics simply claimed to have found the motive which Hamlet declared he was unable to discover. This motive is expressed most clearly by Coleridge when he says:

> Hence we see a great, an almost enormous, intellectual activity, and a proportionate aversion to real action consequent upon it.[14]

Both Hazlitt and Goethe concur in relating Hamlet's procrastination to an excess of intellect or imagination over practical resolve. This is the old view of Hamlet's delay which is still strongly echoed in Bradley, though in place of "enormous intellectual activity" Bradley substitutes his emphasis on Hamlet's brooding and excessive melancholy.

There has been, since the time of Bradley, an understandable reaction against this romantic image of Hamlet. He is no longer seen as an ineffectual angel beating in the void his luminous wings in vain, nor even as a gloomy Dane paralyzed by excessive torpor. Salvador de Madariaga, by contrast, visualizes him as a brutal Renaissance figure of violence.[15] Not everyone agrees with his revision, but by and large spectators and readers now note in him the qualities of energy, resolve, and vigor, and a capacity for sudden and violent action. After all, he not only dispatches Polonius, but in colder blood he sends Rosencrantz and Guildenstern to their deaths; then in the end he displays both fury and tenacity of purpose in giving Laertes his mortal wound and executing judicial punishment on Claudius. Moreover, his posture on the stage throughout is in keeping with this character. The word to describe him is *dangerous*. He uses the word twice about himself, and Claudius—who should know—likewise speaks on two occasions to the same effect. His is a "turbulent and dangerous lunacy" (III. i. 4), and the "hatch and disclose" of his melancholy "will be some danger" (III. i. 175–176). This is surely sufficient to dispose of the notion of a contemplative hero whose powers of action are paralyzed. But the demolishing of the Romantic image of Hamlet is one thing; the refusal to admit the fact of delay is another. Let us agree with Hamlet that he has cause, will, and strength to do it, but let us also agree with Hamlet that he does not do it. The phenomenon which Coleridge and Goethe sought to explain does not disappear when we have found their explanation unsatisfactory.[16] The delay is still there to be explained.

What alternative explanations are there? E. E. Stoll maintains that the delay is merely a dramatic convention, part of the tradition. Hamlet was not a prevaricator but simply a functioning part of the revenge play which required that the final slaughter must be reserved to the end of Act V:

> The audience were accustomed to the revenger beating about the bush . . . In keeping the great deed to the last he was like the heroes of all revenge tragedies . . .[17]

He was like Hieronimo in *The Spanish Tragedy,* and like Atreus, Medea, and Clytemnestra in Seneca. Helen Gardner adds to this the fact that frequently in the revenge-play tradition the revenger does not provide his own opportunity, but waits until it is provided for him by some chance conjunction of circumstances.[18] Stoll acknowledges the fact that Hamlet charges himself with procrastination in his soliloquies, but since the other characters do not accuse him of delay, these self-reproaches are to be considered as simply rhetorical:

> They motive the delay, not in the sense of grounding it in character, but of explaining it and bridging it over.[19]

In other words, Hamlet's self-accusations ("I do not know/Why yet I live to say, 'This thing's to do' . . ." [IV. iv. 43–44]) have a tactical purpose in reference to the plot. They give a specious psychological justification for what is no more than an "artful postponement of the catastrophe." The delay is a *"ficelle"*—a strategy designed to serve the purposes of the revenge plot, as it had come down from antiquity.[20]

Now there is obviously a great deal in all this. The delay, like the Senecan ghost, is something Shakespeare had inherited from the tradition of revenge tragedy. It is there in the earlier Elizabethan analogues. Only in the last act of *The Spanish Tragedy* does Hieronimo stumble upon a method of wreaking revenge on Lorenzo for the death of his son Horatio. Until then he delays. But that is not quite the right word. It would be truer to say that that until then he indulges in a form of suspensive rhetoric which enables him during three long acts to savor the satisfaction of the coming accomplishment of his design and to pour out his fury on his enemies. This was a strategy for imaginatively anticipating the bloody dénouement while deferring its actual execution: at the same time the emotions of the audience could be worked up. This is no true delay but rather a ritual postponement of a foreseen and foreordained act. It is in this sense that delay was—as E. E. Stoll and Helen Gardner have shown—part of the tradition. Now Hamlet too practices this in the second great soliloquy, when he stokes up his venom against Claudius by means of a verbal climax of rhetorical oaths and exclamations:

> Bloody bawdy villain!
> Remorseless, treacherous, lecherous, kindless villain!
> O vengeance!

> (II. ii. 616–618)

A further speech of Senecan revenge rhetoric is provided in the short soliloquy which follows the Mousetrap scene. It contains the expression:

> now could I drink hot blood,
> And do such bitter business as the day
> Would quake to look on.

> (III. ii. 415–417)

Another conventional trick for keeping the play going until the fifth act was the counterplot. And Shakespeare introduces this too. It was a mechanism which provided dramatic interest by diverting attention from the revenger to his intended victims: the latter, getting wind of his intentions, would organize themselves to foil him. Thus Claudius arranges for Hamlet to be shipped to England, and later plots with Laertes to destroy him with the poisoned rapier. This device of the counterplot not only enabled the main protagonist to spin out another act and a half before he need actually perform his deed of vengeance—it also seemed to explicate the delay. You cannot very well kill your enemy if your enemy is busy trying to kill you. If this is not an absolutely logical argument for the study, it is certainly sound and plausible enough in the theater.

Now if this is what the delay in *Hamlet* amounts to, the wonder is why the critics for two centuries should have been so puzzled by it. For what we have been noting is not delay at all but rather, as we have said, a ritual postponement of a foreseen and foreordained act. The delay as a central crux of the play— which it is—belongs to a different dimension entirely: in fact it scarcely belongs to the categories of revenge tragedy at all. We sense it in particular in the four great soliloquies with their hesitant groping and self-questioning. Here more than anywhere else in the play Hamlet expresses the consciousness of there being something to do which he is not doing. And yet it is not a question of suspensive rhetoric, of a *ficelle*, a strategy for holding up the climax, but rather of a search for new directions, an exploration of experience which does not belong to the structure of the revenge plot. To put it simply, it is not the mere deferring of the catastrophe that occurs here: it is rather that he goes off at a tangent, ignoring the revenge situation entirely. For significant stretches of the play, and most particularly in the great soliloquies, Hamlet seems to *forget* what he is in the play for. In a word, it is not the delay as such, but the *forgetting* of the task which is strange, puzzling, and confounding.

One thing is clear: the Senecan revenger, however long he might delay, never forgets what he is in the play to do. He is there sooner or later to kill. He may defer the bloody business for four acts—in fact he must—and he fills the time in either with rhetoric directed to the bloody business itself or with being temporarily foiled by his antagonists. But this does not mean that he forgets. On the contrary, the revenger does not have the capacity to forget.

He does not have the kind of multilayered personality for which such terms as "memory" and "forgetfulness" might apply. Nor does he exist in the kind of "free" time to which memory and forgetfulness are relevant. He is controlled by the laws of his situation. He has never been anything other than a revenger. He has no independent personality apart from that: he has never been a free agent or anything other than a functioning element in a revenge plot.

The problem of *Hamlet* indeed is not the problem of delay pure and simple, but the problem of delay (a technical necessity of the revenge play) complicated by forgetfulness. Here is the dual focus. The last words of the Ghost on his first appearance are "Remember me": his first words on his second appearance are "Do not forget." Hamlet knows very well why the Ghost appears a second time—it is because he is in danger of forgetting his covenant task, the dread command placed upon him in Act I:

> Do you not come your tardy son to chide,
> That lapsed in time and passion lets go by
> Th'important acting of your dread command?
>
> (III. iv. 106–108)

It may be argued that the prime command of the Ghost in his non-Senecan covenant role is to urge Hamlet to remember. It may seem a paradox to say that at this profounder level of the play, Hamlet's primary job is not to kill his uncle but to remember the revelational encounter itself, to bear its meaning within him, to preserve it alive in the heart. And as a corollary to this, the great danger from which he must guard himself is that of forgetting, of allowing the terror, the awe, the sublimity, the challenge, the utter novelty of it to fade from his memory amid the trivial irritations of every day. He is not to sink below the level which that encounter signified, to forget the reality of his election, his summons, his responsibility. It is clear also why the problem of memory and forgetfulness is raised again precisely during the scene between Hamlet and Gertrude, for here Hamlet is in danger of forgetting the truly moral aspect of the Ghost's communication, i.e., that part of it which commanded forbearance toward Gertrude. The forgetting of that implied the forgetting of the essence of Hamlet's covenant obligations as these had been defined in the first act. This is the true meaning of his delay.

It is clear also why memory and forgetfulness should constitute the two poles between which the covenant drama is conducted. Memory and forgetfulness imply real time—historical time. It is only in our real historical time that the Nazi atrocities are forgotten. It requires a moral effort not to forget them. That is the sort of effort which is demanded of Hamlet. There is no such problem in the cyclical time of revenge tragedy. The revenger is swept around in the same circle as his opponent. The doom on the house of Atreus is always there. Cassandra can smell it: the Chorus can sense it. It is festering in the walls of the house like a plague: that is because we are not dealing with history but with myth, not with the dimension of time, but with the dimension of the timeless. The first demand of the covenant is indeed a challenge to historical memory: "I am the Lord thy God who brought thee out of the land of Egypt." The immediate sequel to its promulgation, however, is an act of forgetfulness: the people turn away to the worship of the golden calf. Moses has to ascend the mount again, the covenant has to be recalled, repeated, the fallible human partners lapsed in time and passion have to be recalled to their duty, to their promise. It is notable how often in the covenant-type drama there is this slipping back into forgetfulness, and this subsequent renewal of the covenant bond. Macbeth slips back at the end of Act I and decides that he cannot go ahead: his wife, now herself a witch and dramatically preempting the role of the witches he has seen earlier, recalls him to his "duty," challenging him to screw his courage to the sticking point. Dr. Faustus relapses in face of the importunity of the Old Man and gives signs of repentance. At once Mephistophilis appears and charges him with disobedience: as a result the covenant is again renewed and confirmed once again in blood. Othello tries to forget his solemn vows of Act III in which he had dedicated himself to a "capable and wide revenge" (III. iii. 460). In Act IV he "would most gladly have forgot it" (IV. i. 19), but Iago holds him to his promise like Mephistophilis in Marlowe's play: he reminds him of the handkerchief:

> It comes o'er my memory
> As doth the raven oe'r the infected house,
> Boding to all.

(IV. i. 20–22)

In *Hamlet* the theme of memory is primary, especially in the great soliloquies and meditations which contain the essence of the tragedy conceived as covenant drama. Here there are two themes set off against one another in an acute dialectical fashion, the theme of memory *versus* death. Which is the more real of the two? How long may a great man's memory outlive his life? If time is real, if the dimension of history is the real dimension, then life indeed has extraordinary significance, transcending the accidents of birth and death. Hamlet meditates on this theme in the snatch of conversation with Ophelia in Act III:

> O heavens, die two months ago and not forgotten yet? then there's hope a great man's memory may outlive his life half a year, but by'r lady a' must build churches or else shall a' suffer not thinking on with the hobby-horse, whose epitaph is "For O! for O! the hobby-horse is forgot."

(III. ii. 139–146)

The man who would wish to be bound up in the reality of time after his death must build churches: churches outlast human beings. The discussion continues in Act V. It is in fact the main theme of the dialogue with the grave-diggers which turns on death, time, memory, and forgetfulness. On the other hand, if death is the end of all, if Yorick, the lawyer, the tanner, the buyer of land, Alexander the Great himself, all end up as dust, from which is made the loam which might be used to stop a beer barrel, whence the moral injunction to remember which Hamlet feels as so great, indeed so inescapable an obligation? If death is the ultimate shocking and absolute reality, how comes it that so transcendent a value is placed on human memory? If we ourselves are forgotten after, at the most, nine years—why are we commanded not to forget? Does covenant time measure itself against death itself? Here is a concept of time utterly foreign to classicism in whatever form. The rounded cyclical time of ancient tragedy finds its proper termination in death. Death is the negation of history. For the

covenant view of human life, however, it is almost possible to say
that history is the negation of death. The last cry of Hamlet in the
play is addressed to Horatio: he must live and he must remember:

> O God, Horatio, what a wounded name,
> Things standing thus unknown, shall live behind me!
> If thou didst ever hold me in thy heart,
> Absent thee from felicity awhile,
> And in this harsh world draw thy breath in pain,
> To tell my story.
>
> (V. ii. 358–363)

Horatio is called upon to bear witness. He is to be the historian
of Hamlet's life, for in history the meaning of life finds its transcendent value. When we are dead, history continues. That is why
memory is the supreme command and forgetfulness the supreme
transgression. To forget is easy: it is like death itself: it is to blend
oneself with the cosmos like a beast. "Bestial oblivion" (IV. iv.
40) Hamlet calls it. It is bestial, because the virtue of man is to
remember, the quality of a beast is to forget. Man could not forget
were it not that he is subject to time and mutability: he could not
remember were it not that he was linked by covenant to that which
stands from the beginning of time and endures until the world is
no more. By memory we are held firm in that context of reality
which stretches from Adam to doomsday, but in between there is
a time of forgetting.

CHAPTER IX

All
the World's
a Stage[1]

There is one particular image, or rather strand of images, through which Shakespeare in this play defines the nature of time itself, its frustrations and its promises. Moreover through this image he holds in solution the two contradictory modes of experiencing time which we have just been considering—the cyclical and the historical modes. I refer to the image of the theater and to the many references to acting and the actor's profession scattered throughout the play.[2] As Maynard Mack has correctly discerned,

> The most pervasive of Shakespeare's image patterns in this play is the pattern evolved around the three words, show, act, play.[3]

We recall that at the center of the action is the play-within-the-play, and that in watching it Hamlet mockingly recalls the "short time" of the theater. He bids the actors leave their damnable faces and begin. And they do; they move on rapidly from the climax to the catastrophe, without all the intervening perils, the trials and errors of human life as experienced by Biblical man. In the dumb-show the action of the tragedy is concluded in a few brief moments. The world of the actors is one of make-believe, of art; his own, by contrast is a world of hard and inescapable obligation.

But the situation is not quite so simple. The weeping actor in Act II is also for Hamlet, as we have noted, a warning emblem. He has a moral function in beckoning Hamlet onward to his true destiny, urging him to discover through the medium of the theater, those words, those phrases and gestures which will finally *reveal* the meaning of his task and lead him toward salvation. Sartre's remarks on the revelational power of words[4] find their true ex-emplification in the theater. It is the actors' words which "transfix" the situation and radically change it both for the person "named" and for everyone else who shares the spectacle. In a way there is no substitute for the theater. It is the instrument of moral realism, the means of defining the task itself.

The play is simply full of actors. Polonius, who in his university days had acted the part of Julius Caesar, "looses" his daughter on Hamlet, and waits behind the wings like a stage manager to see how the "act" will work out. He performs the same stratagem in the closet scene with fatal consequences. Claudius is a kind of player-king, "a king of shreds and patches" (III. iv. 102). If he and Gertrude are, as Hamlet says, "hypocrites," then we should remind ourselves that this is the Greek word for actor. Rosencrantz and Guildenstern likewise on their own admission are playing a part, and Ophelia somewhat unwillingly comes on (like that great actor-hero, Richard III) to act her part with a book of devotions in her hands. It is clear that the actors illustrate that text in *Macbeth* which speaks of the "poor player/That struts and frets his hour upon the stage" (V. v. 24–25) as a symbol for life in general. Life is a kind of play, but by the same token, the play "holds the mirror up to nature" and shows life its true image. It is this mingling of reality and illusion which the theater image tries to express. Reality is reflected as by a system of mirrors, one player-king watching another player-king perform, while we ourselves in the audience shift in our seats uneasily, "wondering whether there may not be a Claudius in the house."[5] The prince himself, while urging the actors to leave their damnable faces and begin, is himself acting a part and fooling the rest of the cast to the top of his bent.

The theater image is thus nothing if not complex, and I will suggest that here once again an *agon* or contest takes place within the image itself. By means of the varied and dialectical use made of this image in the dramatic economy, a struggle for a definition of the nature of reality and the nature of time is taking place. That struggle will be resolved as the play proceeds. To understand this *agon* we may study the image in relation to three groups of characters: first, Gertrude, Ophelia, and Claudius; second, the Ghost; and third, Hamlet himself.

II

In relation to the first set of characters, i.e., Gertrude, Ophelia, and Claudius, it may be said that the "show," the "act," and the "play" in which they perform their parts signify a world emptied of reality, an "unweeded garden." It is that state of hypocrisy against which Hamlet bitterly inveighs in his first soliloquy when he says:

> How weary, stale, flat, and unprofitable
> Seem to me all the uses of this world.
>
> (I. ii. 133–134)

This soliloquy strikes the same note of radical disenchantment as the "poor player" speech of Macbeth which speaks of the essential emptiness and futility of existence—time itself having become inauthentic in the world of make-believe:

> Tomorrow, and tomorrow, and tomorrow,
> Creeps in this petty pace from day to day.
>
> (V. v. 19–20)

Hamlet's "unweeded garden" soliloquy gains its full meaning when set beside the parallel outburst to his mother earlier in the same scene in which he had condemned the mere seeming, the "show" of customary false behavior:

> 'Tis not alone my inky cloak, good mother,
> Nor customary suits of solemn black,
> Nor windy suspiration of forced breath,
> No, nor the fruitful river in the eye,
> Nor the dejected haviour of the visage,
> Together with all forms, modes, shapes of grief,
> That can denote me truly. These indeed seem,
> *For they are actions that a man might play,*
> But I have that within which passeth show,
> These but the trappings and the suits of woe.
>
> (I. ii. 77–86)

If these "actions that a man might play" have turned the world into an unweeded garden, futile and disgusting because of its hollowness, it is clear that Gertrude herself is a main culprit. The fruitful river in the eye and the dejected "haviour" of the visage are precisely *her* ways of *showing* her grief: they are "the actions that a man might play," and she played them in following her husband's body "like Niobe all tears." But within a month

> Ere yet the salt of most unrighteous tears
> Had left the flushing in her galled eyes
> She married.
>
> (I. ii. 154–156)

Ophelia is linked in the economy of the play with this same play-acting proclivity, the mere performing of an outward "show":

> God hath given you one face and you make yourselves another, you jig, you amble, and you lisp.
>
> (III. i. 151–153)

And in his savage bawdry in the Mousetrap scene Hamlet makes the same point again:

> OPHELIA: Will a' tell us what this show meant?
>
> HAMLET: Aye, or any show that you will show him—be not you ashamed to show, he'll not shame to tell you what it means.
>
> (III. ii. 154–157)

As for Claudius—the player-king—the relevance of the phrase "for these are the actions that a man might play" is almost too obvious. He is always the consummate actor, the hypocrite mocking the time with fairest show. As he says himself:

> The harlot's cheek, beautied with plastring art,
> Is not more ugly to the thing that helps it,
> Than is my deed to my most painted word.
>
> (III. i. 51–53)

His advice to Laertes in Act IV is that of an experienced actor coaching a less experienced one: the phrase "put on" has the inevitable histrionic connotation:

> We'll put on those shall praise your excellence,
> And set a double varnish on the fame
> The Frenchman gave you, bring you in fine together,
> And wager on your heads.
>
> (IV. vii. 131–134)

And if the staged rapier contest should go wrong, there is another theatrical trick to back it up:

> If this should fail
> And that our drift look through our bad performance,
> 'Twere better not assayed. Therefore this project
> Should have a back or second that might hold . . .
>
> (IV. vii. 150–153)

It is clear that the theater trope is present in the series of quotations just given, and it is just as clear that the characters to whom they apply—along with Rosencrantz and Guildenstern—represent the *hupokrites,* the masked inauthentic figure whose presence in society lights up the essential emptiness and hollowness of the world. Life becomes a walking shadow, a poor player, as in the vision of Macbeth, or as in the drama of Calderon:

> What is life? An illusion, a shadow, a story. And the greatest good is little enough: for all life is a dream, and dreams themselves are only dreams—6

and finally Jaques in *As You Like It*:

> All the world's a stage,
> And all the men and women *merely* players.
>
> (II. vii. 139–140)

This use of the trope is, we may admit, attractively modern. It puts shakespeare into the same skeptical world of theatricality as the drama of Pirandello, Ionesco, and Genet.7 It suggests that all that we know is illusory and insecure, a shifting and unstable reality. But does this really exhaust the meaning of the theater image for Shakespeare? Is he as faithful as this to the canons of the theater of the absurd? When Hamlet tells the actors that the art of the theater "holds as 'twere the mirror up to nature," he may mean that life shares something of the insubstantiality of the stage, but he may also mean that the theater reveals the authentic substratum of reality, the true nature behind the world of appearances. The play image may suggest not a minimum of meaning but a maximum of meaning.8

There is, in short, a possible antithesis to the notion of an illusory world, and in *Hamlet* it is provided, if I am not mistaken, by the Ghost, that most theatrical of figures ("this fellow in the

cellarage") whose presence constantly reminds us of the me-
chanics of the theatrical profession but no less of the inexorabili-
ties of truth and justice. Horatio speaks of the Ghost as a "fantasy"
and an "illusion," and Hamlet likewise uses the vocabulary of
the theater when he says:

> Thou comst in such a questionable *shape*
> That I will speak to thee.

(I. iv. 43–44)[9]

But it is this theatrical visitor who speaks to Hamlet of the four
last things, and of the punishments of vice and the rewards of
virtue. Clearly, if the world of the theater is represented by the
Ghost, this would indicate an advance in authenticity: it would
indicate also a superior evaluation of the profession of actor. In
spite of all the elements of burlesque in his personality, all the
grotesque and melodramatic exaggerations, the Ghost does not
come to support the notion of life being vain and empty of meaning. Quite the contrary, he marks the entry of challenge and
responsibility. He strips the mask from the faces of Claudius and
Gertrude, teaching Hamlet to discern the truth behind the appearances: "that one may smile and smile and be a villain" (I. v. 108).
He comes to oppose the realm of falsehood set up by Claudius,
Gertrude, Ophelia, and the false friends Rosencrantz and Guildenstern; and he does so in the name of truth and justice. Here then
is the antithesis in the heart of the image.

III

Something rather like this happens also in *Macbeth*. Being an
actor, Macbeth is naturally dressed in borrowed robes ("Why do
you dress me in borrowed robes?") which do not quite fit him.[10]
To this the other characters also testify:

> now does he feel his title
> Hang loose about him like a giant's robe.
> Upon a dwarfish thief.

(V. ii. 20–22)

He willingly undertakes this false role, urging his wife to follow
suit:

Away, and mock the time with fairest *show*:
False face must hide what the false heart doth know.

(I. vii. 81–82)

A mocker of time, he tries to create his own time, but it turns out to be futile and empty—the time of a play. Instead of the full and rich existence he had promised himself (Lady Macbeth had spoken of the "sovereign sway and masterdom" which would be the mark of all their "nights and days to come") he experiences time as a meaningless cycle of repetition:

Tomorrow, and tomorrow, and tomorrow,
Creeps in this petty pace from day to day,
To the last syllable of recorded time.

(V. v. 19–21)

His life "is fallen into the sear, the yellow leaf," the image of the theater—powerfully recalled in the fifth act—defining for us an empty and futile career of hypocrisy and wickedness. In this state, time itself has, for Macbeth, been robbed of real significance.

But again there is the opposite use of the same image. We remember the speech of the Porter who imagines, for the space of a long and important scene, that he is the keeper of the gate of hell in the old mystery plays. Here the theater image defines the true reality behind the appearance, for Macbeth's castle has in truth become the gate of hell. Macbeth from this point of view is not a *hupokrites*: he also functions in a theological plot which summons Everyman to heaven or hell as the case may be. And then there are the Weird Sisters: they too help to define his true destiny. Like the Ghost in *Hamlet,* they represent the metaphysical order which surrounds the hero; and like the Ghost in *Hamlet,* they too are figures of melodrama, the stagiest, the most deliberately histrionic figures in the play. Banquo exclaims:

Are ye *fantastical,* or that indeed
Which outwardly ye *show*?   [*my italics*]

(I. iii. 53–54)

It is they who later on produce the play-within-the-play, namely the three apparitions and the show of eight kings. Like Hamlet's father, the Weird Sisters constrain the hero; they attempt to baffle his free will and make him act a part in their supernatural stage play. In response to their soliciting, Macbeth too, like Hamlet, adopts an "antic disposition"[11]—all this in keeping with the summons of his very theatrical visitors from beyond.

But here, in a way, the analogy ends, for the Ghost of Hamlet's father does not manage the performance to the end as do the Weird Sisters in *Macbeth*. Hamlet does not remain controlled by the metaphysical order spelled out by the Ghost in the same way that Macbeth is cribbed, cabined, and confined by the metaphysical system to which the Weird Sisters belong. Hamlet, unlike Macbeth, is launched on a spiritual quest; he seeks through the free exercise of his mind and spirit a wider and more universal stage than that limited medieval *schema* for which the Porter of Hell-Gate is a proper symbol. And in Act V he finds it long after the Ghost has disappeared from view. He will not submit to the mental or religious dominance of the Ghost, though he will look back pityingly to the sufferings of that soul temporarily released from the purgatorial fires of a medieval world-order. For *Hamlet* represents the Copernican revision of that medieval world which is still so vividly complete in *Macbeth*. The individual wayfaring soul will break out of the traditional *schema* and try to discern the providential pattern anew *for himself,* in a more individual as well as in a more universal fashion. The world is still a stage, and the men and women merely players, but the stage is grander than that bounded universe of the Porter speech, and the pathos of suffering humanity seeking salvation more real than that limited pathos of Old Hamlet with his morbid self-reproach and rancors. Hamlet will move into a world of freer spirituality, less static than that of *Macbeth,* less bound to the traditional stage properties, less linked to the theological commonplaces of medieval Christianity. This is the Hamletian synthesis, and it can be approached through Hamlet's own personal use of the theater trope from Act II onward.

IV

Hamlet's search for reality is given its first impetus by the meeting with the Ghost who strips the masks from the faces of the players by whom Hamlet is surrounded. He represents that metaphysical invasion of the mere outward reality and summons Hamlet to discern the truth beneath and beyond the world of appearances. It is from the encounter with the Ghost, with its strong religious, covenantal overtones that Hamlet's meditative and self-questioning effort takes its rise. But this effort yields, in the course of the play, a concept of reality for which the Ghost and his words are no longer the adequate symbol.

The decision in Act II to mount the play-within-the-play marks Hamlet's reaction to the Ghost and his constraining power. He will not rely on the Ghost:

> the spirit that I have seen
> May be a devil, and the devil hath power
> T'assume a pleasing shape.
>
> (II. ii. 635–637)

The word "shape" (a theater word in Shakespeare) reminds us of the Ghost's theatrical character. But Hamlet will have his own play instead of that theatrical *schema* in which the Ghost had invited him to participate—that of heaven, hell, purgatory, and judgment. He, Hamlet, in a spirit of independence of the metaphysical powers, will do his own watching, his own plotting and writing: "I'll observe . . . I'll tent him to the quick . . . I'll have grounds/More relative than this." And he ends by a determined adoption of the mode of drama as the proper method for revealing truth: but he, Hamlet, will be in charge; he will act the overseeing providence:

> the play's the thing
> Wherein *I'll catch* the conscience of the king.
>
> (II. ii. 641–642)

But the plan ends unsatisfactorily: after the triumph in the hall comes the sad dénouement in the closet.

The decisive development in Hamlet's use of the play metaphor occurs in Act V. Now instead of seeking to manage his own play he will humbly collaborate with the power of Providence. It will be a joint dramatic production; there will be neither constraint on the one hand nor the arrogant assertion of a self-conceived design on the other, but a synthesis of human effort and divine leading, a dialogic pattern. He expresses his intuition of this first in a generalization:

> Our indiscretion sometimes serves us well,
> When our deep *plots* do pall, and that should learn us
> There's a divinity that shapes our ends,
> Rough-hew them how we will.
>
> (V. ii. 7–11)

The word "plots" keeps the image of the theater vividly before us; the deep plot by which Hamlet had earlier sought through his own efforts to catch the conscience of the King is here abandoned; and instead there will be a more indirect and hesitant kind of dramaturgy, one that will be ready for all kinds of unexpected twists and developments. Hamlet thereupon provides a concrete example of this from his experience on the ship when he had thwarted the design of Claudius in sending him to England in the company of Rosencrantz and Guildenstern: he expresses the mode of his counterplot through a typical play-image

> Being thus benetted round with villanies—
> Or I could make a *prologue* to my brains
> They had begun the *play*.
>
> (V. ii. 29–31)

The syntax is difficult, but the main idea is clearly that his brains are working almost independently of his will, the play being in a sense written for him in a kind of spontaneous collaboration between himself and that divinity which, he says, shapes our ends, and the ends presumably of all men good and bad.

The play imagery in these lines has also a special reference to Rosencrantz and Guildenstern. On the ship they had believed they were managing their little play-act very well, attending the disaffected prince on his way to England and earning the King's thanks as they did so, but all of a sudden they had become actors in a different kind of play with a more catastrophic ending. We are reminded of Joseph Hall's handling of the trope in a religious meditation of this same decade:

> The World is a stage; every man an actor, and plaies his part, here, either in a Comedie, or Tragedie. The good man is a Comedian; which (however he begins) ends merrily: but the wicked man acts a Tragedie: and therefore ever ends in horrour. Thou seest a wicked man vaunt himself on the stage: stay till the last act, and looke to his end (as *David* did) and see whether that be peace.[12]

Rosencrantz and Guildenstern had thought they were acting in a comedy and would thus end merrily, but they become instead the unwilling actors in a tragedy.

But the description of what happened in the ship is merely a foretaste—the "prologue" to the last "scene" or "act," in which Hamlet takes part, namely the *staged* rapier contest. Here is a play which goes wrong because Providence takes a hand and turns the designs of Claudius and Laertes upon their own heads. The annunciation by Osric—a particularly artificial and histrionic figure—marks the jesting character of the occasion which is intended as a kind of interlude or charade, a court entertainment directly balancing the Mousetrap scene in Act III. The same people (with the absence of Ophelia and Polonius) will be sitting around watching the actors, and Osric, dancing attendance in his absurd costume, will give the proper note of harlequinade. The word "play" with its inevitable theatrical association is used with significant iteration. Hamlet is to "play" with Laertes, and the Queen desires him "to use some gentle entertainment to Laertes before you fall to play" (V. ii. 215–217). A concealed pun connects the play of the theater with sexual play.[13] We had this idea in the bawdy conversation between Hamlet and Ophelia in Act III:

OPHELIA: You are as good as a chorus, my lord.

HAMLET: I could interpret between you and your love, if I could see the puppets dallying.

(III. ii. 259–261)

Hamlet makes the same kind of remark about the "playing" of himself and Laertes in Act V:

You but dally,
I pray you pass with your best violence.
I am afeard you make a wanton of me.

(V. ii. 311–313)

This verbal parallelism helps to underline for us the fact that the duel too is another staged performance, a play-within-the-play— except that now Claudius is trying on Hamlet the trick that Hamlet had earlier on tried successfully on him. But Hamlet has an ally, a providence who takes charge of the "play" and gives it an unexpected twist. Laertes fails to come in on his cue, and Gertrude, who has not been admitted to the producer's confidence, makes the wrong move, and spoils the show. Hamlet, in dying, acknowledges that they have all been taking part in a play—

> You that look pale and tremble at this chance,
> That are but *mutes* or *audience* to this *act* . . .

(V. ii. 348–349)

The "act" here that Hamlet refers to is not the plot of Claudius, or the foolish charade symbolized by Osric, or even that of the ghost, but an act in the drama of salvation, a scene fraught with destiny. Hamlet did not plan it, but in a mood of quiet and attentive expectation, ever ready to come in on his cue, he had collaborated with that Providence which was there guiding it to its proper conclusion: "if it be not now, yet it will come: the readiness is all" (V. ii. 235–236). These words of Hamlet are the best advice that he can give to the actors in the "drama" of salvation, and they may be seen as the completion and summing up of his advice to the actors in Act III.

The stage on which the drama of salvation is enacted is naturally not to be limited by the notion of the play-within-the-play: it is more properly the play-without-the-play. Even the spectators are "mutes," i.e., silent actors. All the deeds of man, all their sports, games, their honest deeds as well as their hypocrisies and play-acting are part of this larger drama of the life of man as governed imperceptibly by the providence of God. All the characters on the stage—and the audience too for that matter—are by the end of Act V seen to be enclosed in it. It is now generally recognized that this larger dramatic ambience, this more universal backdrop is first established for us in the grave-digger scene. Just as the Porter in *Macbeth* through the intuition of his role as the keeper of hell-gate places the world of the play in the context of a medieval morality play, so the grave-diggers in *Hamlet* locate Hamlet and all the inhabitants of the world in that larger dramatic context of which the significant terminal points are creation, revelation, and salvation, that salvation that we must wait for and not anticipate:

> Is she to be buried in Christian burial when she willingly seeks her
> own salvation?

(V. i. 1–2)

They take us back to Adam and forward to doomsday, and remind us of the absolute moral significance of our actions in the interim, for these turn out to be no other than "acts" in a large stage play conducted on the vast theater of the world:

> If I drown myself wittingly, it argues an act, and an act hath three branches, it is to act, to do, and to perform.
>
> (V. i. 10–13)

The great stage play which is ultimately intuited by Hamlet and for which the grave-diggers provide us with the essential terms is no other than the covenant history of the world, considered as a great plan of Providence unfolding in a Biblical dimension of time and place. A little later than *Hamlet* the same notion was to be expressed with a more solemn asseveration in Sir Walter Raleigh's *Preface* to his great *History of the World* (1614):

> For seeing God, who is the Author of all our Tragedies, hath written out for us, and appointed us all the Parts we are to Play, and hath not, in their distribution, been partial to the most mighty Princes of the World . . . why should other Men, who are but as the least Worms, complain of wrongs?[14]

Raleigh too, in his post-medieval fashion, had been much concerned with finding in the great theater of the world, governed as it was by the providence of God, a place for human freedom and effort. He too had started from creation and with a set of Hebrew paradigms worked forward over the vast arena of history, his vision darkened (like Hamlet's) by the approaching last act of his own tragedy.

In the later seventeenth century the idea of a moral drama is enlarged and deepened to form a vision of universal history even more detailed in its references to the theater than that of Raleigh. Henry More in the second of his beautifully conceived *Divine Dialogues* (1668) is concerned with God's providence as revealed in the world of nature. He believes it is a drama proceeding from the beginning of time to the millennium. Behind it there is a divine dramatist: so that this drama is not a meaningless and repetitive cycle as in the speech of Jaques but rather an unrepeatable performance co-extensive with historical time. As a result, each event is important; it is loaded with meaning. There is providence in the fall of a sparrow; every flower is a symbol, every eclipse a dramatic event. We are, he says, to observe

> the admirable windings of Providence in her Dramatick Plot which has been acting on this Stage of the Earth from the beginning of the World.

Nor do we ever see the whole plot. "We cannot," he says, "judge the tendency of what is past or acting or present," but we are to attend patiently for "the entrance of the last Act, which shall bring in righteousness in triumph."[15] This would do also as a somewhat abridged summary of what happens in the last act of Shakespeare's *Hamlet*.

The quotation from Henry More shows us the full religious deployment of the stage image. We are no longer concerned with the individual comedies and tragedies of human life, but with a grand universal pageant in which God, man, and nature meaningfully collaborate. It becomes a metaphor for the history of the world beginning with creation, climaxed by revelation, and culminating in the salvation promised at the end of days. The metaphor of the stage as we have considered it in *Hamlet* is, in fact, *radically* ambiguous. It has both a Hebraic and a Hellenic force. As a Greek metaphor—which is how it began—it suggests the cyclical, repetitive nature of time: it suggests the eternal sameness of things, their illusory quality, the emptiness of mere appearance. But as a Hebraic image—and in More it has been thus Hebraized—it suggests the absolute and portentous quality of history itself as a covenant drama stretching from Adam to doomsday: such a drama has room both for divine action and human freedom, promise and fulfillment. Shakespeare, through the final wisdom which his hero achieves in the last act of *Hamlet,* has leaned toward this later insight. There is no clear message, no confident philosophical assertions, but there is a subtle and shifting conflict within the image of the stage itself, culminating in an ever-increasing emphasis upon the graver, more religious implications of that image. For if man is at the end a poor player merely, he is a poor player in a great and mighty play.

CHAPTER X

The Sight
Is Dismal

We are beginning to approach certain conclusions. One of them will be that *Hamlet* (and by wider implication, Shakespeare's theater) is more radically ambiguous than we had supposed. *Hamlet* reflects both the *closed* time of classical tragedy—it is this which had yielded the five-act structure with its articulated upward and downward rhythm—and also the *open,* free, historical time of the Biblical covenant. It is this latter which had yielded the movement forward by means of trial and error, a movement purposive but irregular. Nor is this metaphysical duality a passive *datum*; it is rather a central factor of the plays, something to be energetically explored by means of a plastic type of organization and by means of dialectical image-structures which enable Shakespeare's characters to bear witness, sometimes to one mode of existence, sometimes to another, sometimes to both.

We have tried to indicate something of the religious mood of *Hamlet* at the end of the play when he feels himself to be participating in a divine stage performance. But we should beware at this point of oversimplification. A. C. Bradley long ago pointed to the "peculiar religious tone" of the play, especially after the sea voyage, and to "the feeling on Hamlet's part of his being in the hands of Providence."[1] But he had been quick to add that "Hamlet cannot be called in the specific sense a 'religious drama.' "[2] Such critical caution has not always been shared by the Christian critics who have been frequently misled by Hamlet's "providential" hints and guesses into reading the play as indubitably a Christian tragedy.[3]

We noticed how in the famous soliloquy in Act III the phrase "consummation devoutly to be wished" echoed both the prayer-book and the skeptical philosophy of Montaigne; "consummation" meant bliss and glory, but we also noted that it signified a total end, a dissolution, an "anéantissement." And such ambiguity is present right up to the end of the play. The phrase "the rest is silence" implies that there is no knowable beyond; it suggests an end in the Montaignian sense, a termination, a bourn from which no traveler returns. But in the phrase which immediately follows "And flights of angels sing thee to thy rest"—the word "rest" implies fulfillment, glory, the *resting* in the bosom of a deity. Shakespeare's verbal texture retains its ambiguity here in these homonyms.

It is necessary to be aware of the full extent of the Biblical theme in this play, the values implied in what I have termed "covenant drama," but it is also necessary to be aware of the limits of that theme, and to realize that in its total economy the play is not indubitably "religious." With this critical reservation in mind, let us see how the last act of the play unfolds on a somewhat closer exegesis.

II

The Christian critics have shown that by the end of the play Hamlet is no longer a mere revenger and that he emerges instead as a redeemer, a divinely appointed purger of the realm.[4] There are hints of this earlier in the play too. There are, for instance, his words in Act III after killing Polonius:

> I do repent; but heaven hath pleased it so,
> To punish me with this, and this with me,
> That I must be their scourge and minister.

> (III. iv. 173–175)

He is the elected vessel of heaven appointed to the thankless task of whipping the follies and vices of mankind. If his own motive had been, at the moment of killing Polonius, less than perfectly religious, this is a sign of that strange collaboration between man and God whereby the ends of Providence are accomplished. The religious insight consists in seeing the process of collaboration *ex post facto*. By Act V of *Hamlet* there is a more spontaneous collaboration, the personal motive and the divine duty perceived as inseparable:

> Does it not, think thee, stand me now upon—
> He that hath killed my king, and whored my mother,
> Popped in between th'election and my hopes,
> Thrown out his angle for my proper life,
> And with such cozenage—is't not perfect conscience
> To quit him with this arm? and is't not to be damned,
> To let this canker of our nature come
> In further evil?

(V. ii. 63–70)

Conscience and instinct are no longer at war, each setting up sovereign claims, as when he sees Claudius at prayer in Act III. The new state of mind involves a genuinely theological dimension, the human and divine realms being effectively joined together without violation of instinct on the one hand or of moral sensibility on the other. With a sense of inner reconciliation, Hamlet summarizes his simple duty by saying:

> is't not perfect conscience
> To quit him with this arm?

It is necessary to point out that there is not the faintest reference here to the prompting of the Ghost, and indeed the whole dimension of Senecan revenge tragedy seems to be lacking. In the revenge tragedies of the period—Chapman's *The Revenge of Bussy D'Ambois* for instance—the "umbra" of the dead father or brother appears properly at this point either to urge the hero on to the catastrophe or to gloat at its near-approach. But in the fifth act of *Hamlet* the word "revenge" occurs only in reference to Laertes and his murdered father—he now becomes the revenger pure and simple—while Hamlet's proceedings against Claudius are seen as part of a providential plan to disinfect the realm, Hamlet being the chosen instrument for the carrying out of that plan. There is strong personal animus in Hamlet's words, but more than that there is an overarching sense of being challenged, of being almost reluctantly forced into action for the sake of Denmark, for the world in general:

> and is't not to be damned,
> To let this canker of our nature come
> In further evil?

At this point the act of disinfection is made real in one of those frequent disease images: Claudius is "this canker of our nature" and Hamlet is the curer of the disease. He is the surgeon of the diseased body politic.[5] As we have noted earlier, the images of disease stem from that moment in the orchard when the venom of Claudius poured into the ears of his brother produced the symptoms of physical horror and decay.[6] In the course of the play, as D. A. Traversi puts it, however, this poison

> has extended its action from the "smooth body" of Hamlet's father to cover the entire court of Denmark grouped for death around the infected person of its usurping king.[7]

Hamlet's task is to purge the realm of this evil infection. In this he would seem much to resemble Malcolm in *Macbeth,* that scourge of God who righteously purges the kingdom of Scotland of the King's evil. In that play the notion of an evil skin disease (actually scrofula) had been presented in the speech of a doctor who—rather in the manner of a morality play—had explicitly described its operation and the peculiar "grace" of God which enabled the righteous king—"Such sanctity hath Heaven given his hand"—to cure it. The same idea is echoed by Macbeth himself in Act V when he pointedly challenges another doctor to

> cast
> The water of my land, find her disease,
> And purge it to a sound and pristine health.
>
> (V. iii. 50–52)

And this is exactly what Malcolm and Macduff will do—they will destroy Macbeth and in so doing will purge Scotland to a sound and pristine health. Are we to say that Hamlet is in the same position as Malcolm and Macduff, the righteous redeemers, instruments of heaven ("the powers above put on their instruments" [IV. iii. 237–238]) who will by the end of the play rid Scotland of its blight, its canker?

Now clearly Hamlet is not in the same position as Malcolm or Macduff. For all his sense of being allied to the will of heaven, those simple acts of dedication which we note in *Macbeth* are lacking in *Hamlet*: the hero cannot and does not say like Banquo

> In the great hand of God I stand; and thence
> Against the indivulg'd pretence I fight
> Of treasonous malice.
>
> (II. iii. 137–139)

If he is a redeemer, he is no simple redeemer in a Biblical-type morality play, nor can he act the part of a doctor or surgeon of the commonweal. And the reason is that the disease that he comes to cure extends to himself!

The regenerative movement in the fifth act of *Hamlet* is more complicated than the parallel phenomenon in *Macbeth,* then, for the very reason that Hamlet has to cure both Denmark and himself: he is the hectic, the cicatrice. The illness from which Denmark suffers is all here about his heart. When Claudius, speaking of Hamlet, says

> Diseases desperate grown
> By desperate appliance are relieved—
>
> (IV. iii. 9–10)

he is saying no more than the sober truth. Hamlet had himself spoken earlier of his enterprises being "sicklied o'er with the pale cast of thought." He is himself a diseased limb of Denmark who must be lopped off, and the sign of this is that he does indeed die at the end, and only with his death is the tragedy satisfactorily consummated. Malcolm, the servant of God, on the other hand, lives on "by the grace of Grace" to plant anew the garden of the commonwealth and restore its pristine virtue.

Ethically, Hamlet is akin to Malcolm or Macduff; he too is a righteous reformer of wrongs; but *existentially, generically,* he is like Macbeth. For both are the heroes of tragedy, and the hero of a tragedy is a man who is doomed. Malcolm and Macduff are not tragic heroes: that is not their structural role. But by the same token, Hamlet, no matter how near he may come to the role of redeemer, is no redeemer pure and simple, but a man doomed, an Orestes, an Oedipus, a Macbeth. His death is the absolute point of fulfillment or of no return—whichever way one likes to look at it—to which the whole play moves. It has that terminal quality of tragedy, and in it is comprised the doom of man, the doom of the world, stricken, lost, and unredeemable. And it is precisely at this point that the application of Biblical categories to Shakespearean tragedy ceases to be possible.

We have earlier remarked on the similarities between *Samson Agonistes* and *Hamlet*—the sense of "divine disposal" is powerful in both plays—but in respect of the way in which the death of the hero is received Shakespeare's play is much more authentically tragic. However hard Milton tries to make the death of Samson a tragedy he cannot do it. The messenger, in telling Manoa of the collapse of the temple of Dagon, tries to produce the effect of overwhelming catastrophe, but Manoa, expressing the sense of the audience, says very properly:

> Sad, but thou knowst to Israelites not saddest
> The desolation of a hostile City.
>
> (1560–1561)

The revelation that Samson has perished in the general cataclysm produces a momentary shock in Manoa, but he soon recovers, and his last lines express the mood of the play at its close:

> Nothing is here for tears, nothing to wail
> Or knock the breast, no weakness, no contempt,
> Dispraise or blame, nothing but well and fair,
> And what may quiet us in a death so noble.
>
> (1721–1724)

We have only to think of *Antigone* or of *Romeo and Juliet* to realize how far away this is from the true mood of tragedy. Samson's death is a triumph: we may truly say, "Death where is thy sting, grave where is thy victory?"

Racine's *Athalie,* governed as it is throughout by the sense of an overarching divine promise, the history of a covenant, an *alliance,* is again no true tragedy. The end of the play, in which the purposes of the covenant are fulfilled in the person of the young Joas, is a triumph. Racine, for the purposes of his chosen genre, strives to focus attention on the doom of Athalie, the monstrous queen who aims to overthrow God's plan, and indeed from time to time he succeeds in investing her with a Cleopatra-like dignity, and with something like the tragic pathos of Milton's Satan. But it cannot be maintained. The triumphant verses of the Chorus looking ahead to the future history of the house of David mark out a different order of eschatological fulfillment, wherein the tragic cycle is abolished, and its close-knit time structure is dissolved. Even the offstage death of Athalie does not fulfil the same function as in classical tragedy. It is not the terminus of the play's action, the final extinction of a meteorlike career on which all our fascinated attention is fixed, but rather a bit of unpleasant business to be disposed of away from the main center of the action so as not to sully the triumph of Joas and of Joiada, the high priest who presides over the covenantal drama. In a sense the death of Athalie is the prelude to the real action intimated in the Choruses, and that real action comprises the theme of punishment, exile, and salvation.

Hamlet is in this unlike *Athalie*. The hero's life is both the center and circumference of his tragedy. And by the same token his death is shocking, total, and inclusive. It occupies the whole stage. We do not contemplate Hamlet's death as we do that of Racine's Athalie or Milton's Samson. It is not swallowed up in victory. Rather is it "a dismal sight." "Proud death" is the victor, and all beyond is unknown and unknowable.

> Proud death,
> What feast is toward in thine eternal cell?
>
> (V. ii. 378–379)

Death has the last word. True, we are satisfied that thus it should be, but it is the satisfaction that comes from assuaging a different wish from that which leads us to desire the triumph of righteousness in the world. It is more like the death wish, the wish to loosen the bonds of mortality, the wish to sink into the grave, to become one with the shades. Hamlet at this level desires to be quit of responsibility, to be rid of all the ills that flesh is heir to.

Behind the death of Hamlet, so inevitable, so subtly satisfying in its tragic sense of doom, we may discern the features of that archetypal myth which in some form or another lurks behind all tragedy old or new. It is, as in *Oedipus Rex,* the myth of a sick

land and a disease which can only be cured by the sacrificial death
(or mutilation and banishment) of the hero. Oedipus had pictured
himself as the righteous judge and redeemer; he is revealed instead as the source of the land's sickness and languishment. As
with the Fisher King, his decline is closely connected with the
wasting of the land.[8] Mysteriously and illogically, Hamlet functions in much this way. The sickness of Denmark has somehow
become rooted in him—perhaps it happens at the moment he
kills Polonius, but in truth its symptoms are with him from the
beginning—and like the King of the Wood in Frazer's *The Golden
Bough* he must eventually die so that fertility and health are restored. The need for this to happen is somehow older than human
memory. And it is this archetypal background which creates the
special complex mood which dominates the close of a true tragedy.

III

There is thus a dual focus in *Hamlet,* a phenomenological paradox
in the very texture of the play. It was present in the encounter with
the Ghost who was both the agent of the Senecan revenge cycle—
and a Christian soul come to turn Hamlet's thought to his highest
duty. From this encounter we have traced the dualistic pattern in
the play as a whole. On the one hand the hero is seen to be swept
around in a circle to his inevitable doom, meeting death with a
tragic self-assertion and the satisfaction (for us and for him) that
the iron wheel of necessity has completed its turn. On the other
hand he is urged forward in a new direction—to seek illumination
and attain a true awareness of that greater destiny, of that life of
dialogue of which the Ghost had given him his first soul-stirring
intimation. We have offered the suggestion that Hamlet abandons
the mode of soliloquy in Act V because he finds that he is not
alone, because he achieves a responsive awareness of that divinity
that shapes his ends, and walks humbly with him: but we could
also say that in Act V he abandons soliloquy because he now
rejoices in that approaching dissolution of selfhood in the impersonal courts of death. The expression "shapes our ends" is
itself ambiguous, for "end" could mean purpose, a historical program or covenant task, but it could also mean termination, death,

the bourn from which no traveler returns. And undoubtedly both meanings are present in Hamlet's words.

The manner of the deaths of the other characters at the end of the play is revealing. Die they must because no otherwise could the land be cleansed, and no otherwise could the vicious circle be terminated and the ritual fulfilled. But the deaths of Claudius and Gertrude are more than ritual deaths. They deeply satisfy our sense of justice—which is something more than the Greek *dike*. The last words of Laertes with their strong Biblical echo underscore this.

> He is justly served,
> It is a poison tempered by himself.
> Exchange forgiveness with me, noble Hamlet,
> Mine and my father's death come not upon thee,
> Nor thine on me!
>
> (V. ii. 341–345)

There is something here of the mood of Jonathan and David again in their covenant of mutual love (I Samuel 20). Hamlet's reply is in the same vein: "Heaven make thee free of it!" (V. ii. 346). Hamlet had done his duty by killing Claudius: he is also morally absolved of the deaths of Laertes and Polonius. In this way our acceptance of him as the religious redeemer is confirmed and strengthened as it must be at this culminating point. More than that, he finally fulfills the religious duty imposed on him by the Ghost through the not-killing of his mother. This we remember had constituted the essential charge symbolizing the radical departure from the standards of pagan-Greek tragedy. Hamlet must prove that he is not Nero, not Orestes, for only thus can he avoid damnation, and qualify for that mode of election, the destiny subsumed under the Biblical categories of salvation. Only thus can he participate in that dialogue with divinity which he desires. Yet until Gertrude is dead by another hand there will be no assurance of Hamlet's successful avoidance of the fate to which the pagan revenge cycle would necessarily consign him. Hamlet's final salvation thus comes, in an important sense, with the accidental death of Gertrude. If in Act III, scene iv, he is opportunely saved from damnation by the appearance of Polonius who pops in between him and Gertrude, his intended victim, he is no less opportunely saved from damnation by the poisoned chalice which Gertrude accidentally drinks off at the end of the rapier contest. She is dead but heaven has made him free of it. Without her death the revenge cycle would not be complete. Forces older than Western civilization demand it; but the whole weight of the Judeo-Christian tradition demands that Hamlet be not responsible for that death: nature must go so far but no further. Hamlet's violent gratification in the killing of his hated foe is only one part of his triumph at the end: the other part comes from the contemplation of Gertrude's death. This can be sensed in the words he speaks as he stabs Claudius—"Follow my mother"—as though to say, "After her with you!" And yet he rejoices that he has had no part in it. Heaven has been ordinant in that too, and the result is that the demands of nature and grace can be simultaneously met. Justice and mercy have kissed one another.

Now that the moral ends of the play have been met, Hamlet may die, for death is that "consummation devoutly to be wished" without which there can be no tragedy. But here too there is the same phenomenological paradox. Tragedy—for that is Hamlet's business—demands that he die; but the tale of redemption and salvation demands that he live. His death is not merely unnecessary, but in an important sense a deflection from the main current of such a tale. The Ancient Mariner, after his career of trial, suffering, repentance, and salvation, lives on to tell his tale. It may be said without distortion that a main purpose of his extraordinary experiences is to enable him to tell his tale. The story he tells to the wedding guest is no adjunct to the events recounted: it is their very raison d'être. For it is his tale which will improve, save, and teach the world. It is for the sake of the tale he has to tell that, like the Wandering Jew in the legend, he must go on living. His survival is of the essence. I am reminded here of the way in which the rabbis expounded *Exodus* 13:8.

> And you shall tell your son on that day, "It is because of this [i.e., the ritual recapitulation of the events] that the Lord did to me as he did when I came out of Egypt."

The whole exodus in a way takes place for purpose of the subsequent narrating of the event. But Hamlet cannot be allowed to tell his tale, for this is not a Biblical drama pure and simple, nor a moral ballad like *The Ancient Mariner.*

Here is Shakespeare's problem, and the strategy he employs to solve it is to be found in that important exchange of roles between Horatio and Hamlet at the end of the play. Horatio, Hamlet's alter ego, wishes to die in the ancient Roman fashion, but Hamlet forbids this, and instead commands him to take on the role of vicarious narrator of the saving events. He becomes the bearer of the historic record. He will guarantee that their full significance is carried forward for those who will hear. The point is stressed:

> O God, Horatio, what a wounded name,
> Things standing thus unknown, shall live behind me!
> If thou didst ever hold me in thy heart,
> Absent thee from felicity awhile,
> And in this harsh world draw thy breath in pain,
> To tell my story . . .
>
> (V. ii. 358–363)

And with the arrival of Fortinbras, Horatio begins faithfully to carry out his task:

> And let me speak to th'yet unknowing world
> How these things came about . . .
>
> (V. ii. 393–394)

The burden must be discharged, for otherwise the purpose of the events as a saving *exemplum,* as a record of divine healing, will be frustrated. Horatio will carry the burden. On him the mantle of the prophet has fallen. Nor is this metaphor alien to the play. Hamlet is a kind of prophet, and it is his prophetic task that he now transmits to Horatio. At the beginning of the play he had spoken of his "prophetic soul" (I. v. 40), and he again uses the verb "prophesy" with a significant emphasis at his last moment:

> I cannot live to hear the news from England,
> But I do prophesy th'election lights
> On Fortinbras.
>
> (V. ii. 368–370)

These important lines carry with them the strong feeling that Hamlet's life is part of a continuing history. Even in death the urgent tasks which history places on us, including the burden of *election,* are not forgotten. For history in the Biblical sense is that which upholds us and challenges us forward. There is no sinking into oblivion either for the individual or for the race of man, and so even at the moment of dissolution, the responsibility for history's onward course and for the preservation of its records may not be abandoned. We recall the doomed victims of the crematoria in Poland and Germany using their last moments to pen a record, a diary, a poem, a letter, burying their words in the earth or in the crevice of a wall. They knew that history would go on. Hamlet is in just that position as he prophesies at the end that the "election" will light on Fortinbras, and as he hands over to his friend Horatio the moral task of narrating his story. In this way he simultaneously fulfils the obligations laid upon him as savior and redeemer in a Biblical drama, and those of a tragic hero performing his archetypal, ritual descent into death.

CHAPTER XI
Shakespeare and the Myth-Makers

To present *Hamlet* in the way we have done, as exhibiting both the death-oriented, archetypal pattern of tragedy and the life-oriented pattern of the Biblical covenant, and to see both these patterns as active in the play's dialectical structure, is to run into serious opposition from the critics.

There is first the myth-ritual school whose position relates Shakespearean tragedy firmly and unambiguously to the archetypal form as we find it in the ancients. Thus E. E. Stoll would refer *Hamlet,* and indeed any other play of Shakespeare, to structures of inevitability. Characters are not free to act as they wish or to discover their own individual destinies: these are laid down for them by the very *form* of the tragedy itself. In entering the world of tragedy, which is essentially the same thing for Greek and Elizabethan, the audience responds emotionally to the "steep tragic contrast" of the "good man doing the deed of horror," of the great man reduced from high estate to misery and death. Moral motivation or commentary is irrelevant.[1] As far as *Hamlet* is concerned, it is not the hero's search through meditation for the meaning of life, not the inner drama in his soul as he seeks to discharge his burden, but the timeworn structure of the revenge tragedy that governs both the hero's behavior and the audience's reaction. The self-questioning, the soliloquizing, the philosophy are all subordinate to this; they are at most sophisticated methods of postponing the awaited and desired catastrophe. The fundamental laws of the revenge plot are supreme and its ends are achieved with a certain aesthetic inevitability.[2]

Northrop Frye is much more wide-ranging than Stoll. For him the formal structure of tragedy is susceptible of infinite variations, yet at bottom, *Paradise Lost, Samson Agonistes, Hamlet,* and *Oedipus Tyrannos* are all varieties of the same archetypal "mythos of autumn."[3] In a dazzlingly synoptic fashion he brings together the Old Testament stories, the passion of Christ, the Greek tragedy of *Philoctetes,* and Ibsen's *Little Eyolf.* Behind them all, he claims, may be discerned the same rituals of communion and propitiation, the same myth of the dying and rising god, the same "sense of cyclical return," and the same ultimate acceptance of an impersonal order which is above man and rooted in the nature of the world:

> Whether the context is Greek, Christian or undefined, tragedy seems to lead up to an epiphany of law, of that which is and must be. . . . In such a world-view nature is seen as an impersonal process which human law imitates as best it can, and this direct relation of man and natural law is in the foreground.[4]

Naturally, such an approach would rule out the possibility of a specific kind of dramatic pattern which we have called the "covenant drama" which is enacted not against the background (or foreground) of an impersonal natural law, but against the background of human history which man helps to create, and with reference to a personal God (or anti-god) with whom the hero enters into a compact. If this is a "myth," its dynamics would seem to be entirely different from those of the "mythos of autumn" which rests ultimately on the rhythms of nature.[5] In the covenant drama there is a linear, exploratory movement, rather than predetermined circular movement, a readiness for new experience rather than an everlasting confirmation of "that which is and must be." And above all, there is a decisive place for human freedom and responsibility.[6]

H. Weisinger approaches the subject more from the direction of anthropology, but his conclusions are similar. There is for him no basic difference between Shakespearean and Greek tragedy, for both go back to a certain archetypal myth-pattern. His choice is the myth of "the fortunate fall." Health and fertility are restored to society at the moment when the tragic hero is destroyed. The

death of the tragic hero functions much as the death of the king
or priest in primitive rituals. We reconcile ourselves to his death—
we even rejoice in it—because we treat him not as an individual
but as the representative of the people or tribe. The collective
well-being (health, fertility, the orderly succession of the seasons)
transcends individual fate. The need for theodicy thus does not
arise, for we are not ultimately concerned with the justice of God's
ways to the individual wayfaring soul, but with the profoundest
needs for survival, for adapting the life of man to the rhythms of
nature. This explains our satisfaction at the death of the tragic
hero, and it also explains its necessity as the proper culminating
point of tragedy:

> The motives for the actual killing of the king centered about the
> desire for control over the processes of nature as they affected man,
> for as I have said, the king symbolized the corporate well-being of
> the people. The king was killed to obtain his magical powers, to
> bring about the restoration in the spring of the dying vegetation
> parched by the summer heat, to participate in the victory of the sun
> over winter . . .[7]

Weisinger has a great deal to say about the cults of Tammuz,
Adonis, and Osiris, and he suggests with some plausibility that
rituals connected with these deities formed the original seed of
that mode of communal mime which later developed as tragedy.
The general theory is familiar to us from the more fundamental
researches of Jane Harrison[8] and Gilbert Murray,[9] but Weisinger
is very much more panoramic. For he includes in his sweep the
whole of Old and New Testament scriptures which likewise, according to him, testifies to the same archetypal mythology of the dying
and resurrected god impersonated by the priest or king of the
tribe. In the so-called enthronement Psalms, the king is a "sublimated vegetation deity"[10] who ritually enacts the death and resurrection of a nature god in order to assure the fertility of the earth
and the orderly progress of the seasons. If this is true it would
tend to abolish the basis of the present book which has argued
for a covenant pattern derived from the Old Testament and be-
queathing to the drama of the Elizabethans a decisive antitype to
the myth of the eternal return, a dramatic form distinct from the

pattern of mythology on which the ancient drama of the Greeks was based.

Now Weisinger has made no original investigations into the field of Old Testament literature and history, and his thesis rests on the work of the so-called myth and ritual school of Bible scholars such as I. Engnell, W. O. E. Oesterley, S. H. Cooke, and G. Widengren (he might have added S. Mowinckel, H. Ringgren, and E. O. James). This group holds that the center of the Israelite experience of God is the "cult." The psalmists and prophets were cult figures and the cult which they practiced was not *essentially* different from that practiced by other people of the ancient Middle East. Indeed the key to the understanding of the Bible lies in the comparative study of other Near-Eastern rituals and beliefs for which traces and analogies are then diligently sought in the Bible. Basing himself on such a syncretistic position,[11] Weisinger argues that the books of Job and Jonah exhibit the same fundamental pattern as that exhibited in the classical prototypes. Jonah is another dying and resurrected god.[12] Jonah descending into the belly of the fish and then being regurgitated onto the dry land is almost too good an example! (The theory does not concern itself with Jonah as mutinous servant, a figure in a debate, a dialogue drama.) He might for this theory be the Fisher King himself all over again. Now if this is true, there would seem to be no sense in setting up a specific antithesis between, say, the revenge cycle in which Hamlet would function as a winter god fated to perish before the arrival of spring, and the covenant drama in which Hamlet would be challenged to save his soul by entering into the life of dialogue. Such an antithesis would simply melt away in the all-inclusive landscape of myth and ritual.

Fortunately for the thesis of this book, however, the panoramic view which would locate the Biblical pattern of belief and experience within a context of nature mythology has not gone unchallenged. There is no need here to become involved in the internal debates of Bible scholars (we have enough to do with the debates of Shakespeare scholars) but mention may be made of Henri Frankfort, J. Pedersen, W. Eichrodt, and G. E. Wright—all of them important scholars in their different specialized fields—who have come to opposite conclusions. Frankfort maintains that:

assimilation was not characteristic for Hebrew thought. On the contrary, it held out with peculiar stubbornness and insolence against the wisdom of Israel's neighbours. It is possible to detect the reflection of Egyptian and Mesopotamian beliefs in many episodes of the Old Testament; but the overwhelming impression left by that document is one, not of derivation, but of originality.[13]

The title of the chapter from which the foregoing quotation is taken is: "The Emancipation of Thought from Myth." That, for Frankfort, is the crucial determinant of the Israelite experience.

G. E. Wright has reached his conclusions on the basis of an even closer and more expert study of the Old Testament literature and its contemporary Mid-Eastern environment. He speaks of

the remarkable fact that the God of Israel has no mythology. Since history rather than nature was the *primary* sphere of his revelation, Israel's effort was to tell the story of her past in terms of God's activity. There was no necessity for nature myths. Yahweh, for example, was no dying-rising God like Baal of Canaan. He was the *living God.* . . . To be sure, in poetry and prophecy of a later period we find allusions to the Canaanite myth of creation, the battle with the dragon of chaos, Leviathan, or Rahab. . . . On the one hand, the myth was historicized and used metaphorically to describe Yahweh's great victories in history, especially that over Pharaoh's army in the crossing of the Red Sea (e.g. *Isa.* 51. 9–10). On the other hand, it was used in eschatology as a description of God's victory over his enemies in the great Day to come.[14]

On this whole question we may perhaps be forgiven for taking the Old Testament at its face value. It records as clearly as such a poetic document can, the decisive rejection of myth, and its replacement by something else. The story of the Flood is a wonderful example of this. In the Babylonian form it has the typical myth-pattern: Utnapishtim, ancestor of Gilgamesh, is the Flood hero. Like Noah he seeks refuge from the overthrow in a ship, and after facing the danger of death he is finally immortalized and deified. It does not require great ingenuity or anthropological scholarship to discern behind this the archetypal myth of the questing hero whose career projects the inner "storms" associated with the growth of the psyche as well as the terrors and perils associated with the passage of the seasons—in particular the frequent and no doubt destructive floods which accompanied the autumn rains. It may be that through the ritual miming of the acts of the legendary hero (Utnapishtim for the Babylonians; Ziusudra for the Sumerians; Deucalion for the Greeks) these ancient peoples sought to propitiate the gods of destruction and deluge. Above all, the story with its alternating emotions of gloom and joy, darkness and light, exactly corresponds to the rhythm of the season of which it is the mythical accompaniment and interpretation.

Now in the Bible there is a decisive turning aside from this pattern. In the Old Testament version of the Flood the conclusion of the story marks also the abandonment of its original basis, the breaking of the vicious circle from which its psychological pattern is derived. When the Flood is over, God resolves that man shall no longer be subject to the degradation and terror of this experience. There will be no need to offer seasonal propitiation, out of terror lest the earth should return to primeval chaos: the order is guaranteed by a Creator-god who subjects the whole to his will:

> While the earth remaineth, seedtime and harvest, and cold and heat, and summer and winter, and day and night shall not cease.
>
> (GENESIS 8:22)

A God who stands above the rhythm of nature will call mankind into fellowship with him; a covenant will be forged between God and his creatures which will free man both from the loneliness of his struggle with the forces of his psyche within, and from subordination to the terrible forces of nature without:

> And I will establish my covenant with you; neither shall all flesh be cut off any more by the waters of a flood; neither shall there any more be a flood to destroy the earth.
>
> (GENESIS 9:11)

He belongs to a different time order from that nature. He walks purposefully along a road which stretches from creation to the end of history. The promise upholds him "while the earth remaineth . . . for perpetual generations." The rainbow is hung in the clouds as a token of this covenant: it is a memory-symbol—a memorial of the past victory over the terrors within and without, and a sign of the promise for the future:

> And God said, This is the token of the covenant which I make between me and you and every living creature that is with you, for perpetual generations . . .

And I will remember my covenant, which is between me and you and every living creature of all flesh; and the waters shall no more become a flood to destroy all flesh.

And the bow shall be in the cloud; and I will look upon it, that I may remember the everlasting covenant between God and every living creature of all flesh that is upon the earth.

(GENESIS 9:12, 15, 16)

Henceforth the word is not nature, but history. Poetic symbols could not possibly speak a clearer language.

But we do not need to confine our attention to symbols and their interpretation. The prophets explicitly attack the fertility religions of their time, and they do so with unparalleled violence. There are the frequent execrations of the worship of Baal and Astarte (e.g., I Samuel 7:3–4), of the cult of Moloch (Leviticus 18:21), and of that of the Babylonian vegetation god Tammuz—a near relation of Adonis (Ezekiel 8:14ff.). The prophet's account of the miscreant women "weeping for Tammuz" (who died in the summer and was reborn in the autumn) shows that he knew all about the "myth of the eternal return" at first hand, and also that his attitude to it was one of unambiguous condemnation. And this is surely the fundamental position taken by the Old Testament Scripture as a whole. The fertility religions existed in the environment, and indeed infiltrated into the life of the people, but it was clearly understood that the distinctive life-experience of Israel was opposed to them. And this is the way Scripture had been understood until the myth-ritual school arose at the end of the nineteenth century to argue for a harmony between the culture of pagan antiquity and that of Israel on the basis of a shared nature mythology. The men of Shakespeare's time may be forgiven for not appreciating this notion. Sir Walter Raleigh, as we have already remarked, sees primarily in the Old Testament a key to the interpretation of history (that of his own time or of any other time). His concern is to preserve the notion of a Creator-god who in his providence stands above, and rules all things—the attitude also of the chroniclers on whom Shakespeare drew in his history plays. But Raleigh goes further in laying down the philosophical basis of his position, and in the *Preface* to his *History of the World* he introduces a long excursus on the ancients, in which he condemns the "monstrous impiety" of confounding God with nature and of speaking of the world as eternal.[15]

The emphasis on history in Raleigh, in the chroniclers, and in Shakespeare himself, the emphasis, that is, on a divine Providence which rules over the affairs of men, rewarding the righteous and punishing the guilty, and preserving the memory of the deeds of men from generation to generation—is not only opposed to the religions of nature but also to certain aspects of medieval Christianity. The ritual drama of the medieval Church, which celebrated in mime the birth, death, and resurrection of Jesus, has evidently more in common—from a structural point of view—with the ancient rituals of Tammuz and Adonis and with the medieval Mummers' play than with the covenant drama that we have here been discussing. This is a consideration worth bearing in mind, and it does help to underline the post-medieval, even the modern character of the type of drama whose importance we are here seeking to establish.

II

We are not yet done with the opposition. If the myth-ritual school conflates the Biblical-type morality or chronicle with the myth pattern of ancient drama, seeing them as being of similar or identical inspiration, another very considerable group of critics maintains an opposite thesis, namely that the Bible, since it deals with salvation, does not yield anything remotely compatible with tragedy, and consequently there is no possibility of a work of art genuinely compounded of the two. A "Biblical tragedy" or a "Biblical-type tragedy" is simply a contradiction in terms! Thus if *Hamlet* is a drama of salvation it cannot be true tragedy, and if it is tragedy it cannot be a drama of salvation.

I. A. Richards had already made this point—though without referring explicitly to the Bible—in *Principles of Literary Criticism* (1924). There is no role for faith in the world of tragedy, neither faith in God nor in the divine government of the world. Tragedy has reference only to the internal ordering of our psyches:

> It is essential to recognize that in the full tragic experience there is
> no suppression. The mind does not shy away from anything, it does

not protect itself with any illusion, it stands uncomforted, unin-
timidated, alone and self-reliant . . . Tragedy is only possible to a
mind which is for the moment agnostic or Manichean. The least
touch of any theology which has a compensating Heaven to offer
the tragic hero is fatal.[16]

George Steiner, in his book *The Death of Tragedy,* takes up this
point of view with specific reference to the possibility of contact
between tragedy and the world of the Bible. Though by no means
sharing Richards's skepticism where religious values are concerned,
he comes to the same practical conclusion, *viz.,* that where there is
a belief in justice at the end of the road, tragedy becomes virtually
impossible:

> Tragedy is alien to the Judaic sense of the world. The book of *Job*
> is always cited as an instance of tragic vision. But that black fable
> stands on the outer edge of Judaism, and even here an orthodox
> hand has asserted the claims of justice against those of tragedy: "So
> the Lord blessed the latter end of Job more than the beginning. . . ."
> God has made good the havoc wrought upon His servant; he has
> compensated Job for his agonies. But where there is compensation,
> there is justice, not tragedy. This demand for justice is the pride and
> burden of the Judaic tradition. Jehovah is just, even in His fury.
> Often the balance of retribution or reward seems fearfully awry, or
> the proceedings of God appear unendurably slow. But over the sum
> of time, there can be no doubt that the ways of God to man are just.
> Not only are they just, they are rational. The Judiac spirit is vehe-
> ment in its conviction that the order of the universe and of man's
> estate is accessible to reason. The ways of the Lord are neither wanton
> nor absurd. We may fully apprehend them if we give to our inquiries
> the clearsightedness of obedience. Marxism is characteristically Jew-
> ish in its insistence on justice and reason, and Marx repudiated the
> entire concept of tragedy. "Necessity," he declared, "is blind only
> in so far as it is not understood."
> Tragic drama arises out of precisely the contrary assertion. . . .[17]

This would seem to stand diametrically opposite the syncretistic
views of Weisinger and Northrop Frye, both of whom refer directly to Job and discern in it the myth pattern of tragedy. Steiner
does not closely analyze any examples, but he lets it be known
that the Elizabethan theater is still fundamentally tragic, while later
on—in the Romantic age—we enter the zone of pseudo-tragedy.
Thus Marlowe's *Dr. Faustus* with its theme of the pride and fall

of the hero, its non-Biblical endorsement of human presumption and sin, is tragedy, where Goethe's *Faust* is "sublime melodrama." The point is that Faust is saved.

> He is borne away amid falling rose petals and the music of angelic choirs. . . . The heavens stream not with blood, as in Marlowe, but with redemptive hosannas.[18]

On this count we may ask Steiner whether perhaps the "death of tragedy" does not set in much earlier. There are vast tonal differences between *Faust* and *Hamlet,* not only at the end but all the way through, and yet Hamlet too is borne away amid the music of angelic choirs! If the theme of salvation and the sense of justice mark the decisive turning-away from tragedy, then it is difficult to see how *Hamlet* can be saved . . . for tragedy.

The disjunctive school has recently received significant support from the Israeli critic, Baruch Kurzweil. He too, like Steiner, stresses the existential incompatibility of the two postures, that of the tragic hero and that of the Biblical hero, doing so on the basis of a somewhat closer analysis of both *Job* and *Faust* than Steiner attempts. His conclusion is that it is Goethe's employment of motifs derived from the Book of Job in the "Prologue in Heaven" which ultimately robs *Faust* of its tragic theme and explains its nontragic end.

> The recourse to the Biblical sources takes the hero, Faust, out of the tragic sphere, and leads to the emphasis upon that weak character, the wretched and mediocre Gretchen. *Faust* represents what the play *Hamlet* might have been had Ophelia and not the Prince of Denmark been the central character.[19]

Ethically, tragedy sets up (as Hegel had said) a world of relative values; the Bible, by contrast, makes a demand for absolute righteousness. The two are thus fundamentally incompatible. The general caution to critics is summarized in the words:

> We are left confronting a boundary line which should not be glozed over, but should rather be recognized for what it is.[20]

These views of the disjunctive school, while clearly more acceptable than those of the myth-ritual school from the point of view of this study, would nevertheless seem to rule out any genuinely fruitful meeting between tragedy (in the case of *Hamlet,* the most typical of tragic forms, *viz.,* the revenge archetype) and the life experience of Biblical man. Our conception of *Hamlet* as an example of such a meeting would then be an absurdity.

To answer this objection pragmatically one could simply abandon all debate about tragic theory and confine oneself to a study of the text. We could agree that perhaps in principle no such work as *Hamlet* should ever have been written. Its double time-scheme which perfectly mirrors the inner duality of its phenomenological structure is doubtless an absurdity. If nevertheless it is artistically achieved, we could say that this is merely evidence of Shakespeare's incomparable strategy. He brings together elements which in fact do not and cannot combine. Shakespeare becomes once again a *lusus naturae,* an ideological freak, and we should enjoy him without drawing from his example any conclusions about the rules of art.

This, however, will not quite do. For one thing this strategy of combining the uncombinable is by no means confined to *Hamlet.* Shakespeare's other plays, as we shall presently see, reveal the same dual focus, the same solution of Hebraic and Hellenic elements, with a different balance in each case, and a different emotional shading. But one can go further than this, for such strategies, such dialectical devices, are by no means confined to Shakespeare. If Western man had not from time to time succeeded in combining the divided parts of his inheritance—the Hellenic and the Hebraic—in spite of their inner incompatibility, his life and art would have become alike impossible. We think of Milton's *Paradise Lost,* of Racine's *Athalie,* and we think of Spenser's attempted reconciliation of the medieval code of courtly love with the Protestant ideal of marriage and family. The effort is too systematic, too continued, and—in spite of inner tensions and irregularities—too successful, to be dismissed as mere artistic sleight-of-hand. Some unity, or at least some illusion of unity there is.

To arrive at a more satisfactory formulation of the problem we may conclude by referring to a discussion by the German-Jewish existentialist philosopher Franz Rosenzweig. This discussion (quoted as a central feature in Kurzweil's essay) is one which no student of tragedy or of Biblical art can afford to ignore. Rosenzweig makes clear the essential differences between the existential role of the tragic hero as revealed by a study of the Greek form and that of Biblical man. The only true language of the tragic hero, he says, is silence. For he "addresses himself only to his innermost self."

> How can this loneliness of his, this rigid defiance be otherwise manifested than by his silence? And this, as the contemporary audience remarked, was the case with the tragedies of Aeschylus. The heroic is dumb![21]

In this choice of silence, says Rosenzweig, the tragic hero "pulls down the bridges which connect him with the World and God."[22] For the self in its pure self-contained character knows nothing outside itself: it is simply alone. And here is the key to the tragic end or "fall" of the hero.

> The hero as such has no alternative but to fall, for his fall makes possible his maximal canonization as hero (*seine hoechste Verheldung*), the utterly locked and closed "enselfment" of his selfhood. He yearns for the solitude of his doom because there is no greater solitude. Yet properly speaking the hero does not die. . . . The character which hardens into an heroic self is immortal. Eternity is exactly what is good enough for echoing back his silence.[23]

By contrast, Biblical man seeks and finds the life of dialogue; and in place of the solitude of doom where proud death holds court in his eternal cell, he is committed to the extraordinary adventure, the perils and challenges of life and history. He is called upon to live.

> I have set before you life and death, blessing and cursing: therefore choose life, that both thou and thy seed may live.
>   (DEUTERONOMY 30:19)

At the point where man, the world, and God enter into a meaningful and purposeful union, the purely aesthetic realm as exhibited in Greek art is transcended, and we enter upon the path of redemption.[24]

So far it would seem that Rosenzweig comes to support the absolute disjunction of the spheres of tragedy and Biblical literature. But this is by no means Rosenzweig's intention. In a profoundly subtle yet quite emphatic way he insists that within the Greek aesthetic itself the yearning for redemption, the will to break out of the cage of the selfhood, is manifest. Monologue strives to transform itself into dialogue. In Sophocles and Euripides the hero no longer maintains his silence: he attempts to speak: he seeks to enter the world of dialogue. And though he is doomed to failure ("they do not learn to speak: they learn simply to debate"), the attempt is significant. The tragic hero in his self-contained existence seeks to become what he can never become—a soul. Over the world of ancient tragedy and ancient art broods the great "perhaps." Perhaps man, God, and the world, divided from one another in total isolation—God imprisoned in mythology, the world a self-generating cosmos, man a lonely tragic hero—can nevertheless join? Perhaps God created the world? Perhaps there is justice in the heavens? Job's questions are posed if not by the tragic hero, then by the tragic author.[25] "There is no certainty, only a ceaseless round of possibilities. . . . If . . . perhaps . . . Who knows?"[26] In fact, the supreme importance for Rosenzweig of the sphere of art, in particular the art of tragedy, is that through its dumb speech it seeks to break out of the vicious circle of the myth world of antiquity. Art is the fundamental bridge between the world of myth and the world of revelation. In it is to be found the first intimation of the truth, the truth of the covenant. It stands upon the threshold before the sphere of reality;[27] it connects myth with faith. In art, and especially in tragedy, is the essential *"Uebergang"*—the point of transition between mystery and miracle, between myth and revelation, between nature and history.

It is clear also that for Rosenzweig post-Christian art has already achieved, in part, this transition from the closed world of ancient tragedy to the open-ended world of Biblical revelation. He does not speak of Elizabethan drama in the same terms that he uses for Greek tragedy. Love, for instance, is alien to Greek tragedy, but not to Shakespearean tragedy:

> In monologue love can at the most appear as unfulfilled desire; the misery of Phaedra's unreciprocated passion is for the ancients possible on the stage; Juliet's love enhanced through the mutuality of possession is not.[28]

But Juliet's achieved love would not have been possible for Shakespeare either, were it not that in the dumb world of ancient tragedy the potentialities of dialogue were already present. It is a world seeking inarticulately to be saved. Thus it is that by the time we reach the drama of Shakespeare the note of salvation may already be clearly heard, and why, in order to sound it, he did not need to abandon the zone of tragedy. Thus Hamlet is both the lonely hero who hammers on the closed doors of the self and the man who, called forth into the life of dialogue, achieves a trembling vision of the star of redemption.

CHAPTER XII

On the Threshold

A cardinal and pregnant ambiguity is thus lodged in the heart of the Shakespearean drama. It is not ultimately an ambiguity of style and image merely, but of something more fundamental, which concerns the very gestalt of the plays, their movement and tendency.

The fifth act of *Hamlet* presents the fall of the hero; from the appearance of the grave-diggers the scene is oriented toward death. And yet there is irony in the very shape of the play, for the last act also celebrates the rise of the hero, his moral ascent. And it is in his life that Hamlet (like Milton's Samson) achieves the victory. The upward curve of salvation is described within the temporal frame of the world we know. It does not belong to the traditional Christian theme of salvation in the afterworld. This will do for Ophelia of whom it is said:

> A ministr'ing angel shall my sister be,
> When thou liest howling.

> (V. i. 263–264)

—a phrase which underlined the traditional Christian concomitants of her personality. But as far as Hamlet is concerned, there is no translation to a better world, no myth of death and resurrection. His salvation, such as it is, is something we may behold in the play: it is part of the dramatic substance. Nor should we think of the hero's newfound stability and power as a kind of lightning before death. On the contrary, it is an achievement for which his whole moral quest has prepared us. In this respect the last act comes not only as a celebration of the hero's death but to crown the upward and onward struggle which had characterized the great soliloquies. He had striven to bring together the three great faculties of memory, reason, and will, and in the fifth act he achieves their necessary coordination and is consequently enabled to apply thought and reflection to the service of an active righteousness. This is the meaning of his salvation. And this is a movement opposite to the "fall" of the tragic hero of antiquity. The tragic fall which in ancient tragedy (according to Rosenzweig) signified the hero's ultimate "enselfment" in the solitude of his doom, occurs in *Hamlet* rather at the moment of maximal *loss* of selfhood. For paradoxically the fifth act celebrates the liberation of the hero from the closed world of monologue and his entry into the life of dialogue. His avowal of love for the dead Ophelia, his earnest words of forgiveness to Laertes, and his appeal to the now-no-longer-stoical Horatio—"If thou didst ever hold me in thy heart" (V. ii. 360) all speak of a new release of the soul in love, affection, and charity. Love, a key word in this act, is no longer the selfish love of the pagan, but the "unselfed love" of Biblical man—as Henry More termed it. It is that "heaven upon earth" which constitutes the Hebraic answer to Hellenism; for "love," as the canticle declares, "is stronger than death."

We have now reached the end of our study of *Hamlet,* but if the insights gained have any value they will serve us also in relation to the rest of Shakespeare's works. Hints of this have been already given, but no frontal treatment of any other play has been attempted. In these concluding pages, therefore, I propose to indicate briefly how the conception of Shakespeare's art as a dialectical compound of Hebraic and Hellenic motifs may apply to three other plays: *King Lear, As You Like It,* and *The Tempest.*

II

King Lear is the story of the fall of the great man. Behind it is the classical gestalt, the circular movement which defines the tragic fall of the hero from high to low estate. Like his predecessor, Richard II, King Lear can say, "Down, down, I come like glistering Phaeton." Using an emphatically classical image, Lear says that he is bound "upon a wheel of fire" (IV. vii. 47). And the image of the wheels occurs with some frequency. Kent, resigning himself stoically to a night in the stocks declares:

> Fortune, good night; smile once more; turn thy wheel.
>
> (II. ii. 180)

The Fool, in this respect as in others, intuits a major theme in the play, for he too speaks of King Lear as a great wheel running down a hill.

> Let go thy hold when a great wheel runs down a hill, lest it break thy neck with following.
>
> (II. iv. 72–74)

And Edmund, the villain, confessing that his star is set, acknowledges before his death that "the wheel is come full circle" (V. iii. 176). The whole shape of the play may be understood under this figure. Lear, at the beginning mounted high on his throne, commands his followers, divides his kingdom, demands love and obedience. In Act III we see him in the storm, "a poor, infirm, weak, and despis'd old man" (III. ii. 20); in Act I imperiously banishing Cordelia from his presence, in Act IV kneeling and begging her forgiveness. The play is governed by images of perpendicularity, the fall of the characters being foredoomed in the figure of a falling movement established from the beginning of the play. Kent testifies to this in the first scene of Act I when he says:

> To plainness honour's bound
> When majesty *falls* to folly.
>
> (I. i. 150–151)

Edmund with a concealed reference again to the wheel declares:

> The younger rises when the old doth fall.
>
> (III. iii. 26)

We realize even when he says this that the alternate rise and fall of the generations carries with it the inevitable implication of his own foreordained descent when the wheel shall have come full circle.

All this is very much on the surface, and yet it is necessary to see the dialectical syntax of the figure of perpendicularity. That figure impresses itself most powerfully on our imaginations in the scene of Gloucester's attempted suicide where Edgar describes the steep drop over the imaginary cliff at Dover.

> I'll look no more,
> Lest my brain turn, and the deficient sight
> Topple down headlong.
>
> (IV. vi. 23–25)

But this is a tragic "fall" to end all tragic falls. The audience is aware that Gloucester is doomed; but it is also made aware that his doom is to be—temporarily at least—denied him. Instead of the wheel, another kind of movement will be established, a horizontal movement of onward labor, of moral responsibility, a pilgrimage through the wilderness of this world in search of salvation. And this substituted movement is given bald physical expression by what happens on the stage. Instead of falling down, Gloucester will fall flat on the boards to be picked up by his son Edgar and gently persuaded to continue his journey through further trials to further vision and further insights. He must not wilfully seek his own salvation. Instead of descent, there will be ascent.

> EDGAR: Hadst thou been aught but gossamer, feathers, air,
> So many fathoms down precipitating,
> Thou'dst shiver'd like an egg; but thou dost breathe,
> Hast heavy substance, bleed'st not, speak'st, art sound.
> Ten masts at each make not the altitude
> Which thou hast perpendicularly fell:
> Thy life's a miracle. Speak yet again.
>
> GLOUCESTER: But have I fall'n or no?
>
> (IV. vi. 50–57)

Gloucester's question defines precisely the structural irony of the entire play: "Have I fall'n or no?" In one sense he must fall: this is the Hellenic pattern. But in another sense such a tragic fall is denied him, for his "life's a miracle." The full theological notion of human fate ordered by God is not far from this scene, concealed though it is behind the grotesquerie and make-believe.

Jan Kott's reading of this scene does not agree with what has just been said. He claims that "Gloucester's suicide attempt is merely a circus somersault on an empty stage." And he compares the scene with Beckett's theater of the absurd:

> The blind Gloucester who has climbed a non-existent height and fallen over on flat boards, is a clown . . . The philosophical parable may be interpreted as tragedy or grotesque, but its artistic expression is grotesque only . . . From the beginning to the end. It is waiting for a Godot who does not come.[1]

This is surely to miss the real point, which is that besides the grotesque circus act, the "play-within-the-play," there is also a "play-without-the-play"—a divine comedy enacted on the theater of the world and overseen by Providence. Gloucester's grotesque circuslike "fall" on the boards does not echo the world's absurdity. On the contrary, it is intended to bring Gloucester to the realization that his life has a purpose:

> Think that the clearest Gods, who makes them honours
> Of men's impossibilities, have preserved thee.
>
> (IV. vi. 74–75)

The stage is by no means empty. Gloucester's somersault is performed within a spiritual ambience in which both love and justice are powerfully represented by Edgar. For Edgar, the loving son of Gloucester who stagemanages the performance, is a kind of messenger of the gods, mediating salvation to both Lear and Gloucester. And this is far enough from the theater of Beckett and Ionesco.

As for King Lear and Cordelia, we notice the same dialectical syntax. They too "fall" in Act V. As Cordelia says, "For thee, oppressed King, I am cast down." But Lear's speech immediately establishes the counterpoint, the horizontal cross-movement:

>   so we'll live,
> And pray, and sing, and tell old tales, and laugh
> At gilded butterflies, and hear poor rogues
> Talk of court news; and we'll talk with them too,
> Who loses and who wins.
>
> (V. iii. 11–15)

The fall and rise of great ones ("that ebb and flow by th'moon") become trivial, even meaningless in the newfound perspective of love which Lear and Cordelia have achieved. They will survive

("we'll live") and learn something of the true meaning of the spectacle of human mutability. Nahum Tate was right to feel that these
pointers in the play to a salvation achieved through the love of
Cordelia and Edgar for their parents demanded a kind of conclusion far different from that which Shakespeare had provided,
a conclusion in which life and love would be permitted to triumph.
But what he had not sufficiently grasped is that the contrary structure, *viz.*, the tragic pattern of the wheel, the stoical readiness for
death, the perpendicular fall of the great man through insanity
and torment, point in another direction, and demand the consummation not of bliss but of total extinction. The absoluteness of the
play's tragic structure is what dooms Lear, Gloucester, and Cordelia. Death is stronger than love. This is the lesson of *King Lear*
as much as it is of *Romeo and Juliet.*

The present theatrical convention (dating from Bradley),
according to which Lear dies of joy in the delusion that Cordelia
is alive, provides a functional compromise between the two patterns, the Hebraic and the Hellenic, whether Shakespeare thought
of it or not. But, in fact, Shakespeare has provided a better means
of interweaving the two patterns, one that is more organic and
more continuous, for it is through the dialectical positioning of
the main plot and the subplot that Shakespeare truly balances the
two *Gestalten* which determine the shape of his play. It is in the
handling of the twin plots that the structural ambiguity of the
play is at once revealed and overcome.´

Much has been said of the two plots in *King Lear* and of
Shakespeare's purpose in developing them so systematically along
parallel lines. Gloucester is betrayed by his wicked son, Lear by
his wicked daughters; Gloucester is visited with blindness, Lear
with insanity; Gloucester is finally cherished by a loving son, Lear
by a loving daughter, both children wronged earlier by their parents. The parallelism is clear and detailed. But more important than
this is the moral and structural *contrast* between the two situations. Lear's trouble takes on, from the beginning, the character of
a natural cataclysm. It is not by chance that at the crisis of his
sufferings he should be the victim of the impersonal forces of
nature. He has functioned all along as the "King of the Wood"

the semi-divine, numenous figure whose triumph and fall obey the rhythm of a vast universal cycle of change. He links himself emphatically from the beginning with

> the sacred radiance of the sun,
> The mysteries of Hecate and the night,
> By all the operation of the orbs
> From whom we do exist and cease to be.
>
> (I. i. 111–114)

If he is therefore the great wheel running down a hill, we know why this should be and must be. There is a necessity at work here as ancient as the most ancient of myths and rituals known to us. And it is fitting that this pattern should be revealed in the fate of the King, for the fate of the King gathers into itself a universal meaning. That is why the King is the central figure in the myth and ritual of the dying god. His fate illustrates the operation of natural law in its universal scope. As Rosencrantz rightly remarks on "the cess of majesty"

> O, 'tis a massy wheel
> Fixed on the summit of the highest mount,
> To whose huge spokes ten thousand lesser things
> Are mortised and adjoined.
>
> (*Hamlet*, III. iii. 17–20)

And with equal precision he concludes:

> Never alone
> Did the King sigh, but with a general groan.
>
> (III. iii. 22–23)

This would do as a perfect summing-up of the celebrations which attended the ritual demise of Tammuz or Adonis. Much the same sense of collective hope and menace surrounds the personality of Lear. And Cordelia too is involved in his fate. The operation of impersonal natural law connects his life with the life and well-being of society, with the operation of the orbs, and the basic functions of the natural world. He also, in his disaster, has an ominous power over the forces which control fertility. He curses Goneril with the curse of childlessness (I. iv. 299f), very properly addressing himself to nature to carry out his orders ("Hear,

Nature, hear! dear Goddess, hear!") and in Act III as he reaches his nadir he spreads disaster over the entire world:

> Crack Nature's moulds, all germens spill at once
> That makes ingrateful man!

(III. ii. 8–9)

Lear as a fertility god is the center of an amoral nature drama, and it is in keeping with this that the evil of his daughters should be both unexplained and unexplainable. They are like sunspots or eclipses, or (as he himself says) like "the roaring sea" (III. iv. 10), and the only proper reaction to their doings is to shield oneself from them as well as may be, adopting at the same time a stoical passivity. There is no moral etiology at work which would serve to link their behavior with the omission or commission of any deed on the part of Lear, nor is there any moral lesson to be learned from their behavior. They are in this respect like the wolf or the bear in the fable, doing what they do by natural necessity; and to this the abundant beast imagery bears witness.[2]

Now King Lear knows all this and recognizes it: indeed he himself authorizes the principal animal images which have reference to his daughters: "pelican daughters," "tigers," "detested kite," "vulture." At the same time he cannot ultimately rest satisfied with his nature religion nor with the structure of inevitability which according to the age-old myth-ritual pattern governs his fate. As his suffering becomes more deeply felt, he begins like Job to question its nature. It demands an etiology. "Is there any cause in nature that makes these hard hearts?" he asks (III. vi. 81). It is not sufficient to speak of escaping the wrath of his daughters as one would seek to avoid the roaring sea. The lives and actions of human beings seem to require to be fitted into some other pattern. His challenge to his daughters is a moral challenge, affirming a transcendent status for man beyond the life of beasts and beyond the instincts of nature:

> Allow not nature more than nature needs,
> Man's life is cheap as beast's.

(II. iv. 269–270)

In the storm he learns not only of the cruelty of nature, but of man's inhumanity to man, and he learns that a king must link himself not to the impersonal forces of nature, but to the justice of the heavens. He cannot tax the elements with *unkindness* (III. ii. 16) but he can so tax his daughters, the laws of human "kind" being determined not by instinct or the rhythm of the seasons, but by that specific "lovingkindness," that covenant bond, which is the distinctive mark of man. It is from this point of view that he can legitimately call them "unnatural hags": they are unnatural in terms of that human dimension of values which transcends the mere instinctual order of animate and inanimate things.

It is precisely at this point that the subplot with its very different moral structure impinges itself on our attention and on Lear's. Attending Lear in the storm is Edgar whose words refer the world's troubles not to a nature mythology but to a Biblical code of crime and punishment, a moral theodicy:

> Take heed o'th'foul fiend. Obey thy parents; keep thy word's justice; swear not; commit not with man's sworn spouse; set not thy sweet heart on proud array.
>
> (III. iv. 79–82)

Here in this brief summary of the second table of the commandments we have the entry into the play of the Judeo-Christian categories. And this is the moral atmosphere which governs the subplot as a whole. Gloucester is no king, no nature god. He is—to stretch a point—a bourgeois citizen functioning in a domestic moral fable. He has what Lear lacks—a pre-history; and this is given us in the first scene. His youthful sins are recalled, and they will influence his fate in old age. Lear has no such moral hinterland—his condition is "long-engraffed": he has never been other than he is; likewise, Goneril and Regan have never been younger than they are. They are part of a changeless natural order, representatives of that which is and must be. Gloucester, by contrast, brings into the world of the play a memory (which will remain deeply imprinted on our minds to be recovered in Edgar's closing speeches) of his early life. Edmund was a knave who "came something saucily to the world before he was sent for, yet was his mother fair." He too has a history: "he hath been out nine years, and away he shall again" (I. i. 21–34). The prose of the first scene emphasizes its quotidian, realistic character. It does not belong to high tragedy but to the "low" genre of the moral fable.³ The mention of significant details from the past already alerts us—as in some novel of George Eliot or Dickens—for what is to come. Gloucester's past will bear down on his future: God will not be mocked.

Here then is the tonal background of the Gloucester-Edmund-Edgar plot, a background very different from that of the main Lear plot. Gloucester has a tendency to forget this, adopting a fatalistic nature philosophy, but his sons—both of them—jerk him back into a proper recognition of his true existential condition. Edmund reminds himself and us that his father was not made an adulterer by planetary influence:

> An admirable evasion of whoremaster man to lay his goatish disposition to the charge of a star!!
>
> (I. ii. 141–143)

At one point, Gloucester states his belief in an impersonal world-order rather like that apprehended by Hardy in *The Dynasts*:

> As flies to wanton boys are we to the Gods;
> They kill us for their sport.
>
> (IV. i. 36–37)

But Edgar sees to it that he becomes conscious of his own part as a moral agent capable of apprehending the nature of his sufferings and of learning from his errors. It is under Edgar's gentle guidance that he takes up his burden in Act IV and seeks out the path of virtue. And it is Edgar who finally sums up with a neat apothegm the grim but salutary lesson of Gloucester's life:

> The Gods are just, and of our pleasant vices
> Make instruments to plague us;
> The dark and vicious place where thee he got
> Cost him his eyes.
>
> (V. iii. 172–175)

It is entirely in keeping with the moral atmosphere of the subplot that Edmund at the end undergoes a process of repentance. His good end marks the completion of a cycle far different from that spelled out by the wheel of fortune. It is a cycle which begins with sin and proceeds through exile and suffering to repentance and absolution. No such moral repentance is possible for Goneril and Regan: they are no more capable of changing their natures than is the roaring sea, the pelican, or the tiger, for they own neither moral history nor growth.

With incomparable art Shakespeare brings these two plots into close and intimate relation with one another, the Lear plot with its myth-ritual structure, and the Gloucester plot with its strong rational and ethical pattern. He introduces Edgar into Lear's ménage (the Edgar-Lear-Kent triangle) and Edmund into that of the wicked daughters (the Edmund-Goneril-Regan triangle). But it is not merely a matter of cunning plot manipulation. Shakespeare is subtly bringing the *pattern* of the one plot to bear on the other. There is a symbiosis of the two. Lear emerges from the myth-ritual pattern to become a figure of moral judgment. The mock trial of Goneril and Regan in Act III, scene vi, is not entirely mockery, for Lear abetted by Edgar ("thou robed man of justice") may legitimately set up to judge the world's evil from his newfound angle of vision. In the fourth act, functioning now emphatically within the Gloucester-Edgar world (and echoing an earlier speech of Edgar's), Lear pronounces his great speech on adultery:

> What was thy cause?
> Adultery?
>
> (IV. vi. 112f)

and he follows it with his great indictment of the abuses of authority:

> A dog's obey'd in office.
> Thou rascal beadle, hold thy bloody hand!
> Why dost thou lash that whore? Strip thine own back;
> Thou hotly lusts to use her in that kind
> For which thou whipp'st her. The usurer hangs the cozener.
> Through tatter'd clothes small vices do appear;
> Robes and furr'd gowns hide all.
>
> (IV. vi. 164–170)

Here he seems to have become the vicarious spokesman of those values and judgments which form the staple of the subplot, and it is of great significance that the mad Lear in speaking these lines is flanked by the blind Gloucester on the one hand and the disguised Edgar on the other. The link-up is complete.

Gloucester, for his part, gains from the proximity of Lear something of the latter's tragic pity and glory. He becomes endowed with the high dignity of the tragic hero. Through him Shakespeare brings about—if one may so put it—the democratization of the theme of tragedy. The most significant effect of the parallelism of the two plots in *King Lear* is one which is so obvious that it has probably never been pointed out, *viz.,* that the tragic figure at the height of his misfortunes witnesses the parallel affliction of another tragic figure. This is the radical departure from the pattern of antiquity. Instead of the single dominant hero locked in the absoluteness of his selfhood, we have Lear and Gloucester linked in their common fate. And it is through this recognition of a common fate and a common humanity, that the moral and esthetic catharsis is achieved. It is like Hamlet's recognition in Act V of his brotherly kinship to Laertes:

> For by the image of my cause I see
> The portraiture of his.

> (V. ii. 77–78)

Gloucester says very much the same of Lear, and Lear of Gloucester; and Edgar, as always expressing the moral essence of the play, gives to this theme its classical formulation:

> How light and portable my pain seems now,
> When that which makes me bend makes the king bow;
> He childed as I father'd.

> (III. vi. 117–119)

As the steep tragic horror of Lear's life and death is mitigated by the saving love of Cordelia, so the common strife of humanity finds its consolation and meaning in the sense of a bond of love by which the lonely monologue of the tragic hero is suspended, and silence gives way to the utterance of man to man, the opening of heart to heart, and soul to soul, in humility and faith.

III

Even if we could all agree that in the tragedies Shakespeare seems to oppose a more strenuous morality to the religion of nature, we would still be left with the comedies and their celebration of the simple pieties of the Forest of Arden. Here, it would seem, is a pastoral world far removed from the harsher responsibilities to time and history which we may detect in the tragedies. Here the characters seem content to slip back into the bosom of nature, enjoying the infinitely comforting change of the seasons. In *The Winter's Tale* the harshness of the mid-winter both in the human sphere and in the realm of nature ("a sad tale's best for winter," II. i. 24) is followed by the mid-summer sheep-shearing:

> Not yet on summer's death nor on the birth
> Of trembling winter.

(IV. iii. 80)

Here all bitterness and misunderstanding melt away in an atmosphere of mellow fruitfulness, the seasonal change defining the rhythm of the action. The same nature religion lurks behind *Twelfth Night,* where the Saturnalian revels, the cakes and ale of Sir Toby Belch and his friends, provide an instinctive defense against the harshness of January with the promise of marriage and fruitfulness to follow in the spring, when the various pairs including Sir Toby and Maria will be duly mated. It is the "good goddess Nature," as Paulina terms her, who presides over this world of romantic comedy—Isis herself in her nontragic capacity—and little profit, it seems, can be gained by searching for a more problematical basis or for a harsher assertion of human obligations. As in Amiens' song, in *As You Like It,* he who loves to lie under the greenwood tree will enjoy the ease of a warm kinship with the birds and flowers:

> Under the greenwood tree,
> Who loves to lie with me,
> And turn his merry note
> Unto the sweet bird's throat. . . .
> Come hither, come hither, come hither:
>> Here shall he see
>> No enemy,
> But winter and rough weather.

(II. v. 1f)

As You Like It, perhaps more than any other comedy, makes this kind of assertion throughout. It comes nearest in its ethical doctrine to what Wordsworth called "the education of nature." The harshness of Orlando's defective upbringing is alleviated when he arrives in the forest and finds tongues in trees, books in the running brooks. A pre-stabilized harmony between man and nature guarantees that goodness and love flourish naturally in the rural setting. Oliver is reformed, finding his natural mate in Celia at the same time. Broken bonds are healed under the beneficent influence of Mother Nature: brother is restored to brother, daughter to father, and lover to lass. The alienation of modern life is at an end, and we are back in the "golden world," the age of Saturn, where all is ordered by natural law. The Duke, we are told,

> live[s] like the old Robin Hood of England: they say many young gentlemen flock to him every day, and fleet the time carelessly as they did in the golden world.
>
> (I. i. 124–127)

Here (with due allowances made for the sunnier atmosphere of comedy) is the same fundamental reliance on the operation of the orbs by which we do exist and cease to be, which we noted in Lear's pagan, unregenerate philosophy. It is a world of teeming fertility where man and beast alike follow the law of their being:

> As the ox hath his bow, sir, the horse his curb, and the falcon her bells, so man hath his desires.
>
> (III. iii. 85)

Above all it is a timeless world without the responsibilities which the irreversible passage of time imposes. The people who join the Duke "fleet the time carelessly as they did in the golden world."

This aspect of the play, however, is in fact no more dominant than the pagan aspect of *King Lear,* and there is, if we care to examine it in the same way, as much fundamental questioning of the natural principle as in the tragedies. There is, in short, the same dual structure. The first indication of this is to be found in the continued and detailed concern with the problem of time. There is in *As You Like It* a dual time-reckoning: on the one hand the time of the clock, on the other hand the cyclical time or rather timelessness which prevails in the forest, the time of the seasons.

> And therefore take the present time,
>   With a hey, and a ho, and a hey nonino:
> For love is crowned with the prime,
>   In spring time, the only pretty ring time,
> When birds do sing, hey ding a ding, ding,
> Sweet lovers love the spring.
>
> (V. iii. 32–35)

Here spring, lovers, and the birds obey the "time" of nature. But against this rhythm of the seasons we have the absurdly meticulous timekeeping of Touchstone:

> And then he drew a dial from his poke,
> And looking on it with lack-lustre eye,
> Says very wisely, "It is ten o'clock:
> Thus we may see," quoth he, "how the world wags:
> 'Tis but an hour ago since it was nine,
> And after one hour more 'twill be eleven,
> And so from hour to hour we ripe and ripe,
> And then from hour to hour, we rot, and rot. . . ."[4]

(II. vii. 20–27)

The life of the greenwood is very fine, except that once a clock is brought into the forest we see that when there is little to distinguish man from the vegetable kingdom, he merely ripens and rots. To bring a clock into the forest is to light up the fundamental deficiencies of Arcadia whether viewed as the Golden Age or as the Land of Cockaigne.[5] Rosalind shares, but with a more serious undertone, Touchstone's concern with time. She is always conscious of the clock:

ROSALIND: I pray you, what is't o'clock?

ORLANDO: You should ask me what time o'day: there's no clock in the forest.

ROSALIND: Then there is no true lover in the forest, else sighing every minute and groaning every hour would detect the lazy foot of Time as well as a clock.

(III. ii. 319–325)

And later she commands her lover to be above all punctual (IV. i. 46f). Like so many of Shakespeare's heroines, her grasp of reality is sure and practical. It is she who will finally bring the dream world of the forest to an end and point the way to a more purposive existence in which marriage and domestic responsibilities will be primary aims.

In fact, one is obliged to question the notion that the Forest of Arden represents the ideal of the play. It is true that the characters there enjoy the long summer of irresponsibility. From the Duke downward they all refer to it in some sense as a golden world; but it is also true that they all refer to it also as "exile." The word is prominent and central.[6] The Duke's very first words in the play are addressed to his "co-mates and brothers in exile." Celia and Rosalind go into exile, and so does Orlando. No amount of Arcadian tranquility quite dispels the harsh Biblical force of this notion. And at this level of the play the banishment from the town and the court are a chastisement which will bring not pleasure but moral profit to those who will patiently endure the hardships involved:

> Sweet are the uses of adversity

$$(\text{II. i. } 12)$$

says the Duke. And when the sharpness of adversity has been brought home to Rosalind in the report of the mortal danger which her lover has just escaped, she says very simply and persuasively:

> I would I were at home.

$$(\text{IV. iii. } 163)$$

The play in fact represents as much the pull away from Arcadia as it affirms the enjoyment of its pleasures.

The antinaturalistic motif is made clear from the moment when Orlando arrives in the forest with his suffering and aged companion:

> If this uncouth forest yield anything savage, I will either be food for it or bring it for food to thee.

$$(\text{II. vi. } 6)$$

Nature is clearly red in tooth and claw. In his subsequent address to the Duke and his friends disported in the forest, Orlando brings them a reminder of the "better days" they have forfeited in their exile:

> But whate'er you are
> That in this desert inaccessible,
> Under the shade of melancholy boughs,
> *Lose and neglect the creeping hours of time;*
> If ever you have looked on better days;
> If ever been where bells have knolled to church;
> If ever sat at any good man's feast;
> If ever from your eyelids wiped a tear,
> And know what 'tis to pity and be pitied,
> Let gentleness my strong enforcement be . . .

$$(\text{II. vii. } 109\text{–}118)$$

He here clearly links together the dumpish oblivion to time ("you that . . . Lose and neglect the creeping hours of time") which characterizes Arcadia with its lack of religion, and of those higher virtues which humanity has painfully acquired through the long centuries of intellectual and moral discipline. Touchstone's words to Corin (III. ii.) are not entirely fooling:

> Why, if thou never wast at court, thou never saw'st good manners; if thou never saw'st good manners, then thy manners must be wicked, and wickedness is sin, and sin is damnation . . .
>
> (III. ii. 42–45)

We may, in short, detect in *As You Like It* the same dialectical presentation of "nature" that we noted in *King Lear*. Viewed in one way, nature may be a Rousseauesque paradise of sweetness uncorrupted by civilization: viewed in another way it may be that Hobbesian "state of meer Nature" where the life of man through the menace of his own undisciplined instincts becomes "nasty, brutish and short." Shakespeare seems to endorse both the Wordsworthian confidence in the spontaneous adaptability of the law of man to the law of the external universe and also the skepticism and fear of a later generation made aware of the dangers of uncontrolled naturalism. At all events he does not deceive himself that one impulse from a vernal wood is all that we need for happiness and virtue. Churches are built in towns, not in the wildwood, and Jaques rebukes Touchstone for his attempted "return to nature" which threatens the whole structure of the family and society.

> And will you, being a man of your breeding, be married under a bush like a beggar? Get you to church, and have a good priest that can tell you what marriage is
>
> (III. iii. 89–92)

The suspicion (to put it no more strongly) as to the possible shortcomings of a naturalistic order of existence is, I would suggest, closely linked to the continuous Biblical echo and allusion in this play. There are recollections in particular of the first chapters of Genesis. The first-named character in the play is the old servant Adam and it is he whose sufferings and exile in the second act first draw our attention to the harshness of a mere natural environment. The theme of the Garden of Eden is later recalled when Oliver, arriving in the forest, is assailed by a "green and gilded snake." It is true that in the course of the Christian centuries the image of the Garden of Eden has been blended with that of the age of Saturn, and the apple of Eve with the golden apples of the Hesperides, but the inner tension, the contradictions between the two traditions, are also clear; and to this the more sensitive writers testify. In Milton's *Paradise Lost*, Eden is a place of moral trial, not of timeless enjoyment. It is also a place of work (IX. 205–212). In the Jewish tradition Eden has never been thought of as a realm of unproblematic enjoyment of nature's bounty: from the very first moment, Adam is subject to certain moral imperatives by which his instincts were to have been curbed. It is precisely the refusal to curb them, the sinking back into the simple enjoyment of "nature," which led to his exile from Eden! One tree had been forbidden, but Adam and Eve following their "natural" instincts had put aside the prohibition, and had thus forfeited the garden state. The Edenic life is thus not the antithesis to the state of civil society but its emblem; it is a state of protection from nature. The total exposure to nature in the wild state (both within and without) was the condition of man *after* he had been exiled from Eden: It was the condition of Cain after he had become a wanderer and a vagabond (Genesis 4:14); and it was also the state of his descendants at the time of the Flood. The Flood indeed symbolizes the state of radical exile: man, having overthrown all restraints and having given himself up to the "evil imagination of his heart" (Genesis 6:5), finally suffers exposure to the terrors of nature in its extreme form. This state of peril is also humorously referred to at the end of Shakespeare's play when the couples seeking refuge in marriage and domesticity from the inclemencies and trials associated with the Forest of Arden are compared to the animals entering the Ark. Jaques is once again the spokesman for the Biblical point of view:

> There is, sure, another flood toward, and these couples are coming to the ark.
>
> (V. iv. 35–36)

The notion of flood and danger leads forward inevitably to the notion of salvation, the salvation through those laws of civil society and obedience which in Hobbes bring the state of nature to an end. In the ninth chapter of Genesis the Flood is the prelude to the enactment of that covenant with the sons of Noah which liberates them from the fear and perils associated with the state of nature. From now on, life will be ordered and forms of civilization will be forged. A similar pattern is symbolically achieved at the end of *As You Like It* through the ceremonies of marriage which at once unite the divided members of society and bring the state of exile to an end. Shakespeare's comedy leads forward to marriage as the redeeming symbol, just as surely as tragedy leads forward to death.[7] Here the marriage of the three couples is very explicitly an act of "atonement" in both senses.

> Then is there mirth in heaven
> When earthly things made even
> *Atone* together
>
> (V. iv. 115–117)

Moreover the song points to civil society, to the town, as the proper environment for the institution of marriage—just as do Spenser's two great marriage poems. Here in Shakespeare the emphasis on the "bourgeois" aspect is lighter, but it is there just the same:

> Wedding is great Juno's crown,
> O blessed bond of board and bed:
> 'Tis Hymen peoples every town.
>
> (V. iv. 148–150)

It is impossible not to be reminded of Milton's great marriage ode with its like emphasis on the "blessed bond," the covenant act which brings to an end the chaos of unrestrained instinct:

> Hail wedded Love, mysterious Law, true source
> Of human offspring, sole propriety
> In Paradise of all things common else.
> By thee adulterous lust was driv'n from men
> Among the bestial herds to range . . .
>
> (*Paradise Lost*, IV. 750–754)

In *As You Like It,* too, the marriage of the three couples is marked with a certain religious solemnity, a sense of dedication. With this happy termination of the play, the Duke and Jaques put on the religious life, and Oliver, who has survived the perils of the wildwood, emerges a penitent and redeemed man. The exile is at an end, and man can return from the dream of a pastoral wilderness to the sober reality and responsibilities of the world we know, supported by love, wisdom, and humility.

IV

In *The Tempest* the ambiguities connected with the contrasting images of nature are even more clearly spelled out than in *As You Like It,* and likewise the redeeming symbol of the marriage covenant ("a contract of true love") is even more powerfully emphasized, held before us from the first meeting between Ferdinand and Miranda in Act I as a solemn promise, aim, and remedy. The whole scheme that we have been seeking to define stands out distinctly in an almost allegorical form, as though Shakespeare had finally decided to give to the hints and guesses of his earlier plays a local habitation and a name.

There is first the idealized past. Gonzalo in his account of the ideal commonwealth presents the notion of a state of nature identical with that of the Golden Age, the Age of Saturn, and reminding us not a little of the Forest of Arden as seen by the Duke in *As You Like It*:

> All things in common Nature should produce
> Without sweat or endeavour: treason, felony,
> Sword, pike, knife, gun, or need of any engine,
> Would I not have; but Nature should bring forth,
> Of its own kind, all foison, all abundance,
> To feed my innocent people.

> SEBASTIAN: No marrying 'mong his subjects?

> ANTONIO: None, man; all idle; whores and knaves.

> GONZALO: I would with such perfection govern, sir,
>   T' excel the Golden Age.

> (II. i. 166–175)

The simple piety of Gonzalo's view of humanity is only matched by its impracticability. As is well known, Montaigne's sentimental vision of primitive society is here the basis for Gonzalo's commonwealth, and the key to Montaigne's discussion in his essay "Of the Caniballes" is the faith in natural law as governing the natural condition of man:

> Those nations seeme therefore so barbarous unto me, because they have received very little fashion from humane wit, and are yet neere their originall naturalitie. The lawes of nature doe yet command them which are but little bastardized by ours, and that with such puritie, as I am sometimes grieved the knowledge of it came no sooner to light, at what time there were men that better than we could have judged of it.[8]

Here in embryo is the optimistic concept of the state of nature derived from the Middle Ages, and later associated with Locke and Rousseau and the eighteenth-century vision of the *beau sauvage*. It is an attractive view, but Shakespeare does not endorse it, any more than he does in *As You Like It*. The mocking commentary of Sebastian and Antonio reminds us of the factors that Gonzalo has ignored—the refractory nature of human instinct, and the need for ethical control, in particular for marriage. Gonzalo also ignores the new economics of the seventeenth century and the new exploitation of natural resources associated with the colonizing of the Western hemisphere. In his island there would be no kind of traffic, nor would there be any use for metal, corn, wine, or oil. Men would be naturally good, and all things would work out for the best through the happy correspondence of the nature of man with the nature of the universe, its cyclical rhythm. Unrealism could hardly be taken further.

The opposite point of view, the antithesis, is implicitly set out in the characters of Sebastian and Antonio who plan to murder Alonso and Gonzalo, and at a lower level by the drunken courtiers Stephano and Trinculo. These show us, in the manner of William Golding's *Lord of the Flies,* what happens when the bonds of normal society are removed and man reverts to his natural condition. Murder, usurpation, and rapine leap out of their covert. "I do begin to have bloody thoughts," says Stephano (IV. i. 221). As Hobbes says of the state of nature, it is a state of war "where every man is enemy to every man." Shakespeare shows something of this same disenchantment. Goneril and Regan represent a savage naturalism and so do the visitors to Prospero's island. More-over, their savagery is made worse by their contact with the "savage and deformed slave" Caliban. Far from introducing him to better ways, they bring him and themselves to greater depravity. Man left alone without obligation to some principle beyond nature will tend to sink, not to the level of the beast, but somewhat lower. This is the insight which Lear reaches, and in less grim and tragic form, it is the insight offered us in *The Tempest*. Man's inner nature is not to be relied on, for underneath every one of us there is a Caliban, and behind every Caliban there is a Sycorax. Even Ariel will not be safe if Sycorax again takes charge. The beneficent influence of external nature (as Wordsworth conceived it, for instance) is not to be relied on either. At first sight it may appear to us to be a Garden of Eden where all things are ordered for our best advantage and where we may simply bask in an everlasting sunlight. But if we attend carefully we see that this is not so. The isle is full of music, but it also resounds with Caliban's subhuman gruntings, with the drunken songs of Stephano and Trinculo, and with the unholy whisperings of the evil conspirators, Sebastian and Antonio. If nature brings out the best in us, it also brings out the worst. It is not only Eden; it is also Cockaigne, a place of de-bauchery and license where (in fantasy) we pick wealth off clothes-lines, and where the food and drink pour themselves unbidden down our throats. The age of Saturn is only one side of the coin—the other is the Saturnalia practiced by the Roman soldiery and ending in death and horror.

V

We have in this play, much as we have in *Hamlet,* a symbolic his-tory of Western man. Long before Western man was Christianized—an event symbolized by Prospero's arrival on the island—the witch goddess Sycorax had ruled. She was a fertility goddess, Circe,[9] the seductive force of nature. And the memory of her rule is not dead. She is alive in her son, the superficially reformed Caliban whom Prospero has conquered, but whose will he has not sub-dued. His mother's pagan religion has been overthrown, and he has been taught how

To name the bigger light, and how the less,
That burn by day and night

(I. ii. 335–336)

The reference to Genesis 1:16 is unmistakable. But Caliban will relapse at the first opportunity. Coincident with the Renaissance there will be a pagan reversion. Led by Stephano and Trinculo, Caliban will become an idol worshipper once again. He kneels to his new god (II. ii. 127) who is Setebos, Bacchus, Mars, and Venus all in one. No more will he serve his old master; he will turn back to the wildwood, to the dark primeval forest from which Prospero had painfully led him out into the light.

The fact is that Prospero's island does not provide an adequate defense against the savageries of nature. The island is one of charm and beauty like the flower-strewn world evoked by Ophelia. "The isle is full of music." It symbolizes that conception of nature as ordered and harmonious; we hear the heavenly music of its cosmic orchestra. It is the world envisioned by Hooker and Sir John Davies: beauty and order are its hallmarks, and it is governed by natural law. Corresponding to this natural law which governs the cosmos is the *logos* or reason of man. Thus Prospero declares:

with my nobler reason 'gainst my fury
Do I take part: the rarer action is
In virtue than in vengeance.

(V. i. 26–28)

Man is "noble in reason, infinite in faculties . . . in action how like an angel, in apprehension, how like a god." This would do as a pen portrait of Prospero (though Hamlet had dismissed it as too flattering a view of human nature). Prospero represents the benevolent and aristocratic view of man which has behind it the whole medieval and High Renaissance tradition. A dignified *pater familias,* he has educated his daughter according to the highest values of Christian humanism, conducting his household rather in the manner of Sir Thomas More. We recall, by the way, that More too had envisaged an ideal island in his *Utopia* which would be governed in a similarly moderate, just, and patriarchal fashion. (There too, incidentally, the ladies had played chess after supper as in *The Tempest,* except that they had chessmen in the form of allegorical virtues and vices.[10]) Prospero's island is nature at its best, seen in the fine mellow light of reason and law, and he himself is the magnanimous man of the Aristotelian ethical tradition.

But this will not last. There is the pagan insurrection of Caliban, of the Machiavellians, of the new colonizers, the exploiters, the adventurers, the manipulators of the new mobile wealth of the sixteenth and seventeenth centuries. All this will threaten the established order of tradition. But it is not only a matter of the lower powers, the *id*; the higher powers of the psyche, the *superego* so to say, will also demand to be liberated. Ariel no less than Caliban yearns to be free from subservience to the wisdom of Prospero, its too rational, too paternal sway. Ariel, representing fire and air, suffers from claustrophobia in the monastic atmosphere of Prospero's cell. It is very comfortable there, very calm, very plausible. No doubt Prospero has, like Thomas Aquinas, a dozen proofs and more for the existence of God. He has a shelf full of books which include Boethius on *The Consolations of Philosophy,* Iamblichus *On the Mysteries*[11] along with the works of Abelard, Plotinus, Porphyry, Aristotle, and Plato. But somehow all this is not enough. Somehow the medieval stained-glass windows, the Tudor casements do not admit quite enough light. Ariel is for the moment "correspondent to command" (I. ii. 297) but he craves freedom: he wishes to be "free as mountain winds" (I. ii. 496), to release his own spiritual intensities unfettered by the limitations of the *logos,* of medieval natural law, those intellectual systems which had guaranteed an orderly world. The rebellion of Ariel is that of Hamlet, of Marlowe, of Donne, of Essex: it is the new republican spirit of the age, the new empiricism, the new exploration.

We err if we suppose this is a play about an ideal island of charm and beauty: it is a play celebrating the farewell to such an island and to its confinements. There is the same valedictory note marking the personality of Prospero that we noted in respect to Ophelia and Othello. Prospero will abjure his magic; he will break his staff and drown his book (V. i. 50f.). The farewell to chivalry, the farewell to the Petrarchan ideal of courtly love, the farewell to the sway of the *logos*—all are part of one composite process of emancipation. Shakespeare is in this the spokesman not of the old but of the new, the new striving spirit of the age turning forward to face what is to come with all its associated risks and dangers. The chief expression in the play of astonishment and delight is not that of the visitors when they first see the island but of Miranda when she turns away *from* the island to gaze upon the real world, the new bourgeois nonsacral world of free men and women:

> How beauteous mankind is! O brave new world,
> That has such people in it!
>
> (V. i. 183–184)

Miranda no less than Ariel seeks her freedom. For in the revolutionary phase of the Renaissance and the Reformation, Prospero will no longer provide the answers that we need. Man, seeking independence for his newly discovered individual personality, will break free; and yet, left to himself, he can govern neither himself nor his surroundings without infinite peril.

VI

Here then are thesis and antithesis, but what is going to be the answer to this? Does Shakespeare offer any kind of synthesis? At this stage I wish to point to an unnoticed Biblical motif, or group of motifs, in *The Tempest* which will indicate the direction Shakespeare takes in his attempted synthesis. If *As You Like It* (as we saw) has reference to some of the earlier chapters of Genesis in its evocation of the Garden of Eden, the story of the emnity between the brothers Cain and Abel, and the account of the Flood, *The Tempest* reminds us continuously of some of the later chapters of Genesis. There are, evidently echoes of the romantic matchmaking between Isaac and Rebecca, and between Jacob and Rachel, and there are strong echoes too of the story of Joseph and his brothers[12] and of Jacob's mourning for his son Joseph. It is worthwhile to set out the parallels. Ferdinand's "prime request" on meeting Miranda is "If you be maid or no" and later he offers to make her his queen "if a virgin" (I. ii. 424, 444). This was a pointed feature in the first appearance of Rebecca in Genesis 24:16. The sense of an arranged meeting, of the presence of a heavenly matchmaker is also powerfully present in the Biblical story (Genesis 24:27). In Shakespeare's play, the atmosphere of promise, of providential dealing, is expressed by Prospero in his asides to the invisible Ariel. The subsequent labor imposed on Ferdinand by his father-in-law-to-be will surely recall to the Biblically-minded auditor the menial tasks which Jacob in a later chapter performs for his father-in-law-to-be, Laban, in the hope of gaining Rachel for his bride:

> And Jacob served seven years for Rachel; and they seemed to him but a few days, for the love he had to her.
>
> (GENESIS 29:20)

And thus Ferdinand:

> The very instant that I saw you, did
> My heart fly to your service; there resides,
> To make me slave to it; and for your sake
> Am I this patient log-man.
>
> (III. i. 64–67)

There follow their mutual vows of love and promises of marriage—the "contract of true love." Prospero's words express the religious dimension of the occasion:

> Heaven rain grace
> On that which breeds between them.
>
> (III. i. 75–76)

But this is not the only Biblical pericope which seems relevant to the situation of Ferdinand and his fellow voyagers on Prospero's island. Prospero's first challenge to Ferdinand is precisely the same as that with which Joseph greets his brothers.

> And Joseph . . . said unto them, Ye are spies, to see the nakedness of the land ye are come.
>
> (GENESIS 42:9)

Prospero levels the same accusation against Ferdinand, knowing like Joseph that it is untrue:

> thou dost here usurp
> The name thou ow'st not; and hast put thyself
> Upon this island as a spy, to win it
> From me, the lord on't.
>
> (I. ii. 450–453)

And then, acting exactly as Joseph did in the Bible narrative, he puts the suspected "spy" in fetters for a period. We should remind ourselves that not only was Joseph also the "lord" of the land of Egypt where his kinsmen had unknowingly put themselves in his power, but he too was a magician who practiced divination (Genesis 44:5). But the most striking similarity relates not to Ferdinand but to Prospero's brother Antonio and his companions who, like Joseph's brothers, had been originally guilty of driving him into exile and thus indirectly bringing about his present situation as lord over a strange land. In the same fashion as Joseph, Prospero conceals his identity and person, and proceeds to subject his brethren to a series of tests and trials which will have the effect of rousing them to thoughts of repentance, of bringing back to their minds their forgotten crime against their brother years before. Thus Prospero causes a banquet to be placed before them but immediately whisks it away, bewildering them with the succession of fortune and misfortune (III. iii). In the same way Joseph first feasts his brothers but then immediately afterward sends his messenger after them to charge them with robbery (Genesis 44:4). The process of repentance, of regeneration is what Joseph had aimed at, and it is that which the various "quaint devices" which he practiced on his brothers were bringing about:

> And they said one to another, *We are verily guilty* concerning our brother, in that we saw the anguish of his soul, when he besought us, and we would not hear; *therefore is this distress come upon us.*
>
> (GENESIS 42:21)

Alonso's repentance is likewise brought about by the bewildering experiences of the tempest, the strangeness and unexpectedness of what is happening to him,

> Methought the billows spoke and told me of it;
> The winds did sing it to me; and the thunder
> That deep and dreadful organ-pipe, pronounc'd
> The name of Prosper: *it did bass my trespass.*
> *Therefore my son i'th'ooze is bedded*; and
> I'll seek him deeper than e'er plummet sounded,
> And with him there lie mudded.
>
> (III. iii. 96–102)

The same process of moral regeneration is at work.

A further Biblical motif from the same pericope is that of Jacob bereaved (or so he thinks) of his son Joseph. Alonso's words about Ferdinand:

> I'll seek him deeper than e'er plummet sounded,
> And there with him lied mudded

will recall the parallel lament of Jacob:

> he refused to be comforted; and he said for I will go down unto my son mourning into *Sheol*.
>
> (GENESIS 37:35)

In the Biblical passage we are discussing, the father's bereavement becomes a powerful stimulus to the moral regeneration of the brothers (Genesis 44:27, etc.), and it is only removed with the happy disclosure at the end of the story of the true identity of the "lord" of the land. Similarly in *The Tempest,* the deception regarding the supposed death of a son has a moral purpose. The belief that Ferdinand is dead forces the more strongly upon Alonso's mind the thought of his wrongdoing, and his relief at the end when he discovers him to be alive is a stimulus to repentance. What Prospero is practicing upon Antonio and Alonso is a ritual of exorcism, the exorcism of guilt and iniquity. With its accomplishment there will be a revelation by the "diviner" of his identity. We should remind ourselves that the great climax of the Joseph narrative is also reached when he "makes himself known to his brothers" (Genesis 45:1–4). It is paralleled by Prospero's "discasing" of himself:

> Behold, sir King,
> The wronged Duke of Milan, Prospero:
> For more assurance that a loving Prince
> Does now speak to thee, I embrace thy body
> And to thee and thy company I bid
> A hearty welcome.
>
> (V. i. 106–111)

The three basic features of the above speech: the declaration of the lost man's identity, the tearful embrace, and the assurance that

"it is my mouth that speaketh unto you" are all to be found in the
Biblical parallel (Genesis 45:3, 4, 12, 15).

These infolded Biblical themes and motifs are not offered here
as a contribution to the study of Shakespeare's sources in *The
Tempest.* If we are going to add the book of Genesis to Montaigne's
Essays and *Purchas his Pilgrimage,* this would be of minor interest
only, at best giving to the editors material for an additional footnote
or two. It may even be argued that this is not strictly a source so
much as a pattern of unconscious allusion, similar to the Biblical
"echo structures" which Louis H. Leiter points to in Conrad's
short story "The Secret Sharer."[13] But what is of interest for our
purpose is the new dimension that all this affords to the play. It
strengthens the impression of the island being not paradise but a
place of exile—the Mesopotamia in which Jacob is exiled or the
Egypt where Joseph is obliged to spend his years—likewise in
exile. From the island of Prospero, the exiles, both the earlier and
the later arrivals, will hope to make their departure and eventually
arrive at the promised land.

This is one basic implication: the other concerns the nature
of Prospero's "art." The Biblical "echo structure" to which we
have pointed obliges us to observe Prospero and his art in a new
light. He is not simply a mage, but a prophet or expounder of
dreams, a Joseph-figure. His task is to cause people to recall forgotten things, to bring sins to remembrance, to reforge broken
relationships between estranged brothers and between father and
son. And above all he presides as "Providence divine" over the
"covenant" of marriage, which in the play represents the final healing and redeeming moment in the lives of the characters—the "salvation" to which the action of the play looks forward. As has often
been pointed out, the romantic attachment between the two young
people is in this play, more than in any other play of Shakespeare,
hedged around with intimations of holiness and with moral restric-
tions. Its "covenantal" character is strongly insisted upon: it is
going to be no pastoral coupling, no spontaneous overflow of
powerful feelings in response to the rhythm of nature, but a serious
and solemn affair, an acceptance of responsibility. Prospero makes
the point twice:

> take my daugher; but
> If thou dost break her virgin knot before
> All sanctimonious ceremonies may
> With full and holy rite be minister'd
> No sweet aspersion shall the heavens let fall
> To make this contract grow.

(IV. i. 14–19)

The end of the religion of fertility, and its replacement by some holier principle of regulated instinct, is humorously announced by Iris in the Masque of Hymen which follows: Venus, she says, has been dismissed:

> Of her society
> Be not afraid. I met her deity
> Cutting the clouds towards Paphos; and her son
> Dove-drawn with her: here thought they to have done
> Some wanton charm upon this man and maid,
> Whose vows are that no bed-rite shall be paid
> Till Hymen's torch be lighted; but in vain
> Mars's hot minion is returned again.

(IV. i. 91–98)

It is through this "contract of true love" (IV. i. 84), raised through moral self-limitations and "sanctimonious ceremonies" to the level of a religious act of self-dedication, as in Spenser's *Epithalamion,* that the spiritual life of man is to be reintegrated. Caliban, representing unrestricted naturalism, is to be brought under control, and at the same time room is to be found for the Ariel principle, for love, imagination, and the free spirit of man.[14] Grace and nature are brought into a new unity, and the exile of man is at an end. Critics have shown themselves aware of the centrality of the marriage theme in *The Tempest* and of its spiritual significance. Thus Roy Walker:

> The poetic crisis in the struggle to integrate sensuality into a fully human wisdom was endured by Shakespeare at the turn of the century, and resolved in the chaste marriage in *The Tempest.*[15]

The marriage of the two characters symbolizes the solution of a fundamental problem with which Shakespeare's whole dramaturgy is concerned, namely the integration of sensuality with wisdom, of nature with grace. He achieves this under the aegis of a covenant or contract, that of marriage.

Such a "solution" is in keeping with the Biblical consciousness of the age, especially with its vivid awareness of the power
and pathos of the Old Testament Scripture. In *The Tempest* we
are reminded of Isaac and Rebekah, of Jacob and Joseph and
Rachel; and Prospero in bringing the young people together and
warning them of their responsibilities becomes an image of that
"providence divine" (I. ii. 159) who leads the troubled race of
man back to paradise. But this is not a peculiarity of *The Tempest*.
I hope to have shown in this study that such a scriptural environment is characteristic of Shakespeare's tragedy and comedy as a
whole, to a degree that has not been hitherto sufficiently recognized.

But a further conclusion arises out of this study: and that is
that Shakespeare's "solutions" are radically modern solutions. The
paradise to which he beckons us, both in *The Tempest* and in other
plays, is not the magic island of medieval Christianity with its songs
and sweet airs, its orderly subordination of spheres, its harmony
of natural law. It is altogether more strenuous, more real, more
close to our everyday problems. There is in it neither illusion nor
enchantment. "Their words are natural breath," says Prospero at
the end (V. i. 156); and their destination as we know is Naples,
not Utopia. There will be no medieval *logos* there to support the
young people, no hierarchies, no feudalism, no magical correspondence between man and nature. Instead, there will be all the
problems that we know in the modern world: Stephano and Trinculo will have to be kept in check, houses will have to be built
with hands and not in the heavens, there will be a new cash nexus.
And man, now suddenly very much alone in his newfound indi-
viduality, will have to learn through trial and error to understand
the nature of his freedom and obligation. If his discovery of mutual
love in the covenant of marriage provides him with one essential
key to this understanding, it is because behind that covenant stands
a larger and more embracing covenant, that enacted on the great
stage of the world from the beginning, and pointing forward by
promise to the end of days.

Appendix

Julius Caesar AND THE BLEEDING STATUE*

In her pioneering work on Shakespeare's images Caroline Spurgeon noted that *Julius Caesar* was bare in style and had "relatively few images." She went on to claim that, apart from a significant number of references to animals (Caesar a wolf and a snake, Lepidus an ass, Cassius a horse, etc.), "there is no leading or floating image in the play; one feels it was not written under the particular stress of emotion or excitement which gives rise to a dominant image."[1]

It may be argued that here, as with other plays of Shakespeare, Miss Spurgeon's statistical methods of counting and classifying images prevented her from seeing the great visionary statements which underlie the speeches of the characters and the events which befall them. We are now accustomed to finding dominant images where Miss Spurgeon missed them, often in hints and guesses or in images of only infrequent occurrence but which nevertheless have a certain centrality. In this respect the later work of G. Wilson Knight, A. E. Armstrong, and many others has carried us further and deeper into an understanding of the imaginative structure of Shakespeare's plays. In relation to *Julius Caesar,* however, later commentators have been almost as negative as Miss Spurgeon herself. A recent editor, T. S. Dorsch, has agreed that "there is no single dominating image [in *Julius Caesar*]" such as may be found in *Othello* or *Romeo and Juliet*.[2]

* First published in *Bar-Ilan Volume in Humanities and Social Sciences,* edited by M. Z. Kaddari (Jerusalem, 1969).

One particularly illuminating thread of images has nevertheless been pointed out by a number of present-day critics: this relates to metal objects and tools.[3] There is a double-entendre in Cassius's summing-up of Brutus's character:

> yet I see
> Thy honourable mettle may be wrought
> From that it is dispos'd.

(I. ii. 313–315)

"Mettle" here signifies both *metal* and *temperament*. There is a certain contradiction between these two meanings: the latter suggests something pliant, human, malleable; the former suggests something rigid and inhuman. In spite of the first meaning (metal rigidity), Cassius thinks that the "metal" of Brutus "may be wrought from that it is dispos'd." He becomes the blacksmith who, through his skill and power, can bend the metal–mettle of Brutus any way he wishes. Brutus himself seems to echo the same notion:

> Since Cassius first did *whet* me against Caesar,
> I have not slept.

(II. i. 61–62)

The concealed metaphor here is of a metal instrument or tool which has to be *whetted* or sharpened in order to do its work. Brutus is in a sense identified here with the knife with which he will later stab Caesar. He abdicates any human feeling, and by deliberate choice becomes a mere implement or tool of the conspiracy. The same (or a similar) concealed motif is found earlier in Cassius's remark,

> I am glad
> That my weak words have struck but thus much show
> Of fire from Brutus.

(I. ii. 174–176)

The reference is to striking fire out of a flint or rock or from a piece of metal in a smithy. In the opening scene of the play, Flavius after lecturing the people on their faithlessness to the memory of Pompey says,

> See where their basest mettle be not mov'd.

(I. i. 65)

Again, the play on the two meanings of metal–mettle, both of which could be spelled alike in Shakespeare's day.[4] According to the first sense, the people are immobile, frigid, incapable of true feeling (one of them was a cobbler who jokingly describes his work with an *awl*—another metal instrument) and this would explain their unthinking devotion to Caesar: according to the second sense, they are essentially changeable, fickle, violently unpredictable, like a "mettlesome" horse or other animal.

All this, fascinating and revealing though it surely is, seems nevertheless to be no more than the outer shell of the play's central system of imagery. I would suggest that such a system is to be found in a much more dramatic motif, that of stone statues as active participants in the drama. In the context of the last-quoted line from Act I, scene i, the main interest is focused on the "images" or statues of Caesar which had been adorned to celebrate Caesar's triumphal procession. Flavius and Marullus are determined to strip the statutes of their festive "scarves" or diadems in order to strike a blow against Caesar himself. These details come from Shakespeare's source in Plutarch's *Life of Julius Caesar*. Nor is this the only reference to statues in Plutarch's "Lives" of Caesar and Brutus. At every turn in the history of these two main characters, as told by Plutarch, there is testimony to the Roman interest in statuary. Caesar ostentatiously displays the images of his uncle Marius; a palm miraculously springs up beside Caesar's statue in the temple of Victory at Tralles; Caesar generously sets up Pompey's statues after they are thrown down: under the statue of Brutus's ancestor Junius, Cassius and his friends place a message urging him to rise against the dictatorship; statues have an active role in ceremonies of state and demonstrations of political power: above all, the image of Pompey presides over the culminating act of the drama as described both by Plutarch and by Shakespeare:

> Even at the base of Pompey's statua
> (Which all the while ran blood) great Caesar fell.
> (III. ii. 193–194)

In Plutarch, the statue of Pompey does not only bleed; it seemed to "take just revenge of Pompey's enemy."[5] Moreover,

Some say that Cassius, casting his eyes upon Pompey's image, made his prayer unto it, *as if it had been alive.*[6]

The stone image that bleeds, takes revenge, and to which prayers are addressed becomes for Shakespeare, it would seem, a dominant symbol. Taking a deep imprint from these suggestive passages in Plutarch, Shakespeare introduced the same motif by anticipation also in Calphurnia's dream where the bleeding statue had become that of Caesar himself

Which like a fountain with an hundred spouts
Did run pure blood.

(II. ii. 77–78)

It will be seen that the image is essentially dialectical: it presupposes stony figures incapable of human feeling and yet both remarkably active and amazingly subject to human casualty. "When you prick us, do we not bleed?" they seem to be saying. And from this central dialectical symbol there seems to extend outward into the play a system of opposed and yet interconnected references to metal, stones, and flints on the one hand, and to tears, blood, and feelings on the other. In the opening lines of the play, Marullus addresses the people as,

You blocks, you stones, you worse than senseless things!
O you hard hearts, you cruel men of Rome.

Here again with explicit reference to stony hearts is the puzzling ambiguity of metal–mettle. The violence, mobility, and fickleness of the crowd are revealed as a function of their stony immobility. They are "senseless things." At the moment of Brutus's supreme success as an orator, the people shout out

Give him a statue with his ancestors!

There is irony in the fact that Antony is about to rouse up the mob to a violent counter-revolt, while the people's conceptions are still governed by the Roman obsession with lifeless statuary. At the climax of his funeral speech in the marketplace, Antony warns the people against the dangers of hearing the will—this is likely to turn them from stony monuments into mad, flaming, and weeping beasts:

> You are not wood, you are not stones, but men;
> And being men, hearing the will of Caesar,
> It will inflame you, it will make you mad.
>
> (III. ii. 148–150)

The opening line of the second major speech of Antony—

> If you have tears prepare to shed them now

—may be glossed as, "If, in spite of your presumptive quality of wood and stone, you nevertheless are capable of shedding tears just as Pompey's statue sheds blood, then do so now." Wilson Knight has drawn attention to the emphasis on weeping in the play; nearly all the characters, Brutus and Cassius included, weep at some time or other.[7] This is almost as impressive as the number of references to blood in this particularly blood-drenched play.[8] These two features are, however, equally ironical. They gain their peculiar force from the fact that the weepers seem not to be the weeping type, and the bleeders seem to be peculiarly bloodless, frigid, and stony, like veritable statues—and yet they bleed and weep.

This nerve of imagery significantly links together the main characters and episodes of the play. It applies both to the people and their leaders, and to both the political factions, the party of Caesar and the party opposed to him; it is a comment on Romanism as a whole. The wound which Portia makes in her thigh (Act II, scene i, 300), and the "ruddy drops" which surprisingly visit Brutus's heart testify to the ironical conjunction of warm blood and cold stoic frigidity. Caesar is compared to the greatest statue of all—the bronze image of Apollo at Rhodes:

> Why, man, he doth bestride the narrow world
> Like a Colossus, and we petty men
> Walk under his huge legs . . .
>
> (I. ii. 134–136)

Cassius's intention in so describing Caesar is basically ironical. He is the Colossus with feet of clay; he reports on his physical weaknesses, as when he cries to Titinius for some drink "as a sick girl." And at the climax of the play Caesar is stabbed to death by his enemies and his blood visibly flows out in the Capitol—this is the visual confirmation of the fact that the stony immobility of the Colossus–Caesar is ultimately a mere illusion. In his own speech prior to the murder, Caesar comes near to denying that there is blood in his veins at all. He aspires to the quality of a veritable statue, "unshak'd of motion":

> Be not fond
> To think that Caesar bears such rebel blood
> That will be thaw'd from the true quality . . .

(III. i. 39–41)

The "true quality" of his blood is to be unthawed, i.e., to be like ice or stone. Thus at least he is in his own conceit. The sight of his flowing blood provides us with the means of judging this claim—the statue bleeds.

Cassius and Brutus in their quarrel scene (Act IV, scene iii) ring the changes on the various dialectical possibilities of blood and tears, *versus* metal and stone. Brutus had rather "coin my heart/And drop my blood for drachmas" (i.e., silver coins) than take money from the peasants. Cassius makes the same point about his own heart. If Brutus stabs it, he will find it is solid metal within:

> There is my dagger
> And here my naked breast; within a heart
> Dearer than Pluto's mine, richer than gold.

(IV. iii. 99–101)

The comparison of Cassius's heart to stone or metal is later on belied when we witness his tragic end in the next act—

> So in his red blood Cassius' day is set

(V. iii. 62)

—another bleeding statue.

The above remarks by no means do justice to the frequency and multiform character of this central image through which Shakespeare articulates his fundamental criticism of Rome and the Romans. In Plutarch, the episode of the bleeding statue had given a gruesome touch of melodrama to the story of Caesar's assassination with a hint of its being a righteous revenge for Pompey's death. In Shakespeare's play it becomes the focus for an ironical reading of the nature of Roman civilization as a whole. All the characters, Antony, Brutus, Caesar, Cassius, and the mob are seen in the searching light of its irony. The question addressed to them all is, "Are you stones or men?" And through the insistent force of this central image, the spectator is made to apply this question to each and every episode of the play, even in places where the image and its variants are not explicitly evoked. When Lepidus consents to his brother's death, when Brutus dismisses Portia's death in three lines, when Antony coldly sends the mob about its business after rousing it to fury—in all such instances we echo the question—"Are you stones or men?" Shakespeare is conscious throughout the play of the limitations of Romanism, and he communicates that consciousness to us.[9]

Shakespeare does not spell out the Judeo-Christian categories in this play as he does, for instance, in *Antony and Cleopatra* or *Hamlet* or *King Lear*: the spectator is afforded an unrelieved image of paganism, an image unsweetened by any gentler ethic, by any nobler concept of man's purposes. Yet the paradoxical image which paganism itself presents carries within it the question of its basic adequacy as a way of life for breathing men and women. Here is perhaps Shakespeare's main departure from Plutarch, for whom the fundamental values of Greek and Roman civilization had remained unquestioned. Shakespeare's vision is infinitely more detached and critical. He beholds everywhere men and women with hearts of stone, but he finds it impossible to conceive this except as an absurdity, and the consciousness of this absurdity causes us instinctively to desire that some divine hand will "remove the stony heart out of their flesh, and give them a heart of flesh."

Notes

INTRODUCTION

1. Harold Fisch, *Jerusalem and Albion* (London and New York, 1964).
2. John Vyvyan, *The Shakespearean Ethic* (London, 1959), p. 57.
3. *Shaw on Shakespeare,* edited by Edwin Wilson (London, 1961), p. 76.
4. Roy Walker, *The Time Is Out of Joint* (London, 1948), p. 106.
5. Sir Walter Raleigh, *The History of the World,* 1614 (edition of 1687), p. ix.
6. Cf. I. Gollancz, *The Sources of Hamlet* (London, 1926), p. 259.
7. All scene and line references for Shakespeare are to W. G. Craig's one-volume Oxford edition of 1904.
8. This and subsequent Biblical quotations are from the King James version.
9. Cf. W. R. Elton, *King Lear and the Gods* (San Marino, 1966), pp. 108–109.
10. Sir Walter Scott, *Ivanhoe,* Chapter XXXIX.
11. J. C. Powys, *The Enjoyment of Literature* (New York, 1938), p. 6.
12. Cf. Lily B. Campbell, *Divine Poetry and Drama in Sixteenth-Century England* (Cambridge, 1959), p. 142.
13. Cf. Murray Roston, *Biblical Drama in England* (London, 1968), pp. 71, 108.
14. *Ibid.,* p. 104.
15. G. Wilson Knight, *The Wheel of Fire* (London, 1930 and 1957), Chapter IV, etc.
16. *The Tempest,* edited by Frank Kermode (Arden edition, London, 1954), Introduction, p. xxx.
17. Jan Kott, *Shakespeare Our Contemporary* (New York, 1964), p. 104.
18. Roy W. Battenhouse, *Shakespearean Tragedy: Its Art and Its Christian Premises* (Bloomington, Indiana, 1969), pp. 88–95, 270–276, etc.

Chapter I—A CRY OF CRITICS

1. See Eleanor Prosser, *Hamlet and Revenge* (Stanford, 1967), Chapter IV *passim*. She ends the chapter wherein these treatises (and a great many more of the same kind) are discussed with the remarkable statement that "the majority of Hamlet's original audience is likely to have been familiar with most, if not all, of the material we have considered in the present chapter" (p. 117).
2. Jan Kott, *Shakespeare Our Contemporary* (New York, 1964), p. 62.
3. Konrad Swinarski's production had a brief run in Tel Aviv, commencing April 3, 1966.
4. D. G. James, *The Dream of Learning* (Oxford, 1951), pp. 35, 90, 119.
5. L. C. Knights, *An Approach to Hamlet* (London, 1960), p. 55.
6. Cf. Hiram Haydn, *The Counter-Renaissance* (New York, 1950), *passim*.
7. C. S. Lewis, "Hamlet, the Prince or the Poem," in *Proceedings of the British Academy,* Vol. XXVIII (London, 1942), p. 72.
8. Cf. Irving Ribner, *Patterns in Shakespearean Tragedy* (London, 1960), p. 84.
9. Cf. H. Granville-Barker, *Prefaces to Shakespeare* (London, 1963), Vol. I, p. 276. See also Roy Walker, *The Time Is Out of Joint* (London, 1948), p. 143.
10. Ribner, *op. cit.,* pp. 68, 90.
11. Miriam Joseph, "*Hamlet,* A Christian Tragedy," *S.P.* LIX (1962), 125–126.
12. Salvador de Madariaga, *On Hamlet* (London, 1964), p. 33f.
13. *Ibid.,* pp. 34, 144.
14. John Vyvyan, *The Shakespearean Ethic* (London, 1959), p. 27f. Cf. also Knights, *op. cit.,* pp. 46, 58.
15. Vyvyan, *op. cit.,* p. 55.
16. Geoffrey Bush, *Shakespeare and the Natural Condition* (Cambridge, Massachusetts, 1956), p. 115.
17. *Ibid.*
18. Roy W. Battenhouse, *Shakespearean Tragedy: Its Art and Its Christian Premises* (Bloomington, Indiana, 1969), pp. 81–82, 265, etc.
19. *Ibid.,* p. 245.
20. *Ibid.,* p. 250.
21. *Ibid.,* p. 263.

22. *Ibid.*, p. 264.
23. *Ibid.*, p. 245.
24. Cf. F. M. Krouse, *Milton's Samson and the Christian Tradition* (Princeton, 1949).
25. It may be noted that Mr. Battenhouse's model is derived in approximately equal measure from the Middle Ages and the moderns, his discussion of Shakespearean tragedy being punctuated by quotations from St. Thomas Aquinas, Augustine and T. S. Eliot. Little account is taken of the Elizabethan Age and its indigenous mode of "realism."
26. Erich Auerbach, *Mimesis*, translated by Willard R. Trask (Princeton, 1953), pp. 201–202.
27. Cf. *ibid.*, p. 212f.

Chapter II—HAMLET AGONISTES

1. A. C. Bradley, *Oxford Lectures on Poetry* (London, 1950), pp. 69–95.
2. From the translation of Hegel's *Aesthetik* by F. P. B. Osmaston, as reproduced in *Hegel on Tragedy*, edited by Anne and Henry Paolucci (New York, 1962), p. 3.
3. *Ibid.*, pp. 73–74.
4. *Ibid.*, pp. 60, 83f.
5. "Nunnery" has sometimes been explained as slang for "bawdy-house," but there is no proof that this is what Hamlet intended. The straightforward meaning is accepted by H. D. F. Kitto, *Form and Meaning in Drama* (London, 1956), p. 280.
6. I am anticipated in this thought by W. Empson; see *"Hamlet When New," Sewanee Review*, LXI (1953), 187.
7. John Donne, *The Indifferent.*
8. Caroline Spurgeon remarked on the contrasting imagery in *Hamlet* (*Shakespeare's Imagery and What It Tells Us*, Cambridge, 1965, pp. 319–320), but she draws no conclusions from this as regards the nature of the conflict so intimated, nor does she pay attention to the flower imagery.
9. Cf. also W. H. Clemen, *The Development of Shakespeare's Imagery* (London, 1966), p. 113.
10. See Appendix, *"Julius Caesar* and the Bleeding Statue," *infra,* p. 224f., and Chapter III, *infra,* p. 50.

11. Cf. Hiram Haydn, *The Counter-Renaissance* (New York, 1950), pp. 405–409.
12. Francesco Guicciardini, *Counsels and Reflections* (translated by Ninian Hill Thomson), as abstracted in *A Renaissance Treasury,* edited by Hiram Haydn and John Charles Nelson (New York, 1953), pp. 158, 161.

Chapter III—MY BROTHER JONATHAN

1. See especially, Hiram Haydn, *The Counter-Renaissance* (New York, 1950), pp. 619–636.
2. *Meditations,* Book IV, 3, translated by G. Long, in *The Stoic and Epicurean Philosophers,* edited by W. J. Oates (New York, 1940), p. 508.
3. *Ibid.,* Book II, 13, pp. 499–500.
4. Haydn, *op. cit.,* p. 620.
5. Cf. *Ethics,* Book IX, Chapter 8, "Of Self-Love."
6. Henry More, Dialogue IV, in *Divine Dialogues* (1668).
7. See Appendix, "*Julius Caesar* and the Bleeding Statue," *infra.,* p. 224f.
8. Joseph Hall, "Heaven upon Earth: or of True Peace and Tranquillity of Mind" (1606), a Christian revision of Seneca's treatise, *De Tranquillitate Animi.*
9. Arnold Hauser, in an interesting discussion of the relations between literature and the visual arts in this period, sees in Hamlet the typical sign of alienation, *viz.,* narcissism: "the psychological root of his renunciation of outside reality is always narcissism." (*Mannerism: The Crisis of the Renaissance and the Origin of Modern Art,* New York, 1965, Vol. I, p. 126.) But Hauser fails to appreciate the equally strong pull in Hamlet's psychology in the direction of selfless attachment.

Chapter IV—FROM MONOLOGUE TO DIALOGUE

1. William Empson, "*Hamlet* When New," *Sewanee Review,* LXI (1953), 24, 39.
2. Harry Levin, *The Question of Hamlet* (New York, 1959), p. 72.
3. The literature on this topic includes G. C. Taylor, *Shakespeare's Debt to Montaigne* (Cambridge, 1925), especially pp. 40, 41;

G. Brandes, *William Shakespeare: A Critical Study* (London, 1902), pp. 354–355; J. Feis, *Shakespeare and Montaigne* (London, 1884), *passim*. J. D. Wilson points out many echoes in his edition of *Hamlet* (Cambridge, 1948); cf. pp. 191, 240, 249.

4. Book III, Chapter xii. Florio's translation was first published in 1603, but it seems certain that Shakespeare had access to it in manuscript before that date.

5. I am indebted here to an unpublished paper by Hunter Kellenberger entitled " 'Consummation' or 'Consumation' in Shakespeare."

6. This suggestion was first made in an essay on *Hamlet* contributed by the present author to *The Shakespearan World*, edited by M. Roston [Hebrew], (Tel-Aviv, 1965), p. 115f.

7. Cf. John Donne's *The Divine Poems*, edited by Helen Gardner (Oxford, 1952), Introduction, p. L.

8. L. L. Martz, *The Poetry of Meditation* (New Haven, 1954), pp. 137–138; 324. See also, Eleanor Prosser, *Hamlet and Revenge* (Stanford, 1967), p. 220f.

9. From *The Christian Directory* (1582), quoted by Christopher Devlin, in *Hamlet's Divinity* (Southern Illinois, 1963), p. 40.

10. Cf., by the present author, "Bishop Hall's Meditations," *R.E.S.*, XXV (1949), 210–221.

11. Martz, *op. cit.*, p. 39.

12. *Occasional Meditations*, No. 1, in Joseph Hall, *Works*, edited by P. Wynter (Oxford, 1863), Vol. X, p. 121.

13. *Ibid.*, p. 186.

14. See below, Chapter IX, p. 153f.

15. Geoffrey Whitney, *A Choice of Emblems* (1586), p. 179.

16. For a fuller discussion, see, by the present author, "The Hero as Jew: Reflections on *Herzog*," Judaism XVII (New York, 1968), 42–54.

17. The parallel passage in Florio reads:

> A man should ever, as much as in him lieth, be ready booted to take his journey, and above all things, looke he have then nothing to doe but with himselfe . . . what matter is it when it commeth, since it is unavoidable. . . . Nothing can be grievous that is but once. (Book I, Chapter xix)

But the echo from Montaigne blends with another source, the gospel of Matthew 10:29, "Are not two sparrows sold for a farthing? and one of them shall not fall on the ground without your father." Another example of literary "perspectivism."

18. Cf. D. A. Traversi, *An Approach to Shakespeare* (New York, 1956), p. 99.

Chapter V—SPIRIT OR GOBLIN?

1. Christopher Devlin, *Hamlet's Divinity* (Southern Illinois, 1963), p. 50; Miriam Joseph, "*Hamlet,* a Christian Tragedy," *S.P.,* LIX (1962), 119–140.
2. John Vyvyan, *The Shakespearean Ethic* (London, 1959), p. 27f.
3. L. C. Knights, *An Approach to Hamlet* (London, 1960), p. 58.
4. G. Wilson Knight, *The Wheel of Fire* (New York, 1957), p. 39.
5. Cf. "*Hamlet* Reconsidered," *ibid.,* p. 300f.
6. Devlin, *op. cit.,* p. 48.
7. Roy Walker, *The Time Is Out of Joint* (London, 1948), p. 106.
8. William Empson ("*Hamlet* When New," *Sewanee Review,* LXI [1953], 194) opines that this feature was already present in the earlier *Hamlet* of Kyd. This, however, does not affect my point. I am not trying to establish Shakespeare's copyright in the ideas discussed in this and the subsequent chapters; at the same time, it does seem that Shakespeare has given these ideas a particular emphasis which is his own.
9. *The Complete Roman Drama,* edited by G. F. Duckworth (New York, 1942), Vol. II, pp. 715–716.
10. Hippolyte Taine, *The History of English Literature,* translated by H. Van Laun, from the Introduction to Part VI.
11. Jacob Burckhardt, *The Civilization of the Renaissance in Italy,* translated by S. G. C. Middlemore (London, 1945), pp. 265–266.
12. Cf. Erich Kahler, *The Tower and the Abyss* (New York, 1957), p. 54f.
13. For an early, seminal treatment of this topic, see Gilbert Murray's essay "Hamlet and Orestes," (*The British Academy,* 1914; revised 1920), and see Chapter X below, *passim.*

Chapter VI—THE COVENANT TASK

1. Martin Buber, *Koenigtum Gottes* (edition of 1956), p. 100f. For a brief introduction to the Israelite notion of covenant, see G. E. Wright, *The Old Testament against Its Environment* (London, 1950), pp. 55–73.

2. Roy Walker, *The Time Is Out of Joint* (London, 1948), p. 24.
3. T. F. Driver (*The Sense of History in Greek and Shakespearean Drama* [New York, 1960], p. 119) emphasizes the Biblical overtones of the "commandment" mentioned here, but does not explicitly relate it to the notion of covenant. For the link here with the Sinaitic revelation, see also Roy W. Battenhouse, "The Ghost in *Hamlet*: A Catholic 'Linchpin,' " *S.P.*, XLVIII (1951), p. 176.
4. For a more complete treatment of the topics handled in the remainder of this section, the reader is referred to my *Jerusalem and Albion* (London and New York, 1964), Chapters VII and XIV.
5. Cf. Perry Miller, "Preparation for Salvation in New England," *J.H.I.*, IV (1943), 254–255; *The New England Mind* (New York, 1939), Vol. I, p. 419f.
6. Later, in the Restoration comedy, we may note how the marriage contract, or at least the agreement to arrive at such a settlement between two partners, as in the famous contract scene between Millamant and Mirabell in *The Way of the World,* serves to bring an end to the social and moral anarchy of the "state of meer nature" in which everyone follows his lusts and appetites without regard to others. The "covenant" here functions in precise analogy to the Hobbesian contract of society.
7. See concluding section of Chapter XII below.

Chapter VII—THE BOOK OF THE COVENANT

1. Jean Paul Sartre, *What Is Literature?*, translated by Bernard Frechtman (London, 1967), pp. 12–13.
2. Francesco Guicciardini, *Counsels and Reflections* (translated by Ninian Hill Thomson), as abstracted in *A Renaissance Treasury*, edited by Hiram Haydn and John Charles Nelson (New York, 1953), p. 162.
3. His *Cabinet Council* and *Discourse of War* are particularly Machiavellian, as is also much of the political theorizing in *The History of the World*. Political cunning and sagacity have their part to play in history as "second causes"; however, the "first cause," i.e., the overall control of events, is in the hands of God. Justice ultimately prevails, but one does one's own part by delving one yard beneath one's enemies' mines. Cf. E. A. Strathmann, *Sir Walter Raleigh: A Study in Elizabethan Skepticism* (New York, 1951), pp. 102, 168, 275.

Chapter VIII—A TIME OF FORGETTING

1. Goethe's *Faust,* Part I.

    > The giddy whirl be mine, with agonized delight,
    > With loving hatred, quickening despite.

    (Translated by A. G. Latham, London, 1908, p. 80.)
2. *Ibid.*

    > Headlong we'll plunge in the turmoil of Time,
    > The roll of circumstance sublime;
    > And then let Pain and Delight,
    > Fruition and Despite,
    > Each with each interchange as they can.
    > 'Tis action alone attests the man!

3. Tom F. Driver, *The Sense of History in Greek and Shakespearean Drama* (New York, 1960), p. 38.
4. *Ibid.,* p. 39. From the considerable literature dealing with the history–consciousness of ancient Israel, mention may be made of Paul Tillich, *Biblical Religion and the Search for Ultimate Reality* (Chicago, 1955), E. Voegelin, *Order and History* (Louisiana, 1956), and Karl Loewith, *Meaning in History* (Chicago, 1949).
5. *Ibid.,* p. 40 (quoting James Muilenberg). Driver, however, fails to relate these insights clearly to *Hamlet.*
6. This is either a case of paronomasia or of folk etymology. Cf. also Jeremiah 33:25. The true etymology of *berit* has been much discussed. It may originate from the verb *barah,* meaning "to eat (the covenant meal)."
7. Cf. Driver, *op. cit.,* pp. 129–130.
8. Henri Frankfort, *Before Philosophy* (London, 1951), Chapter VIII, pp. 244–246. (Conclusion). This section was actually composed jointly by Henri Frankfort and Mrs. H. A. Frankfort.
9. Erich Auerbach, *Mimesis: the Representation of Reality in Western Literature,* translated by Willard Trask (New York, 1957), p. 9.
10. *Ibid.,* p. 15.
11. *Wilhelm Meister,* Book V, section 4, translated by Thomas Carlyle (London, 1888), Vol. II, p. 14.
12. Aristotle, *On the Art of Poetry,* translated by Ingram Bywater (Oxford, 1920), Section 8.
13. On the two time-schemes, see *Hamlet,* edited by H. H. Furness (*The Variorum Shakespeare,* Philadelphia, 1877), Vol. I, pp.

xiv–xvii (quoting Christopher North); also, Salvador de Madariaga, *On Hamlet* (London, 1964), pp. 111–113.

14. Samuel T. Coleridge, *Lectures and Notes on Shakespeare and Other English Poets* (London, 1902), p. 344.
15. de Madariaga, *op. cit.*, pp. 33, 100–105.
16. E. Prosser (*Hamlet and Revenge*, Stanford, 1967, p. 144) maintains the remarkable thesis that there is no delay to be explained. But then she rejects the whole notion of the longtime scheme.
17. E. E. Stoll, *Art and Artifice in Shakespeare* (Cambridge, 1933), Chapter V. Reprinted in *Interpreting Hamlet*, edited by R. E. Leavenworth (San Francisco, 1960), p. 107.
18. Helen Gardner, "The Historical Approach: *Hamlet*," in *The Business of Criticism* (Oxford, 1959), pp. 35–51.
19. Stoll, *op. cit.*, p. 107.
20. *Ibid.*, pp. 113, 115.

Chapter IX—ALL THE WORLD'S A STAGE

1. This chapter develops a point made by the present author in an earlier essay, "Shakespeare and the Theatre of the World," in *The Morality of Art: Essays Presented to G. Wilson Knight by His Colleagues and Friends*, edited by D. W. Jefferson (London, 1969), pp. 76–86.
2. The fullest general treatment is that of A. Righter, *Shakespeare and the Idea of the Play* (London, 1964), *passim*. See also Harry Levin, *The Question of Hamlet* (New York, 1959), pp. 50, 84, 161, etc., and F. Fergusson, "The Meaning of *Hamlet*," in *The Idea of a Theatre* (Princeton, 1949), Chapter IV.
3. Maynard Mack, "The World of *Hamlet*," *The Yale Review*, XLI (1952), reprinted in *Shakespeare: Modern Essays in Criticism*, edited by L. F. Dean (New York, 1957), pp. 251–252.
4. See above, p. 121.
5. Levin, *op. cit.*, p. 163.
6. *La Vida es sueno*, translated by Edward and Elizabeth Huberman, in *Spanish Drama*, edited by A. Flores (New York, 1962), p. 225. On this aspect, see also Arnold Hauser, *Mannerism: The Crisis of the Renaissance and the Origin of Modern Art* (New York, 1965), Vol. I, pp. 113, 326.
7. Cf. Fergusson, *op. cit.*
8. The actor image is used to indicate the highest reach of man in his role as imitator of the gods in Vives' "A Fable about Man."

(See *A Renaissance Treasury,* edited by Hiram Haydn and John Charles Nelson [New York, 1953], pp. 224–229.)

9. On the histrionic associations of "shape" see M. M. Mahood, *Shakespeare's Wordplay* (London, 1957), p. 123.
10. On this aspect, see V. Y. Kantak, "An Approach to Shakespearean Tragedy: The 'Actor' Image in *Macbeth,*" *Shakespeare Survey,* XVI (1963), 42–52.
11. Cf. *Macbeth,* IV, i, 130. On the theatrical associations of "antic" in reference to *Richard II* (III. ii. 162), see Mahood, *op. cit.,* p. 85.
12. Joseph Hall, *Centuries of Meditations,* Book II, Section 30. (In *Works,* 1634, p. 22.)
13. Cf. Mahood, *op. cit.,* pp. 154, 159, but she does not discuss the passages cited here.
14. Edition of 1687, p. xxi.
15. Edition of 1713, p. 172.

Chapter X—THE SIGHT IS DISMAL

1. *Shakespearean Tragedy* (London, 1949), pp. 172–173.
2. *Ibid.,* p. 174.
3. Cf. H. S. Wilson, *On the Design of Shakespearean Tragedy* (Toronto, 1957), p. 46: "The catastrophe of *Hamlet* is clearly Christian in its implications." And see also, Chapter I, above, p. 18f.
4. Cf. G. R. Elliott, *Scourge and Minister* (Durham, North Carolina, 1951), p. 181f; I. Ribner, *Patterns in Shakespearean Tragedy* (London, 1960), p. 78f; Bertram Joseph, *Conscience and the King* (London, 1953), p. 130f.
5. The disease imagery was first noted and commented on by Caroline F. Spurgeon (*Shakespeare's Imagery,* pp. 316–319).
6. W. H. Clemen, *The Development of Shakespeare's Imagery,* p. 113.
7. D. A. Traversi, *op. cit.,* p. 105.
8. Cf. Jessie L. Weston, *From Ritual to Romance* (New York, 1957), pp. 12–14, 60–63.

Chapter XI—SHAKESPEARE AND THE MYTH-MAKERS

1. This is Stoll's basic position, expressed in numerous books and articles. The quoted phrases are culled from "Source and Motive

in *Macbeth* and *Othello*" in *From Shakespeare to Joyce* (New York, 1944), pp. 295–306.

2. Cf. E. E. Stoll's essay on *Hamlet* in *Art and Artifice in Shakespeare* (Cambridge, 1933), and see Chapter VIII above, p. 146f.

3. Northrop Frye, *Anatomy of Criticism* (Princeton, 1957), pp. 206–223.

4. *Ibid.*, p. 208.

5. Scholars who acknowledge the distinction between the historical consciousness of Israel and the myth-consciousness of other peoples are nevertheless apt to speak of the former as "the fundamental Jewish myth" (cf. R. J. Z. Werblowsky, "Hanouca et Noël, ou Judaïsme et Christianisme. Note phénoménologique sur les rapports du mythe et de l'histoire," *Revue de L'Histoire des Religions,* Paris, CXIV [1954], p. 53). This is a matter of linguistic taste. In this study I prefer to restrict the term "myth" to patterns of belief and experience based on the rhythms of external nature and the inner drives of the psyche. Neither of these covers the Israelite covenant experience for which the categorical terms are: challenge, meeting, event.

6. Frye is nothing if not subtle, and he has a way of anticipating objections. In his discussion he does, for instance, allow for the history play as a specific form, and there the emphasis is on continuity rather than the cathartic death of the hero. *Hamlet* and *Macbeth* partake of this mode. "Fortinbras and Malcolm, the continuing characters, indicate the historical element in the tragic resolution" (*op. cit.,* p. 284). The reservation is helpful and does seem to allow for the kind of emphasis on historical rather than cyclical time that I have been urging. But there is no doubt that for Frye the decisive informing principle is not history *per se,* but myth.

7. H. Weisinger, *Tragedy and the Paradox of the Fortunate Fall* (East Lansing, 1953), p. 37.

8. Cf. Jane E. Harrison, *Themis* (Cambridge, 1912), *passim.*

9. Gilbert Murray, "Ritual Forms in Greek Tragedy," in appendix to Harrison, *op. cit.* Also, by same author, *Five Stages of Greek Religion* (London, 1925), pp. 48–49.

10. Weisinger, *op. cit.,* p. 135.

11. But Weisinger is careful to point out that the Hebrew myth-ritual pattern attains a higher spirituality than that of the surrounding peoples. The Hebrews came to conceive of a God who does not

die but imposes an intelligible and just order on chaos. His conclusion is that "the Hebrew cult did employ the practices of the
other Near Eastern rituals, but always transformed and spiritual-
ized." (*Op. cit.*, p. 152.) Weisinger, it seems, would like to have
it both ways, but the basically syncretistic position is clear.

12. *Ibid.*, p. 174.
13. Henri Frankfort, *Before Philosophy* (London, 1951), p. 241; and
    see Chapter VIII above, p. 133f.
14. G. E. Wright, *The Old Testament against Its Environment* (Lon-
    don, 1950), pp. 26–27. On the Israelite tendency to use mythic
    motifs and apply them to concrete historical situations, see, by
    the present author, "Hebraic Style and Motifs in *Paradise Lost*"
    in *Language and Style in Milton*, edited by R. D. Emma and J. T.
    Shawcross (New York, 1967), pp. 40–45. Milton was particularly
    receptive to this demythologizing tendency and reacted to it in
    his poetry.
15. Sir Walter Raleigh, *The History of the World, ed. cit.*, pp. xxv–
    xxviii.
16. I. A. Richards, *Principles of Literary Criticism* (London, 1930),
    p. 246.
17. George Steiner, *The Death of Tragedy* (London, 1961), pp. 4–5.
18. *Ibid.*, pp. 134–135.
19. Baruch Kurzweil, "Is There Such a Thing as Biblical Tragedy?"
    in *An Anthology of Hebrew Essays,* selected by I. Cohen and
    B. Y. Michali (Tel Aviv, 1966), Vol. I, p. 107.
20. *Ibid.*. p. 99.
21. Franz Rosenzweig, *Der Stern der Erloesung* (Berlin, *anno mundi,*
    5690 [1930]), Part I, p. 101. Rosenzweig's discussion at this
    point evidently owes something to earlier discussions by G. Lukacz
    (*Die Seele und die Formen,* Berlin, 1911).
22. *Ibid.*
23. *Ibid.*, pp. 103–104.
24. His full discussion of this aspect is in Part III of *Der Stern der
    Erloesung.*
25. *Ibid.*, Vol. I, p. 103.
26. *Ibid.*, pp. 112–113.
27. *Ibid.*, Part II, p. 132. For discussion of Rosenzweig's doctrine of
    the "threshold," see M. Scwarcz, *Language, Myth, Art* [Hebrew]
    (Tel Aviv, 1966), pp. 368–369.
28. Rosenzweig, *op. cit.*, Part I, pp. 102–103.

Chapter XII—ON THE THRESHOLD

1. Jan Kott, *Shakespeare Our Contemporary* (New York, 1964), pp. 105–107.
2. Like most students of this play I have learned much from J. F. Danby's *Shakespeare's Doctrine of Nature* (London, 1949) as well as from Robert B. Heilman's *This Great Stage* (Baton Rouge, 1948). This debt, I hope, is evident in this and the following paragraphs.
3. A similar effect is created by the vulgar prose of the "Countryman" in the last act of *Antony and Cleopatra* when he brings Cleopatra the asps in a basket of figs. His speeches, with their veiled allusions to the serpent of Eve and to the sinful woman marred by the Devil, introduce a note of Biblical realism and serve to refocus the whole myth-ritual pattern on which the play is so largely based. Cleopatra ceases to be Isis or Venus and becomes the erring female who leads man into sin. The tragedy takes on, for the moment, the character of a Biblical drama of sin, trial, and damnation. See by the present author *"Antony and Cleopatra*: The Limits of Mythology," in *Shakespeare Survey*, Vol. XXIII (Cambridge, 1970), pp. 63–64.
4. Cf. Harold Jenkins, *"As You Like It,"* *Shakespeare Survey*, VIII (1955), 49.
5. I have in mind the distinction made by Roy Walker in his valuable study, *The Golden Feast* (London, 1952), *passim*. But orgy and abstinence are often, as Walker himself shows (pp. 79, 101), but two sides of the same coin. At its best, Western literature has sought a point of reference beyond both types of naturalism.
6. Cf. Helen Gardner, *"As You Like It,"* in *Shakespeare: The Comedies*, edited by Kenneth Muir (Englewood, New Jersey, 1965), pp. 64–66.
7. *Ibid.,* p. 61.
8. Montaigne, *Essays,* translated by John Florio (London, 1904), Vol. I, p. 245.
9. See *The Tempest* edited by F. Kermode (London, 1954), note to I. ii. 258 on p. 26.
10. Sir Thomas More, *Utopia,* The Seconde Booke, "Of Sciences, Craftes and Occupations."
11. On Prospero as a practitioner of the art of "theurgy" and on its medieval antecedents, see W. C. Curry, *Shakespeare's Philosophical Patterns* (Baton Rouge, 1937), p. 183.

12. This link was first noted by Roy W. Battenhouse, "Shakespeare and the Bible," *The Gordon Review,* Vol. VIII (Fall, 1964), p. 20.

13. Neil D. Isaacs and Louis H. Leiter, *Approaches to the Short Story* (San Francisco, 1963), p. 188f.

14. It is important to recognize that this sharpening of the ideological basis of the play to the extent of giving both to the characters and the plot a certain allegorical clarity is perfectly in line with the art of the masque by which this play is much influenced throughout. Some of the titles of Jacobean masques are suggestive: "Pleasure Reconciled to Virtue" and "Time Vindicated to Himself and to His Honours" (both by Ben Jonson); the masques of Fletcher, Carew, and later Milton all have this same abstract moral tendency.

15. Roy Walker, *The Golden Feast* (London, 1952), p. 157.

Appendix—Julius Caesar AND THE BLEEDING STATUE

1. Caroline Spurgeon, *Shakespeare's Imagery and What It Tells Us* (Cambridge, 1965), p. 346.

2. *Julius Caesar,* edited by T. S. Dorsch (London, 1955), Introduction, p. lxv.

3. *Ibid.,* p. lxvii, Dorsch quoting John Crow; see also G. Wilson Knight, *The Imperial Theme* (London, 1954), pp. 35, 52.

4. See also I. ii. 292, on Casca:

   > What a blunt fellow is this grown to be!
   > He was quick mettle when he went to school.

   Here the idea of metal is linked by association with the word "blunt" as of a knife.

5. *Four Lives from North's Plutarch,* "Life of Julius Caesar," translated by Sir Thomas North (edited by R. H. Carr, Oxford, 1932), p. 107.

6. *Ibid.,* "Life of Marcus Brutus," p. 126. [*my italics*]

7. G. Wilson Knight, *Imperial Theme,* pp. 43–44.

8. Cf. *ibid.,* p. 47; Maurice Charney, *Shakespeare's Roman Plays* (Cambridge, Massachusetts, 1961), pp. 51–59; L. Kirschbaum, "Shakespeare's Stage Blood," *PMLA,* LXIV, 520.

9. Cf. Mrs. E. Beit-Halahmi, "Shakespeare's Criticism of Rome" (Bar-Ilan University, unpublished thesis, 1963).

Index

Adonis, 133, 186
Aeschylus (see *Oresteia*)
Alabaster, William, 66
Antigone (Sophocles), 27–28
Antony and Cleopatra, 40–41, 230, 243
Aquinas, Thomas, 35, 216, 233
Aristotle, 35, 49, 138, 238
Armstrong, A. E., 224
Arnold, Matthew, 2, 39, 88
As You Like It, 157, 204–212, 213
Athalie (Racine), 4, 172–173, 189
Auerbach, Erich, 25, 136–137, 233, 238
Augustine, 21, 100, 233
Aurelius, Marcus, 45

Bacon, Francis, 1, 10, 17, 60, 65, 68, 106
Battenhouse, Roy W., 9, 23–25, 231, 232, 237, 244
Beckett, Samuel B., 15
Beit-Halahmi, Esther, 244
Belleforest, François de, 3
Bellow, Samuel, 74–75
Bible (see *Old Testament, New Testament*)
Blake, Robert, 1–2, 88
Boccaccio, Giovanni, 25–26
Boethius, 216
Bradley, Andrew C., 27, 40, 78, 102, 145, 167, 198, 233
Brandes, Georg, 235
Brecht, Bertolt, 144
Buber, Martin, 101, 236
Bunyan, John, 1, 63, 108, 110

Burckhardt, Jacob, 87, 236
Bush, Geoffrey, 20–23, 88, 232

Calderon de la Barca, Pedro, 157
Calvin, John, 21, 35
Campbell, Lily B., 231
Chapman, George, 47, 169
Charney, Maurice, 244
Cicero, 45
Claudius, 42, 93, 96–97, 98, 117, 118, 121, 155, 156, 170
Clemen, Wolfgang H., 233, 240
Cockaigne, Land of, 207, 214
Coleridge, Samuel T., 145, 146, 239
"Counter-Renaissance," the, 17, 54
Covenant idea, 9–10; as Israelite mode of understanding history, 130–131, 241; marriage as symbol of, 116, 211, 221–223; c. with Noah, 184–185; use of c. in period, 107–109, 113, 114; in Hobbes, 109, 237; in *Athalie*, 172–173
Crow, John, 244
Curry, Walter Clyde, 243

Danby, John Francis, 243
Dante Alighieri, 25, 26
Davies, Sir John, 215
Devlin, Christopher, 66, 78, 79, 235, 236
Donne, John, 33–34, 66, 233, 235
Dorsch, T. S., 224, 244